Venture Girls

Venture Girls

Raising Girls to Be Tomorrow's Leaders

CRISTAL GLANGCHAI, PhD

HARPER

NEW YORK • LONDON • TORONTO • SYDNEY

HARPER

FIRST EDITION

Designed by Jamie Lynn Kerner

Library of Congress Cataloging-in-Publication Data has been applied for.

ISBN 978-0-06-269755-4 (pbk.)

18 19 20 21 22 DIX/LSC 10 9 8 7 6 5 4 3 2

To my loving and supportive husband, Pat Condon; my four wonderful children, Javier Glangchai, Cate Condon, Maribel Glangchai, and Carter Condon; and to all of the girls around the world who dream, dare, and do.

CONTENTS

INTRODUCTION

My Dream, Our Dream—a World of Empowered Young Women

IMAGINE A GIRL WHO AT FIVE IS AN ENTREPRENEURIAL WONDER. SHE scores at the genius level for thinking outside the box, collaborates beautifully with her friends to solve problems, and spends her time making new toys with whatever resources she has. She's intrigued by science, math, and technology, and while she may find these subjects challenging at times, she tackles the tough questions persistently until an answer finally emerges. She's visionary, creative, innovative, resilient, and, most important, unafraid to take risks to get what she wants. This kind of person is in desperate demand across the global economy and in our own society, which is striving to maintain leadership in a hypercompetitive world. The most extraordinary thing is, I'm actually describing nearly every five-year-old girl. At this age, according to one expert,

98 percent of children are naturally brilliant in these remarkable traits.[1]

But then something terrible happens. The genius takes a precipitous dive. These bold, imaginative powers are conditioned out by societal pressure and educated out by a system designed to create the boundaries valued by the old world, not the new. The girls who dared to dream big—who were empowered to be curious and follow their passions, who dreamed of creating technologies, careers, and businesses with the potential to solve the grand challenges of our society—begin to opt out.

Each year, millions of girls who are vital to our nation's future abandon their dreams. The social forces that discourage girls from pursuing their full potential begin to affect them before kindergarten, become cruel in middle school, and erode their confidence further as they mature.

It can happen when a girl finds her school's computer club dominated by boys who subtly or overtly exclude, taunt, or reject her, or when an aspiring female entrepreneur is continually ignored or interrupted in the business classes at her high school. By the time they are eighteen, young women who choose to major in fields like math, engineering, or business find themselves seriously outnumbered.

If young women look at the makeup of the workplaces they might enter, they see that the ratios are often worse. They cannot help noticing that the leadership positions are largely held by men, and they find themselves asking, "Where are the women?" No wonder so many girls quietly give up on the dream of being among the future innovators and change makers of tomorrow.

I want to change this, and I hope you do, too.

What if this didn't happen to girls? What if there was a window in a girl's life when just the right dose of learning at the just right time could snap the downward spiral, and produce a girl whose gifts were available for the rest of her life? What could this new kind of girl—an undiminished girl, a VentureGirl—become?

I am an engineer, a nanoscientist, a professor, and an entrepreneur. So I've approached the problem in the spirit of a scientist intent on discovery. Why do some women forge ahead in science, technology, engineering, and math—the so-called STEM fields—and rise into leadership positions, while others give up? What interventions might change this pattern? What can we do that will really work?

The challenge is to bring STEM to life for girls—to make it relevant to them. We can no longer afford to live in a world where more than one-half of the population is essentially excluded from the cutting edge. We need those brilliant minds at work. Furthermore, we can no longer cheat so many young women out of the pride and joy that come from finding a vocation in innovation. It's critical for our girls and for our future as a society to attract girls to the STEM fields, and to create a world where both men and women actively participate in building the future.

Through my experiences, I have found that the key to lifting up the next generation of girls is to blend STEM with entrepreneurship. And we can't just teach girls—we must teach boys at the same time, so that they understand that girls are equally capable of achievement, creativity, and leadership.

I believe in this approach because I'm a product of it. I've experienced how empowering and fulfilling technology and entrepreneurship can be.

Ever since I was a kid, I've loved building things and taking things apart to figure out how they worked. I remember as a child picking up a screwdriver and taking apart my family's mustard-yellow rotary telephone to see what made it work. (If you don't remember what a rotary telephone was, it had lots of gears and moving parts.) I found the dozens of parts inside the phone pretty amazing.

At first, my parents were upset. In those days before cell phones and e-mail, the home phone was a family's only means of communication. But here's the extraordinary thing: Rather than scolding me and stifling my excitement, they let me experiment. They tried to explain how the phone worked and then helped me put it back together.

My parents' approach to life was about curiosity and unfettered expression. More important, they were *not* focused on what I should and shouldn't do as a girl.

My father himself had overcome difficult times. He grew up on the streets in Mexico, not knowing where his next meal would come from. His parents both had only elementary school educations, and his dad died when my father was young. When his shoes became torn, he would put cardboard in them to cover the holes. Nonetheless, he had the drive, ambition, and fearlessness he needed to make a better world for himself. Penniless and knowing little English, he came to the United States to study, and that is where I was born.

I was raised to do anything a boy could do. My Sunday dress was just that. The rest of the week, I was free to play in the mud or tinker with broken appliances in the garage. It was a hands-on childhood that included cardboard imaginary castles, GI Joes, and Legos. Back then, girls were more likely to be given pink toys, miniature stoves, irons, and Barbie dolls to play with instead. But my sisters and I were allowed to get messy, dirty, and greasy. If we wanted a tree house or even a dollhouse, we watched our dad build it and helped him. We were highly involved in sports, and our dad taught us everything from electrical wiring to tiling floors to changing brake pads in the car—and we loved it.

We often joked that our dad treated us like boys because he wished he'd had some sons, too. But we shouldn't have! Today, studies show that by playing with those stereotyped "boy" toys at an early age, we girls were developing the spatial relation skills we'd need for our education and future careers in STEM.

Dad encouraged us in math and science, often bringing home science and electronics kits. If we had trouble with math in school, instead of telling us that maybe it just wasn't for us, he would get us a tutor. We were lucky to be able to afford these luxuries, but the most important thing he gave us was free: He always told us we could do and be whatever we wanted if we worked hard and followed our passion.

In all these ways, my dad gave me the tools I needed to be comfortable being the only girl in male-dominated classes at school—and, later, in male-dominated workplaces. His curiosity and fearlessness got baked into my personality. It was a natural progression for me to get involved in science projects and contests at school. I was a math-and-science–smitten girl, almost oblivious to the fact that most of my fellow geeks were guys. I thought I could do anything as long as I put my mind to it. And I did, winning science fairs and scholarships.

In college, going into mechanical engineering was a natural choice for me. I enjoyed the thrill of learning about new technologies and creating inventions of my own. After graduating, I became a product development engineer at 3M. In the late 1990s, I read the news reports about genetic engineering and Dolly, the first cloned sheep. In 2003, I decided to transition to biomedical engineering, despite the fact that I'd had little background training in biology or chemistry. While in grad school, I learned the importance of technology commercialization and entrepreneurship. I realized that it was extremely important to apply research to create goods and services that benefit society.

By the age of twenty-seven, I was pursuing a PhD in biomedical engineering focused on drug delivery and nanotechnology, a field in which materials, tools, and devices are measured in nanometers—a unit so tiny that the paper on which these words are printed is about seventy-five thousand nanometers thick. I had developed a new way to manufacture disease-responsive nanoparticles, and I decided to build an enterprise around my research. I launched a new company, NanoTaxi, with the dream of delivering cancer-curing treatments and reducing side effects for chemo patients. I pitched my business concept to prospective investors on both coasts and began participating in "angel investing" programs that provided seed money to startups. I immersed myself in technology-oriented entrepreneurial culture.

I had become one of the few women tech entrepreneurs. During those years of study and startup, I never encountered another Hispanic female technology entrepreneur, and I joyously celebrated whenever I met another woman CEO, inventor, or scientist. So imagine how exciting it was for me to be invited to join Springboard Enterprises, a nonprofit resource hub of entrepreneurs and investors dedicated to building high-growth, technology-oriented companies led by women. In Springboard, I finally found a vibrant network of peers, role models, and advisors who were elevating women entrepreneurs. Experiencing the thrill of a supportive community inspired me to try to close the gender gap for women in technology and entrepreneurship.

Eventually, my career took me back to academia. It was while I was leading the Center for Entrepreneurship and Innovation at Trinity University in San Antonio, Texas, that the problem crystallized for me. I observed striking differences between male and female students in class. Young women whom I saw strolling around campus fully engaged and outgoing became, in a predominantly male classroom, somewhat timid. Most of the young men would take a stab at answering any question, seemingly without worrying about embarrassing themselves if they were wrong. Young women who actually knew the answer wouldn't venture it unless they were entirely certain, and even then they often responded sheepishly.

The pattern was consistent, unmistakable, and aligned with what I'd experienced as an engineering student a decade earlier. The young women lacked confidence and feared failure. One hesitant student confided in me that she was dropping her computer science class because she was earning Cs. To me, making a C in a tough subject was simply an educational rite of passage; it suggested the need for tutoring or other help. But this student considered each C she received as a ruling on her abilities. It might as well have been an F.

Talking to her sparked something within me. In my own life, I'd learned what virtually every entrepreneur knows—that failure is a step on the ladder of success. That insight opened doors for me to a world of achievement and freedom. What if girls could learn such entrepreneurial lessons long before college? Could girls in elementary school, or even earlier, be taught to approach learning and life with an entrepreneurial mind-set? Could they be taught to persevere through failures and setbacks in pursuit of their goals? Might this be the key to unleashing their self-confidence?

In search of answers to these questions, I created VentureLab, a nonprofit dedicated to teaching entrepreneurial skills to children—with a particular focus on teaching girls.

In the entrepreneurial setting of VentureLab, girls are free to take risks and make mistakes without hurting their grades. They learn to work with teams on problems that interest them, tackling projects that they themselves define.

We eliminate the scariness so that even girls who think they are "not good at math" can reconfigure how they think of math and numbers, seeing them as useful tools. They learn the steps involved in research and development—analysis, hypothesis, testing, prototypes, and findings. They learn about teamwork, markets, audiences, buyers, sales—and, of course, profits. This empowers girls to discover that people will *pay* for the products they design and create—that their work has value and meaning.

In dozens of camps and class modules we've conducted since then, we've found something remarkable. When girls are exposed to entrepreneurial thinking, a profound change takes place. They become more aware of opportunities around them, develop powerful problem-solving skills, and improve their abilities to think critically and creatively. What's more, the fear and insecurity they may associate with subjects in the STEM fields often disappear as they discover that these tools can be used to solve problems that fascinate them and may ultimately help society.

A magic triangle emerges that connects three sources of power: girls, entrepreneurship, and STEM. As girls learn more about imagining and creating business ventures of their own, they discover the ability of science and technology to help make their dreams possible. And the greater their knowledge about entrepreneurship and STEM, the more imaginative and far-seeing they become. The ultimate effect is that girls become steadily more confident and fearless about their ability to tackle and conquer challenges of all kinds. Like I did.

They become VentureGirls.

As an engineer, a nanoscientist, a professor, and an entrepreneur—but also as a mom of four, including two girls—I want my kids, and especially my daughters, to be confident in their abilities and to follow their passions, even if they are different from those of other girls. I want them to believe they can be astronauts or doctors, auto designers or bridge builders, programmers or chemists or company founders.

The entrepreneurial mind-set was the best gift I ever received from my parents. I want to pay it forward and teach girls to create their own future.

That's why I've written *VentureGirls*. I believe early entrepreneurial training should be a part of every child's education, and especially that of girls. My goal is to provide those who love girls—parents and grandparents, teachers and counselors, professionals, mentors and advisors—with the knowledge, insights, techniques, and tools they need to help them become VentureGirls: confident, resilient, creative, and smart, no matter what fields of endeavor they may choose to enter as adults.

The book is divided into three parts. Part One, "The Problem," explains the three interlocking challenges that girls and women face in today's world—attitudes that create barriers that discourage them from pursuing their interests in science, technology, engineering, and math; from developing their skills as entrepreneurial problem-solvers and creators of organizations; and from achieving leadership positions in business and in society as a whole.

Part Two, "The Solution," explains why learning and

practicing entrepreneurial skills is an invaluable key to solving the three-part problem and thereby unleashing the creative powers of girls and women for the benefit of all humankind.

Part Three, "How to Raise a VentureGirl"—the longest section—offers specific advice to parents, family members, teachers, community leaders, and anyone else who wants to help a girl develop to her full potential. The chapters in Part Three include inspiring stories, insights from experts and leaders in the worlds of business and STEM, and fun activities you can enjoy with girls of all ages.

Because it's likely that you may also be the parent or friend of a boy whose future is just as important, the book concludes with some tips about how to raise a VentureBoy, as well as a selection of resources for further learning, including organizations, websites, and tools that offer even more information, activities, and ideas.

Thank you for opening this book and thereby taking your first steps on this exciting journey. Every girl should have a chance to learn the incredible lessons of entrepreneurship—lessons that can help them hold on to their five-year-old genius and confidence, and never let them go.

If you share my dream of a world filled with powerful, creative, and inspiring young women who are using their talents to help create a better future for all of us, then, please, read on!

Luz Cristal Glangchai

SEPTEMBER 2017

Part One

The Problem

1

Where Are All the Girls?

IT AMAZES ME THAT FOR ALL OF OUR ADVANCES AS A SOCIETY, GENDER BIases are still a problem in the twenty-first century. If anyone doubts that girls face discouragement because of their gender, consider the experience of Nick Hahn. Nick is a software designer at IBM and what I call a "tech dad." He's had a lifelong fascination with all things digital and is deeply committed to sparking his daughter's interest in computing. He recently shared a story with me that involves Minecraft, the hugely popular video game that has introduced millions of kids to the basics of computer coding through its digital-style game commands:

> *When my seven-year-old daughter was just getting into Minecraft, she was excited to share her new interest with another seven-year-old girl whose family was visiting us. Her friend's mom overheard our conversation*

as I brought my laptop out and turned the game on. She seemed surprised that I'd been showing my daughter Minecraft. Right there in front of us all, she said to her daughter: "Oh, honey, that game is for boys, you don't need to bother with that." Then she looked at me and laughed, like I didn't get this either, and said, "Why do you show this to your daughter? It's not for her!"[1]

The mom in Nick's story didn't intend to limit or hurt her daughter. She probably knew almost nothing about Minecraft and had thought very little about the social or intellectual content of video games. That's the nature of insidious bias. Its invisible influence permeates our culture so deeply that it can go unrecognized until someone blurts out such a jarring statement. (And yes, as the story illustrates, women, too, can be infected with insidious forms of bias that limit and hurt the opportunities for girls.)

It probably doesn't come as news to you that girls and women face gender bias that can limit their opportunities and discourage their participation in many activities. But not everyone understands the subtle ways that gender bias holds women back—and the ways that three interrelated forms of bias reinforce one another. I'm referring to the belief that science is for boys, not girls; that entrepreneurship comes naturally to men, not to women; and that leaders in general are male rather than female. All three of these stereotypes are false, despite the fact that they are deeply ingrained in our society—so deeply, in fact, that many of us are influenced by them without even realizing it. And all three are closely intertwined, each bias strengthening and supporting the others, and thereby creating a wall against female achievement that is surprisingly difficult to overcome.

That pattern of interlocking gender barriers is the big problem I've devoted my life to solving. It's a pattern that stands in the way of empowering girls and women in our society . . . which means it not only deprives women of the opportunities to succeed and strive for what they deserve and want, but it also deprives our society as a whole of the talent, creativity, and energy that half our population can contribute.

I learned how these interlocking biases work in the most painful way possible—by experiencing them firsthand.

As I explained in the introduction, I was a very lucky young girl. I grew up with parents who nurtured my curiosity and my interests in science and math. They inspired my confidence and self-esteem by encouraging me to dream big and follow my passion. They encouraged me to fly by refusing to clip my wings; they made it feel safe to explore my ideas and try new things. As a result, I never saw a difference between boys and girls and I was not afraid to ask silly questions or go down the unpaved roads. I had the opportunity to reach my fullest potential and develop the talents that have helped me enjoy a successful career as an engineer, a professor, and an entrepreneur.

Unfortunately, not everyone in the world is as accustomed to seeing girls in STEM, entrepreneurship, and leadership.

And like many women, I've experienced my own share of gender bias, whether unconscious, explicit, or institutionalized, throughout my journey.

I'll never forget my years in grad school, working late hours doing research in the lab and handling toxic bone-eating chemicals in order to create a new way to treat cancer patients. I was twenty-seven and weighing the tough choice between starting a family and waiting until I finished my PhD, as many women in academia do. After much deliberation, I decided not to wait, and I got pregnant at age twenty-eight. I worked in the lab until the day my water broke and returned just five weeks after my son was born.

Shortly after I resumed working, I was scheduled to make a presentation at a scientific conference in Europe. I'd been warned that if I missed this opportunity, I might forfeit ownership of my research project. So here I was on a plane to Vienna with my five-week-old son, nervously trying to breastfeed him under the disapproving stare of the male business traveler sitting next to me. Thankfully, the stewardess was a cordial British woman who responded to the businessman's complaints by explaining that breastfeeding is "very natural," and allowed him to move to an empty seat in the back of the plane. I spent the conference in Vienna, seeking quiet corners in which to breastfeed my son between sessions spent preparing and presenting my talk.

Things weren't much better in my own lab. At the time, there was no such thing as a lactation room at the university. I had to use the janitor's closet, where I would turn on a red light that could be seen from the outside, then jury-rig a chair to jam the door shut for fifteen minutes while I pumped breast milk, surrounded by mops and cleaning supplies.

Not all women in male-dominated fields experience moments like that—but far too many do. And while each incident on its own doesn't seem like a big deal, they are like small paper cuts that build upon one another. No wonder countless women have chosen to step away from science-oriented or entrepreneurial fields for which they have a natural affinity and talent. It's our job as parents, educators, and mentors to catch these women while they're still young, and to give them the confidence and encouragement to push through the paper cuts and follow their passions.

To play this supportive role for the girls in our lives, it helps to understand the three forms of interlocking gender bias and the ways they work together to discourage women from becoming scientists, entrepreneurs, and leaders.

PROBLEM 1: "SCIENCE IS FOR BOYS"

THE FIRST PIECE OF THE PUZZLE IS THE CULTURAL BIAS THAT DISCOURAGES girls and women from pursuing their interests in science, technology, engineering, and math—the all-important STEM fields.

We live in a world that is shaped by scientific technologies. In the last century alone, we've had unprecedented innovations, giving us the ability to easily travel and communicate across the globe, to get goods and services delivered almost instantly on demand, and to enjoy fingertip access to the knowledge of all humankind. Advances in agriculture have dramatically reduced the number of people living in poverty, and medical miracles have extended life spans and enabled millions to live more productive and happier lives. All of these innovations are based in STEM.

Furthermore, STEM is still increasing. According to experts at the World Economic Forum, we are at the beginning of a Fourth Industrial Revolution.[2] Developments in artificial intelligence, robotics, genetics, and big data are all amplifying one another and building upon each other. Breakthroughs like nanobots that can diagnose and cure diseases, nonpolluting and renewable energy sources careers, and driverless cars are all on the horizon.

As a result, careers are changing rapidly. Experts predict that roughly 65 percent of children entering primary schools today will work in jobs that don't currently exist, with titles like organ designer, virtual reality architect, drone programmer, and genetic administrator. Entrepreneurship and STEM skills are increasingly being recognized as *the* skills required for success in today's increasingly challenging, fast-paced, unpredictable world—and not just in business, but in every field imaginable. Whether you are an artist, an attorney, a teacher, or a physician, your future career will be shaped and empowered by technology.

This is all very exciting, but there is a big problem. We are leaving girls behind. Almost half the population is effectively cut off from full participation in the future simply because of insidious gender biases that discourage girls from engaging with science and technology.

As early as preschool, girls in our society begin to absorb unconscious stereotypes. There is an entire industry built around princesses—toys, costumes, posters, decor, and bedroom furniture. Girls are set on a particular, narrow track when they're given Barbie dolls and quietly discouraged from playing with Lego blocks or other building toys. The funneling can be as subtle and unintentional as the holiday and birthday presents chosen for girls by well-meaning relatives and friends.

The track is reinforced when girls see boys depicted in the media as leaders, science whizzes, and problem-solvers, while they are usually relegated to the role of damsels in distress. It begins as soon as they start watching YouTube, TV shows, or movies with their parents. These early influences are crucial. Studies of the brain show that neural pathways affecting the way girls and boys perceive the world are created at a very young age.[3] That's why subliminal messages kids begin to absorb as toddlers really matter.

Like a lot of America, I laugh at the popular sitcom *The Big Bang Theory*. It's nice to see a hit TV show that is about physicists and scientists. But I also wonder: Does it have to focus on four geeky male scientists and Penny, the cute, blond, "babe-alicious" waitress and aspiring actress who lives next door? (*Babe-alicious* isn't my word. It's how the publicists at the CBS television network describe Penny's character in promoting the show.)

Admittedly, after the initial seasons of *The Big Bang Theory*, the show's producers did add some female characters who are involved in science and technology. They include Amy

Fowler, a neurobiologist played by actress Mayim Bialik, who actually has a PhD in neuroscience (earned at UCLA in 2007). Unfortunately, though, strong female characters like her have remained relatively rare in media, and don't give girls the confidence that normal, everyday women can become scientists.

Furthermore, the treatment of science in movies follows the same insidious pattern, as numerous research studies have shown. For example, a 2015 study sponsored by the Geena Davis Institute on Gender in Media found that in 120 popular films recently produced in countries around the world, the ratio of male to female characters depicted as having STEM careers was greater than seven to one (88.4 percent to 11.6 percent). In case you are wondering, films made in the United States were not noticeably better than those produced in other countries—just 12.5 percent of characters with STEM careers in US-made pictures were female. And this gross imbalance can't be excused by saying that the filmmakers are merely reflecting an unfortunate social reality. In fact, the gender imbalance in movies is worse than that in real life, since in the United States about 24 percent of STEM jobs are held by women.[4]

Once girls and boys start school, the subliminal messages tend to lead to hardened biases. We know from research that girls begin their education with the same potential as boys to be leaders and innovators in math, science, and technology fields—and with virtually the same level of interest and enthusiasm. Yet, over time, the picture dramatically changes. Girls begin to make determinations about their own math and science aptitude as early as second and third grade. Many are steered away from these subjects by well-meaning but biased and unthinking teachers or counselors. When boys suffer setbacks in mastering tough math and science topics, they're often provided with encouragement, support, and resources (like tutoring). When girls hit the same roadblocks, they're often allowed to quit or told that math isn't for them. As a result, they imbibe the message "I'm just not smart at math and science."

By their teens, girls may lack the confidence to push forward in math and science. They are often discouraged. They may lack a mentor. Chances are, they've never met a woman in science, technology, or math. In STEM classes, they exhibit what I call a "nurtured apprehension" that prevents them from standing up and speaking up. Many have been taught to drop out instead of having the confidence to pursue their interests.

By the time girls reach high school, the damage is done. For example, while roughly half of high school students taking physics are girls, they are taking fewer Advanced Placement (AP) courses and AP tests. And even when they are sitting for AP exams, they are scoring sharply lower than their male classmates, suggesting that they are unlikely to continue with physics. Of US teens polled in a 2013 survey by the Department of Labor, just 16 percent of girls expressed possible interest in STEM careers, compared with 30 percent of boys—and the imbalance has gotten worse rather than better in recent years.[5]

GIRLS AREN'T THE ONLY VICTIMS OF THE STEM GAP

In the United States, females aren't the only group shortchanged when it comes to opportunities to study and pursue STEM subjects. There are big gaps that also impact various racial, ethnic, and socioeconomic groups. Research by the National Science Foundation shows that white and Asian/Pacific Islander students and those from higher-income families consistently score higher than their counterparts who are black, Hispanic, or American Indian/Alaska Native, as well as those from lower-income families.

High school students enrolled in beginning-level science courses in 2012 at comparable rates, regardless of sex and race and ethnicity. However, students with less-educated parents or of lower socioeconomic status were less likely to take these courses. Furthermore, black and Hispanic students are much less likely than white students to enroll in advanced science and math courses. Unfortunately, these gaps start in kindergarten and multiply and expand at higher educational levels.[6]

The problem of racial and economic disparities in achievement is beyond the direct scope of this book. But it compounds the challenges faced by female students who may also be members of ethnic minorities or economically disadvantaged—challenges that become more difficult at higher rungs of the achievement ladder. Thus, for example, in 2012, while minority women earned 11.2 percent of bachelor's degrees in science and engineering, they earned just 4.1 percent of doctorate degrees in the same fields.[7] This is a real problem in a world where advanced training is often a ticket to the best jobs and the greatest opportunities.

College brings a new set of challenges for young women. One pervasive problem is so-called gateway classes, designed to weed out less-talented students by breaking them down. They are supertough courses that by design will cause at least one-quarter of the students to feel so incompetent, so ill prepared, so dumb, and so hopeless that they flunk, drop the course, or change to an easier major. You may have glimpsed scenes from gateway courses in popular culture: Think of the movies in which a professor standing before a large classroom tells the nervous freshmen, "Look to the student on your left. Now look to your right. One of the three of you will not be here at graduation."

Gateway classes are especially prevalent in science and engineering departments and, combined with discouraging social cues and a lack of role models, often serve as a barrier to aspiring young women. Maria Klawe, a computer scientist and the president of Harvey Mudd College, notes that "in many colleges these courses are seen by female students as a way to prove that you belong."[8] Gateway courses capitalize on the fear of failure and nullify love of learning. They are based on the old thinking of a "fixed mind-set," the belief that intelligence is fixed and you can't do much to improve it. It's a self-limiting belief system, and one I'll discuss further later in this chapter.

Computer science and engineering are tough, rigorous majors for virtually everyone. It's no different for men than women. But for women, it's hard to continue fighting their way upstream when there are few other women and few role models, and their own instructors are saying, in essence, "You're not good enough and never will be." It's a lot for a young woman to take on alone, or nearly alone, when other fields are more inviting.

I've interviewed many students who've experienced the emotional impact of gateway classes. Grace Frye, a bright and motivated undergraduate at Trinity University in San Antonio, Texas, said:

> *I got an e-mail from my professor on August 1, a month before school started, saying, "You need to do this pre-work. People who don't do the pre-work typically withdraw or fail." The way we talk about computer science classes is a little morbid. People say things like, "That assignment killed me" or "I died." I had a stone pit in my stomach. Whenever I thought about that class, I felt sick. It doesn't create an environment where I feel like I can go to my professor to ask questions, or where I can feel comfortable not knowing the right answer.*[9]

According to Maria Klawe, many institutions are trying to identify where gateway courses exist and change them. At

Harvey Mudd, for example, students collaborate as teams, knowing that each of them has the potential to learn and succeed.

But evidence suggests that gender bias in sciences continues to be a major problem at US universities. A 2012 Yale University study found that science professors at American universities widely regarded women undergraduates as less competent than men with the same skills and accomplishments. As a result, professors were less likely to mentor women students. When presented with two imaginary job applicants of equal education and achievements, one male and one female, the professors were more likely to choose the man, and those job offers that women did receive were for salaries on average four thousand dollars lower than those offered to the imaginary men. The study concluded that the bias was an "outgrowth of subconscious cultural influences."[10]

As a result of these and other factors, women with interests and talents related to science tend to drift away from the STEM fields during their college years. The consequences have been perverse. While opportunities for technology careers have exploded since 2000, the percentage of young women majoring in engineering has hovered, unchanged, at about 20 percent for a generation. Even more startling, *fewer* women today are pursuing computer science degrees than in the 1970s and 1980s, when women made up one-quarter of all computer science students in the nation's colleges and universities. Today, women make up just 18 percent of the computer science majors.[11]

Matters don't get any better when young women enter the workforce. A study of more than a thousand women in engineering by the Anita Borg Institute, a nonprofit dedicated to advancing women in technology, shows that the main reasons talented women drop out of technology careers are related to deeply ingrained cultural practices and prejudices against women. They include:

- Poor working conditions: no advancement, too many hours, low salary (30 percent)
- Poor work-life integration: inadequate time with family, conflict with family, or too much travel (27 percent)
- Unattractive work opportunities: uninteresting work or unappealing daily tasks (22 percent)
- Negative organizational climate: unsupportive culture, boss, or coworkers (17 percent)

Sometimes subtle systemic problems make career choices especially difficult for women. Graham Weston, cofounder and former chairman and CEO of Rackspace, says that one of the challenges in hiring women for high-ranking positions in his technology company is the so-called trailing spouse problem. Since most of the female job candidates he interviews are married to men with equally demanding careers, a job offer that requires a woman to make a geographic move—not uncommon in today's highly mobile business world—is likely to conflict with her husband's work. In past generations, when men held nearly all of the high-powered jobs, it was assumed that a wife would simply pull up stakes whenever her husband's job required a move. Now the trailing spouse can be of either gender—and too few men have yet developed the willingness to sacrifice their own career preferences in support of their ambitious wives. "We sometimes end up making offers to five highly qualified women," Weston says, "only to get turned down by all five because their husbands weren't willing to move."[12]

In some cases, old-fashioned male chauvinism is alive and well, even in our supposedly "politically correct" era. The Nobel Prize–winning British biochemist Tim Hunt caused a scandal when he spoke more frankly than most about his "problem" with women in science in a 2015 speech before the World Conference of Science Journalists in Seoul, South Korea. "Let me tell you about my trouble with girls," Hunt said. "Three things happen when they are in the lab: You fall in love with them, they fall in love with you, and when you criticize them they cry."[13] He offered this as a justification for his policy of maintaining an all-male environment for his own scientific studies.

Hunt's statement was quickly disavowed by the British Royal Society, the country's most prestigious science organization. It also led to a global backlash that included hundreds of Twitter posts using the hashtag #distractinglysexy, in which female scientists posted photos of themselves in lab coats, hard hats, and safety goggles. Still, most women in science will tell you that Hunt probably speaks for many male colleagues who are simply more cautious about expressing what they really think about women in the lab.

If anyone still doubts that young women face discouragement because of their gender, consider the story of Barbara Barres, who was a prominent female neurobiologist at Stanford University.

As a female student at MIT, Barres experienced the usual subtle and not-so-subtle forms of bias most STEM-oriented women have faced. For example, when she solved a particularly tough math problem in an advanced class, her professor remarked, "Your boyfriend must have solved it for you."

Barres's perspective on the problem deepened in a unique way when she got breast cancer in her forties. In the wake of her illness, confronting the fact that being a woman had been a lifelong agony for her, she decided not only to have a double mastectomy, but also to change gender. Today Ben Barres is chairman of the Neurobiology Department at Stanford University School of Medicine, a top-drawer scientist by any measure. Thus Barres has had the rare experience of living both as a woman and as a man, and has known life and work in all kinds of scientific circles and situations from both perspectives.

To his surprise, Ben Barres found that living as a man dramatically changed the way people react to him. "Shortly after I changed sexes, I gave a seminar about my research at MIT. One of my friends told me that afterward, as they were leaving, one of his colleagues said, 'Gee, that Ben Barres's work is so much better than his sister Barbara's!' "

Barres can testify from firsthand experience that society treats men and women differently solely based on their gender. His conclusion: "In general, society assumes a man is *competent* until proven otherwise, and a woman is considered *incompetent* until proven otherwise. This creates terribly unfair barriers for talented women in science." Barres now devotes part of his time to helping women get a foothold in science.[14]

The picture is a sadly consistent one, from preschool through adulthood: At every stage in their lives, talented females with an aptitude for math, science, and technology face cultural and psychological barriers that block the road to achievement.

This is a problem that I and many other like-minded leaders are working to solve. And it is compounded by the way it is linked to two other problems.

PROBLEM 2: "A BUSINESS FOUNDER IS A GUY"

THE CULTURAL BARRIERS THAT DISCOURAGE WOMEN FROM COMMITTING TO math and science also send discouraging messages about women and business. This leads to the second problem—the lack of women business founders and the resulting dearth of women-led businesses contributing to economic growth and dynamism.

Cultural stereotypes tell girls that business leaders are men, not women. Here, as with science and technology, media messages reflect the problem and help to perpetuate it. For example, the same study I cited earlier that shows the paucity of female film characters with STEM careers also documents the overwhelming prevalence of men depicted as business leaders in films. In movies from around the world, women constitute less than 14 percent of characters shown as members of corporate "C-suites"—that is, chief executive officers (CEOs), chief financial officers, and other "chiefs." The same bias applies to the depiction of other high-powered business leaders—investors, financiers, law partners, and the like. In many cases, the percentage of women shown as leaders in specific industries in movies is even lower than the low numbers found in real life.[15]

Unfortunately, the real-life business world is another place where women find it terribly difficult to make headway. One small, shocking illustration: Not only is the number of women who serve as CEOs of big corporations appallingly low, but it is also actually smaller than the number of CEOs who are men named John! (To be precise, of the giant companies listed in the Standard & Poor's Composite 500 Index, 4.1 percent are headed by women . . . while Johns are in charge at 5.3 percent. By the way, Davids also outnumber women, with 4.5 percent of the top spots.)[16]

Boards of directors are barely better. A study by Ernst & Young found that only 16 percent of the board seats for the fifteen hundred companies in the S&P 500 are held by women. Among smaller companies, it is even worse. Women hold only 15 percent of the board seats at the S&P MidCap 400 companies, and only 12 percent at the S&P SmallCap 600. While smaller than those in the S&P 500, each company in the MidCap group is valued at well over $1 billion, and some are household names.[17]

Once women get a toehold in business, they often find they are judged by unfair and unequal standards. One study of 248 performance reviews shared by 180 people in twenty-eight different companies, from large technology corporations to smaller businesses, found that reviews of women were sharply more critical than of men. For example, 71 percent of women's reviews included critical feedback, compared with just 2 percent of men's reviews.[18] Did the women truly merit *that much* more criticism? How did this affect the future career advancement of the employees involved?

The culture of discouragement is expressed in countless less-formal ways. I don't know a single woman in the technology industry who hasn't experienced unconscious gender bias. Sometimes it seems as if combating bias is like a game of Whac-A-Mole. Just when you've eliminated a bias, another instance pops up where you weren't looking.

It is particularly troubling when bias masquerades as cultural sensitivity. Business executive Catherine Crago describes her experience of being shut out for fear a woman wouldn't be accepted. "When I was working for a US-based consulting firm," she says, "they didn't let a woman lead the team because they thought their Taiwanese clients couldn't handle it . . . so men with less experience and knowledge were put in charge."[19] Yet at the time, women in Taiwan actually headed several leading companies in the same industry, giving the lie to the excuse offered by the American consulting firm.

Women joke about the pervasiveness of gender bias in business with lines like "Whatever women do, they must do twice as well as men to be thought half as good. Luckily, this is not difficult." But beneath the humor is raw, painful truth.

PROBLEM 3: "A LEADER LOOKS LIKE A MAN"

THE THIRD, BROADEST PART OF THE PROBLEM IS THE PERVASIVE LACK OF self-confidence among too many girls and women—a hesitance to assert our leadership abilities due to the fact that our society overwhelmingly assumes that leadership positions of all kinds naturally belong to men.

Here, again, media stereotypes play a powerful role. Think for just a moment about the way girls are depicted in literature, children's movies, and TV. It's great that there are female heroines in so many of the stories we tell our kids—except that, in too many cases, the princesses are depicted as passive victims reliant on the princes who rescue them.

Many of the most popular and oft-repeated fairy tales would have us believe that girls are delicate and sensitive. In "The Princess and the Pea," the real princess can be recognized by her ability to sense, and be disturbed by, a pea beneath her mattress. Can you imagine the powerful tennis pro Serena Williams being disturbed by a tiny pea? Or women's rights activist Malala Yousafzai? Or astronaut Sally Ride? Or business leaders and entrepreneurs like Facebook's Sheryl Sandberg or Sara Blakely, the inventor of Spanx?

Unfortunately, harmful gender stereotypes are so pervasive in our mass media that avoiding them is almost impossible. I challenge you to try to think of a few female leads in cartoons or shows that children watch. How many can you come up with? Almost none. If you came up with the Powerpuff Girls, congratulations. Unfortunately, they're portrayed as cute little girls with abnormally large doe eyes, creations of an evil professor who attempted to create perfect little girls using "sugar and spice and everything nice," until his experiment went awry. *Dora the Explorer* works for a year or two, but my kids stopped watching the show around age three. Then there is Johnny Test and his genius scientist sisters; however, the premise of the cartoon is that he is the hero, and his sisters' experiments often cause problems that he must resolve.

Can't television and movie producers develop a girl character who is as inventive, brave, and adventurous as the boy characters? Or how about as inventive, brave, and adventurous as girls I know? And how about counterbalancing princess stories with a gritty alternative?

One of my favorite children's books is *The Paper Bag Princess*. Instead of the princess being rescued by the prince, she fights off a dragon and saves them both. When her finery is scorched and her skin made sooty by the dragon's fiery breath, the resourceful princess cuts openings in a brown paper bag and wears it. This turns off the prince, who cannot even acknowledge that she saved his life. But by then she sees him for what he is—a nitpicking, entitled, ungrateful coward—and goes off happily on her own.

The 2017 *Wonder Woman* movie, starring Gal Gadot and directed by the female director Patty Jenkins, is another positive exception. It portrays a strong, curious, and brave female lead who saves the world, defeating an evil female scientist along the way.

Unfortunately, TV shows and films depicting strong

women leaders are few and far between. The impact of this pervasive stereotyping becomes apparent in the early grades of school.

You may know Amy Cuddy from her widely viewed TED Talk, "Your Body Language May Shape Who You Are." Quite by accident, she and her colleagues began studying the role of gender in children's body language when they launched a social developmental study "to identify the age at which kids start to associate expansive body posture with power and contractive postures with powerlessness." They showed sixty children—thirty four-year-olds and thirty six-year-olds—images of gender-neutral dolls. What they found was a startling increase in "male-power bias" by age six. "[W]hile both groups showed a strong male-power gender bias, compared to the four-year-olds, the six-year-olds were about three times as likely to see every powerful doll as male and every powerless doll as female. And there were no differences between the scores of girls and boys—they were equally biased," according to Cuddy.[20]

As girls enter puberty, the effects of stereotyping express themselves in a gradual loss of self-confidence and self-esteem. Girls tend to defer to boys in class, even when they know as much or more. Their body language is hesitant. When they do raise their hands, it's often timidly. And when they don't get called on, they tend to shut down even further.

A study by the American Association of University Women found that around the age of nine, girls were confident and assertive, but by the time they reached high school less than a third of girls felt this way. The survey also showed that boys lost some sense of self-esteem, but far less than the girls.[21]

Part of the problem, says Londa Schiebinger, author of *Has Feminism Changed Science?*, is that "girls are raised to be modest, while boys learn to exaggerate their intelligence, their successes, their prospects in life, and even their height. Girls who have been trained to underestimate their talents encounter boys who overestimate their talents; the girls take the boys' estimations of their skills at face value and think even worse of themselves."[22]

What is the cost of women's lack of confidence? Schiebinger calculates that it takes four hundred ninth-grade boys, but two thousand ninth-grade girls, to produce one PhD scientist.

By the time they get into college, says Dr. Bruce Porter, professor and former chairman of the Computer Science Department at the University of Texas at Austin, "the men have two qualities that most women lack. They are cocksure. They speak out with confidence, even when it's unwarranted. And they have Teflon baked into their fiber. When they're mistaken, when they get a critique that would devastate most women, the men don't take it personally. They bounce right along and keep going."[23]

The American Association of University Women study I discussed earlier supports Dr. Porter's assertion, demonstrating that when girls perform poorly in math, they internalize it as personal failure, whereas boys brush it off as a subject that was not useful. This internalization demonstrates something that I also touched on briefly earlier—the attitude that renowned psychologist Carol Dweck calls a *fixed mind-set.*[24]

A person with a fixed mind-set believes that she only has a "fixed amount of intelligence, a certain personality, and a certain moral character." According to Dweck, having a fixed mind-set "creates an urgency to prove yourself over and over. . . . It simply wouldn't do to look or feel deficient in these most basic characteristics."

Dweck's research shows that, over time, girls and boys develop different views about what they can accomplish, and that difference is often rooted in the way girls and boys are praised. Girls are frequently praised for being "good" or "smart" or "pretty" (that is, for their innate qualities), while boys are often praised for "trying hard" (that is, for their effort). Girls are told to be good girls and not to get their dresses dirty, while boys are told to play in the mud and be adventurous.

While these compliments from parents and loved ones are well-meaning, they are counterproductive and put an expectation on girls to believe in their labels. Many girls believe that they have to do well to prove they are smart. They start believing the media messages telling them to diet and wear makeup in order to prove they are beautiful. And when challenges arise, they play it safe in order to live up to their labels and to avoid being seen as failures.

The differing levels of self-confidence in boys and girls continue to impact women throughout their lives and even affect the ability of women to simply ask for what they need. Speaking up about what you want doesn't appear on any list of academic subjects or professional skills, yet it's a skill that can make an enormous difference in a girl's prospects for life.

"Just the prospect of asking is assertive," observes Nick Hahn:

> *It requires confidence, and there's an element of risk. You may ask for things and get turned down. So asking for things is an issue for girls. There's a good chance you'll fail. But you also might prevail. If you see asking as part of what you do, you can become good at it and go shoulder to shoulder with anyone.*[25]

Depending on the kind of environment you grow up in, being assertive and asking for what you want may seem almost impossible or may seem to be the most natural thing in the world. Graham Weston, chairman and CEO of Rackspace, reflects on this using an example from his own family life:

> *Recently my son told me about how he'd bought a thirty-dollar ticket to some event, then realized he couldn't go. Of course, he didn't want to waste the thirty dollars, but the ticket said "nonrefundable" on it. Still, he didn't take that for an answer. He called up the box office, explained the situation, and asked whether he could get his money back—and the manager at the other end of the line agreed to give him a refund.*
>
> *When I asked my son how he'd gotten the idea to do that, he said, "Dad, you taught us to ask for what we*

want." I never did it consciously. But I guess my kids grew up watching me behave that way, and they saw that it worked. So now it comes naturally to them.

If they'd grown up in a different kind of family, that's a lesson they might never have learned. It's certainly not something you learn in school. School isn't about making exceptions—it's about enforcing the rules. So in school, you're taught that asking for what you want is kind of rude. It's a problem for a lot of kids—and especially for girls.[26]

All too often, the battered sense of self-confidence that girls develop even before they start school persists through high school and college, and into their work lives. When the time comes for leaders to step forward—on the job, in the community, in politics, and in every setting—men are more likely to push themselves ahead, while women with greater talent tend to hang back and are often hesitant to ask for the resources they need to succeed.

Not only the women, but also society as a whole suffers profoundly as a result.

COMBATING THE PROBLEMS

Jason Seats is a tech entrepreneur and a partner at Techstars Ventures. Most important, he's the father of a daughter, Isla, and a son, Gus. Seats has done a lot of thinking about the gender gap in tech and categorizes gender biases in two buckets: biases that repel women from attempting STEM and entrepreneurial paths and biases that cause them to be unsuccessful within these paths.

The first bucket involves messages and language, and Seats describes it as " 'easyish' to quantify and fix—correcting folks to say 'women' instead of 'girls' when referring to adults; making sure that the marketing material for startups or tech jobs doesn't have all white males in the photos; teaching recruiters that job ads for 'expert rock star ninja programmers' repel many women candidates."

The second bucket is more insidious, unconscious, and opaque. "It has to do with individual behaviors and power structures," Seats explains:

> *People tend to choose other people to work with or promote who are most similar to them. Without correcting for that, a majority group in control turns into a super majority very quickly. A group of male executives running a company are extremely likely to put policies and patterns in place that will feel more familiar to people who are similar. It shouldn't be surprising that a male-dominated company is easier for a man to navigate politically than it is for a woman.*[27]

As Seats observes, changing people and their behavior is hard work that takes a long time. But many groups and individuals are working on the problem. The Girl Scouts is the original organization for empowering girls. While it once offered awards, badges, and patches mainly for typical "girl" activities, it has expanded to promote girls' STEM and innovation activities. In July 2017, the Girl Scouts announced a new batch of twenty-three badges dedicated to science and outdoor subjects.[28] Girl Scouts can now earn recognition for STEM-based activities like Design a Robot, Animal Habitats, Digital Photographer, Inventor, and the Model Car Design Challenge. Meanwhile, the Girl Scouts' classic cookie sales remain the most widespread entrepreneurial experience for girls in the United States.

Another group leading the battle for change is Girls Who Code. Since its start in 2012, it has brought relevant computer science experiences like summer immersion to the lives of tens of thousands of young girls nationwide to inspire them to pursue studies in technology and engineering.

Then there's the most visible, rollicking STEM event in the world, the Grace Hopper Celebration of Women in Computing, held annually since 2006. It now draws more than ten thousand women and six hundred presenters from more than fifty countries in a glorious exchange of ideas, inspirations, camaraderie, and entrepreneurial energy. It's where college students go to become part of the next wave of women to embark on STEM careers.

Still, groups like these are continuing to fight an uphill battle. The three forms of bias I've described are deeply intertwined and firmly embedded in the culture and mores of our society. It isn't hard to see how they work together in producing the female empowerment gap.

In a world where technology is driving most of the major changes in business, in economics, in lifestyles, and in society as a whole, the exclusion of women from science and math means that they are condemned to relative powerlessness. The scanty numbers of women in STEM fields are an underlying cause of the lack of women as business founders and leaders. With so many businesses today based on technological breakthroughs—and with the mathematical disciplines of economics, finance, and investing playing such a key role in the world of business—the exclusion of women from STEM leads almost inevitably to a lack of women in the ranks of corporate leaders.

And both of these trends are closely interwoven with the third problem—the lack of self-confidence that plagues so many women in our society. When you see relatively few role models who resemble you in the ranks of STEM leaders and business leaders, it's understandable that you will suffer from self-doubt and a sense of inadequacy. And the hesitancy and timidity that these feelings produce only make it more difficult for young women to break through the cultural barriers and assert themselves as potential leaders—a vicious cycle that perpetuates the second-class citizenship of women.

Through my research and my experiences, I have found that we must take a bottom-up approach and address this when girls are young. If we really want to create a culture change we must start by giving girls confidence and showing boys that girls are equally as capable.

Because these three problems are so tightly connected, tackling just one of them isn't likely to be effective if we want to close the female empowerment gap. Instead, a real solution must address all three, and do so in a way that transforms the vicious cycle into a virtuous cycle of self-reinforcing, positive change. That's the kind of solution I'll describe in Part Two of this book. It will serve as the foundation for a detailed, step-by-step recipe you can use to implement the solution in your own family, school, or community, which I'll provide in Part Three.

Part Two

The Solution

2

Daring, Risking, Growing:

The Entrepreneurial Spirit at School, at Work, in Life

THE CONCEPT OF ENTREPRENEURSHIP IS CRUCIAL TO CLOSING THE FEMALE empowerment gap and to our country's future in the global economy. To understand why, you need to know what I mean exactly by entrepreneurship.

Let's begin by looking at the story of Bri Connelly, a millennial (still in her twenties) who has fearlessly followed her passions and mapped one of the more remarkable entrepreneurial career stories I know.[1]

Connelly studied computer science at the University of Texas and was lucky enough to intern during her school years with three of the world's leading information technology companies—IBM, Apple, and Google. She also got to be part of a class project powered by Watson, the IBM supercomputer that is exploring the potential of artificial intelligence (and became famous in 2011 when it won a groundbreaking competition on the TV quiz show *Jeopardy!*). After graduating, she joined Google as an associate product manager, where she works on projects that include Gboard, Google's name for the keyboard it has created for its smartphone operating system.

It's an impressive high-tech resume that probably makes Connelly sound like a classic techie. But computer science wasn't on Connelly's radar as she was growing up in Portland, Oregon. Her father worked in software, and like most kids, she wanted to do something different than her parents. She was good at math and science, but she also loved reading, making short movies, and performing and recording music. She fantasized about being a rock star.

Above all, she was a dancer. At the age of three, she began dancing and never stopped. As she grew older, she joined a dance company and danced every day after school—often for three hours at a stretch—before turning to her homework. To accomplish this while leaving time for school, hanging out with friends, and the other things kids like to do, she developed time management skills that would rival those of any corporate executive.

Dance shaped her life. She learned to accept constructive criticism of the thousands of microfailures on the way to mastery. "Nothing is as bad as some of the things that are said during dance class," she recalls. "When your ballet teacher is yelling at you while you're looking at yourself in the mirror in a leotard, it's personal."

Dance helped Connelly learn to stretch her abilities and

challenge herself. "I looked up to the older girls in the dance studio," Connelly says, "and saw them do all these tricks. I would practice over and over again. Even if I didn't have a class, if there was an open studio, I would be there practicing that move that I couldn't do. Practicing and being able to be bad at those tricks in front of a room of girls made me less afraid to try things that I think I won't be good at. I learned not to say no just because I was afraid of things."

Competitive dance strengthens not only the body but also the brain, blending thoughts and sensations with muscle memory for peak performance. Neuroscientists tell us that dancers use and strengthen the sense of *proprioception*, a function centered in the cerebellum that guides the position and strength of a body in motion.

"When you're learning a routine, sometimes you have to learn it really fast," Connelly says. "You learn a two-minute routine in an hour. That ability for fast memorization still helps me today. It's a mental puzzle and it keeps your mind fully engaged. I find myself being really good at memorizing and remembering small details, and I think a lot of that ability comes from dance."

By the time Connelly left home for college, her cumulative time spent practicing dance had exceeded the magical number of ten thousand hours, which author Malcolm Gladwell identifies in his bestselling book *Outliers* as a key to attaining mastery of any difficult skill.[2] She also spent hundreds of hours in high school on social activities like student council and the drill team—and just a few hours on the single, one-semester computer class she took.

But having developed an array of powerful achievement-driving abilities—including self-discipline, drive, concentration, problem-solving talent, and sheer grit—Connelly was ready for the spark that would ignite her career aspirations. It turned out to be a movie—*The Social Network*, filmmaker Aaron Sorkin's 2010 story of Mark Zuckerberg and his founding of Facebook.

The movie reminded Connelly of the fun she'd had more than a decade earlier when she, like thousands of other girls, had connected with friends old and new by creating her own space on MySpace (the pioneering social network that would ultimately be displaced by Facebook). But more than that, she was inspired by the way the movie captured the excitement of creating something entirely new. "I thought, 'Wow, I want to be able to do that, too, whether it's starting a company, or just making an app or a website that people use—a cool project that involves lots of different skills. The best way was to get a degree in computer science.' "

Connelly figured that mastering computers would be relatively easy. Until college, she hadn't truly, utterly failed at anything. Even tough subjects had always been easy for her.

"There was a shock of going from being one of the smartest kids in your school to being what I interpreted as the dumbest kid at school. I was part of the honors program at UT [the University of Texas], so it was really tough. And I'd just started programming, while everyone else had started when they were twelve." And, of course, Connelly's classmates were overwhelmingly male.

Connelly flunked her first programming project and

went sobbing to her advisor, telling him she was going to drop her major. He advised her to stick with it for one more project. She did, and she failed that one, too. Connelly was sorely tempted to quit. Like so many women, she was suffering from what psychologists Pauline R. Clance and Suzanne A. Imes dubbed the *impostor syndrome*. Katty Kay and Claire Shipman, authors of *Womenomics*, describe the *impostor syndrome* as the deep-seated belief that you're a failure and fraud with no business even trying to succeed.

Again, Connelly's advisor convinced her to ride out her tears and to stay in for just "one more project." And somehow she found herself beginning to shake off the chains imposed by the impostor syndrome. "I began to realize that everyone else was doing badly, too," she recalls. "They just didn't tell me. Especially the boys would act like they knew everything, and if you failed a project, *you were so dumb*. But in reality, they were all failing their projects, too."

Within a semester, Connelly found her grounding force—the network of female role models, mentors, and colleagues who wanted to support her in her personal quest. She got involved in the group Women in Computer Science and became president of her university's local chapter. She traveled to Houston to attend the annual Grace Hopper Celebration of Women in Computing, where she saw thousands of women from around the world who, like her, were hoping to change the world through computing creativity.

In 2015, IBM invited students from ten universities, including the University of Texas at Austin, to "develop something cool" using genius computer Watson. That semester,

Connelly happened to be taking a class taught by the UT computing department chairman, Bruce Porter. She quickly found herself the only female participant on the Watson project and, just as quickly, becoming project leader. Connelly says that, even as a child, she was "a bossy little girl," the kind of negative characterization often used to describe girls who would be simply called "leaders" if they were boys. Now she had a chance to show her leadership skills without being faulted for them.

Her team studied different societal problems that they could solve with vision, algorithms, and software, and they settled on her original idea, "to do something that impacted people outside of our privileged technology world." They came up with a plan for using the tremendous intelligence of Watson to help low-income people to navigate the confusing array of social service bureaucracies to find the help they needed.

IBM flew each of the ten teams in the competition to New York, where the winning team would be announced and would receive $100,000 to fund its project in the form of a real startup business. It was Connelly's responsibility to choose the five students who would represent the UT team in New York. "I was nervous about seeming rude," she recalls, "so I made a Google poll and had everyone vote on the five hardest-working people." Luckily the vote matched her own choices.

Connelly honestly didn't know what to expect in New York. "UT was one of the few schools with a team that was all computer science majors. The other teams had designers, engineers, and business majors all working together. When we won the competition, we were shocked. It didn't sink in until later that night. We came back to our hotel room and were planning to go out and celebrate. But instead we just sat in a room together and thought, 'Wow, what are we going to do?' We went from being just students to founders of a funded startup with six figures in the bank."

Upon graduation from UT, Connelly was offered—and accepted—one of forty places in a highly selective Google class of new college graduates. Within the next five years, she hopes to be an entrepreneur running a startup business of her own, or, perhaps an "intrapreneur" within Google—a company employee charged with developing and launching new business ideas.

At its Silicon Valley corporate offices, Google encourages employees to spend 20 percent of their time on projects unrelated to their present work. For Connelly, the choice of how to spend that time was easy. She teaches a dance class for Google employees.

ENTREPRENEURSHIP—THE ART OF OPPORTUNITY

FOR ME, PEOPLE LIKE BRI CONNELLY EPITOMIZE ENTREPRENEURSHIP—NOT just in her current work at Google; not just as the leader of the Watson team at the University of Texas, creating a business idea that earned $100,000 in funding; but in her entrepreneurial mind-set and her relentless pursuit of opportunity.

Entrepreneurship is not just about starting a business.

It can happen in many contexts. It's about recognizing opportunities, asking questions, developing skills, taking calculated risks, and solving problems. An entrepreneur is someone who achieves more than other people because she is curious, high-energy, eager to explore the world, continually learning, and willing to make mistakes along the way. Perhaps above all, entrepreneurship is about courage—the courage you need to try new things, to challenge conventional wisdom, and to take the road less traveled.

If you've never worked in Silicon Valley or on Wall Street, you may think that entrepreneurship has nothing to do with you. Think again.

Have you ever taken on a challenging assignment—at school, at work, in a social group, in your local community, at the PTA or the Girl Scouts or your church—and figured out a way to make it work?

Have you ever conceived a new method for handling some aspect of your job and found a way to implement it, thereby improving customer service, saving time and money, or otherwise making things just a little better than before?

Have you ever brought together a committee or team to tackle a tough task and figured out how to get people to overcome their differences and work together for a common cause?

Have you ever come up with a surprising solution to a tricky problem that left other people feeling baffled?

Have you ever agreed to try something you never did before, knowing you'd have to experiment, make mistakes, and probably fail a number of times before discovering the winning formula?

If you've done any of these things, you may well have a touch of entrepreneurial genius—even if you've never written a business plan, raised a dollar of investment capital, or signed a payroll check. You've shown the ability to recognize the opportunity hiding in what others consider merely a problem—and found a way to convert that opportunity into an accomplishment. And that's what you have in common with those whom the world recognizes and admires as entrepreneurs, from Thomas Edison to Henry Ford, Estée Lauder to Bill Gates, Oprah Winfrey to Mark Zuckerberg, Martha Stewart to Arianna Huffington.

What's more, entrepreneurial skills like yours are increasingly being recognized as *the* skills required for success in today's increasingly challenging, fast-paced, unpredictable world. And not just in business, but everywhere.

Artists, writers, performers, designers, and other creative people must use the entrepreneurial mind-set to figure out how to create and market products and services that will delight audiences and turn them into willing customers.

Leaders in nonprofit organizations and government agencies must employ the spirit of entrepreneurship to find ways to streamline their operations, provide meaningful help to people and communities in need, and accomplish great things on limited budgets.

Teachers, professors, academics, and scholars must develop the entrepreneurial ability to find new ways to use, share, and communicate the knowledge they have so that more and more people will recognize its value.

Doctors, nurses, therapists, and others in the healing professions must become entrepreneurial in seeking out innovative methods of bringing cures to the suffering, combining high-tech efficiency with high-touch compassion.

In a world awash with serious problems—income inequality, climate change, political conflict, global terrorism, rampant unemployment, crumbling infrastructure, racial discord, health care disparities, and so many more—we're desperately in need of people who can bring the spirit of entrepreneurship to *every* walk of life. We need millions of young people with the drive, creativity, and grit of Bri Connelly to help us tackle these challenges and develop the innovative approaches we need to solve them.

ENTREPRENEURSHIP AND THE GROWTH MIND-SET

WHEN KIDS—ESPECIALLY GIRLS—ARE EXPOSED TO ENTREPRENEURIAL thinking, a profound change takes place. They become more aware of opportunities around them. They begin thinking more critically and creatively. Most important, they become more confident and adventurous in their ability to solve problems and tackle challenges.

I've already suggested some of the key traits that make up the entrepreneurial character. At VentureLab, we help girls learn to embody the following eleven traits:

- Courageous—recognizing that they can make great things happen if they dare to step outside their comfort zones.
- Unafraid to fail—able to redefine failure as an opportunity to learn and a launchpad for the next success or discovery.
- Persistent—characterized by the quality that bestselling author Angela Duckworth has called *grit,* a powerful blend of passion and resilience that enables people to overcome obstacles and achieve their goals.
- Opportunity-seeking—continually thinking about things that go wrong in society and in the world at large, and looking for ways to make them go right, viewing problems as challenges waiting to be met.
- Problem-solving—actively exploring creative solutions to the challenges they see around them.
- Curious—continually asking "Why?" and "What if?" and seeking new ways of learning and doing.
- Empathetic—able to understand and share the feelings of others, and ready to think about their needs and problems.
- Optimistic—prone to focus on the positive potential in any situation rather than emphasizing the negatives and the possibility of failure.
- Resourceful—able and willing to "do a lot with a little," finding ingenious solutions to problems based on whatever is available, without becoming discouraged over the lack of resources.

- Adaptable—ready to change directions and try new approaches while working on a project rather than rigidly clinging to an idea that appears flawed or incomplete.
- Equipped with a growth mind-set—aware that they have the power to stretch their brains and sharpen their minds, which enables them to achieve practically anything.

Think about this list of eleven traits. Doesn't it capture some of the qualities that you have used when achieving any important success in your own life? And doesn't it describe the attitudes and behaviors you would like to see in the young people you care about—including your own daughters, granddaughters, students, friends, and any others whose lives you touch?

Notice, too, that these entrepreneurial traits are relevant to so much more than just launching a business. These are traits that underlie success in practically every area of life. A young woman with these traits will be equipped to do well in the world of the twenty-first century no matter what path she chooses. She might start a new company, like those we commonly refer to as entrepreneurs. But she might also become an exceptionally valuable contributor to an existing business, or an unusually talented and productive artist, nonprofit manager, government employee, researcher, scientist, teacher, physician, lawyer, or anything else you can imagine—as well as a deeply engaged, informed, and caring citizen. That's why I believe that bringing these eleven traits to the young women in our world is an essential element of solving the female empowerment gap.

One of the most important qualities on this list of eleven entrepreneurial traits is the idea of *the growth mind-set*—the idea formulated and described by the brilliant psychologist Carol Dweck that I mentioned in Chapter One.[3]

The growth mind-set is the opposite of *the fixed mind-set*—a set of attitudes, assumptions, and beliefs that all too many people, including young women, share. The fixed mind-set says that a person's intelligence, personality traits, emotional attributes, and abilities are basically set in stone, determined and limited by some combination of genetic inheritance and childhood influences. Children who are trapped in the fixed mind-set may think of themselves as "bad at math," "not smart," "lousy at chemistry"—and they believe that their shortcomings are innate and unchangeable. Even children who believe they are intelligent can be resigned to being failures in certain subjects.

The fixed mind-set is often reinforced by environmental, familial, or cultural forces. A teacher who classifies and categorizes students as either "bright" or "dumb," or who lowers the standards of achievement for kids who she assumes are doomed to failure, helps to spread the fixed mind-set. So does a parent who projects his or her own problems in school or disappointments in life onto a child, discouraging attempts to break the mold. And so do misguided messages from the media or from artifacts like the talking Barbie doll from the 1980s that told little girls, "Math class is tough!"

By contrast, the growth mind-set recognizes the reality that human behaviors, attitudes, and abilities are *not* fixed and unchangeable. In fact, they are capable of change, growth, and development to a degree that scientists are only now beginning to fully appreciate.

The growth mind-set concept incorporates what neuroscientists have been discovering about the ability of our brains to grow and evolve over time—a trait sometimes referred to as *plasticity*. Here is how Professor Lise Eliot of Rosalind Franklin University explains the concept:

> *[P]lasticity [is] an admittedly ugly term used to describe the very beautiful fact that the brain actually changes in response to its own experience. . . . Every physical feature of the human nervous system . . . responds to life experiences and is continually remodeled to adapt to them. . . .*
>
> *Plasticity is the basis of all learning as well as the best hope for recovery after a brain injury. And in childhood, the brain is far more plastic, or malleable, than it is at any later stage of life—wiring itself in large measure according to the experiences in which it is immersed from prenatal life through adolescence.*
>
> *Simply put, your brain is what you do with it.*[4]

People who understand and internalize the truth of the growth mind-set develop a different attitude toward themselves and their own abilities. They realize that any flaws or weaknesses they may have (or that others may perceive in them) are subject to change. When they make a mistake or fail at something, they don't consider it evidence of their own immutable limitations; instead, they view it as an opportunity to learn, make adjustments, and improve, with the hope of succeeding next time.

And this attitude tends to be self-fulfilling. Those who adopt the growth mind-set usually find that it's correct—because the optimism, energy, and determination that they bring to life and its challenges help to bring about the long-term success they foresee.

The big question, then, is this: Can children be induced to adopt the growth mind-set?

Carol Dweck and her colleagues set out to answer that question. They wanted to develop an intervention that they hoped could shift—maybe even transform—a fixed mind-set into a growth mind-set. So they devised an eight-week series of workshops that taught middle school children study skills, the workings of the brain, and how the brain can become stronger when they tackle challenging tasks. In other words, children learned that *their brains can change,* and *they can get smarter.* Meantime, a similar control group of students were taught only study skills.

The results of this experiment were astonishing. Children in the control group continued the downward decline in math grades that the majority of students experience in middle schools. But students who learned about how the brain can change earned better grades throughout the remaining school year by a factor of 0.3. In simple grade language, that means a student who might have made a C-plus now made a B-minus, and an A-minus became a solid A. Even months after the specific memories of the lessons had dimmed, children continued to apply what they'd learned about the potential of their own brains.

The lesson is clear: Students who learn that intelligence is not fixed, that they can grow their abilities with effort, not only perform better and become smarter, but can also become tougher, "grittier." The growth mind-set is about believing in oneself, even in the face of failures and setbacks.

The growth mind-set is a crucial component of the entrepreneurial personality. In fact, *an entrepreneurial mind-set is an accelerated growth mind-set*. After all, what entrepreneur has ever accomplished something new without believing it is at least possible? The growth mind-set is about *possibilities*—and that's why it caps our list of the most important entrepreneurial traits.

ENTREPRENEURSHIP AS A NATIONAL CHALLENGE

YOU MIGHT THINK THAT ENTREPRENEURSHIP IS SO CENTRAL TO CAPITALism, that the United States—the world's largest and most powerful capitalist economy—must lead the world in teaching entrepreneurial skills to youth. Unfortunately, that's not the case.

Some traditionally trained educators and school administrators are only vaguely aware of the importance of entrepreneurial traits in achieving life success. Others, who understand the value of entrepreneurial skills, bemoan the fact that standard school curriculums leave little or no time for teachers to focus on them. Under political and parental pressure to do more with less, and already forced by budgetary constraints to reduce the time and resources dedicated to "peripheral" activities like music and art, school officials are understandably resistant to any proposal that requires devoting more classroom time to subjects beyond the traditional basics. Good intentions have led many American educators to obsess about raising standardized test scores—sacrificing broader learning, and still failing to meet testing targets.

As a result, we've been overlooking a key insight—the fact that entrepreneurial education can *enhance* student performance in every field of study. It gives students reasons to aspire, improves their self-confidence, stimulates their curiosity, teaches them to fail wisely, and makes all the other subjects—including math and science—more relevant.

The fact is that there are educational systems elsewhere in the world that are already incorporating this reality into their school programs.

Consider the modest country of Finland. With fewer than 5.5 million people, its population is smaller than that of New York City. Yet Finland is one of the world's most successful entrepreneurial economies—as well as a nation that consistently ranks near the top in student achievement. Perhaps it's no coincidence that Finland has set a national goal of making entrepreneurial skills a core competence of its citizens. Entrepreneurial learning is embedded in Finland's educational system. No one complains that entrepreneurial education is taking time away from teaching basic skills. The Finns understand that entrepreneurial learning is not in competition with other subjects—rather, it complements and enriches them.

Finland became serious about entrepreneurial education when its economy crashed in the 1990s. National leaders recognized that they needed to raise more young people who were innovative, resilient, proactive, growth-oriented, and self-reliant. In 1994, entrepreneurship education was introduced as a new theme in Finnish school curriculums. Entrepreneurial skills were seen as a lifeline—not just for young people, but for the country.

The shift in direction received a serious test in 2007, when Finland's economy suffered a serious blow. Nokia, a respected maker of cell phones, accounted for about 4 percent of Finland's economy. Its business was going well until the day Apple unveiled its game-changer, the iPhone. Watching Steve Jobs's live demo of the device, Nokia executives were dismayed. They quickly recognized it would be impossible for Nokia to catch up with the iPhone and futile to try. It was as if a genetically modified horse with unprecedented strength and speed had entered the Kentucky Derby. No jockey could close the gap.

But scrappy Finland used Nokia's demise to further propel the country's entrepreneurial initiatives. Fortunately, the groundwork had been laid, with nearly a generation of Finns already schooled in entrepreneurism. Quickly, Nokia and Finland went to work helping Nokia employees spin out new entrepreneurial ventures, finding capital and talent to support the launch of many new businesses. So far, former Nokia employees have produced three hundred startups, ranging from Valkee, maker of a bright-light headset to combat the winter blues, to ZenRobotics, which automates recycling. The startup you've surely encountered is Rovio Entertainment, maker of the worldwide sensation Angry Birds and a supporter of Finland's Startup Sauna, an accelerator program that helps to jumpstart the growth of new businesses, with coworking space in Helsinki and connections to Silicon Valley.[5]

That's Finland's story. The story of the United States, unfortunately, is one in which entrepreneurship has been neglected as a school subject. As a result, US economic performance has lagged. In the words of Jim Clifton, CEO of Gallup, whose company closely watches social trends, "True entrepreneurs are rare—and getting rarer. Yet it is crucial to our economy and national security that we find them. Without a growing entrepreneurial economy, there are no new good jobs. . . . We are focused on innovation. *But what we need are entrepreneurs* to turn innovations into products, revenue, jobs, and economic growth."[6]

Statistics bear out Clifton's warning. In fact, US entrepreneurship as measured by business startups has recently neared a forty-year low. In 2014, the last year for which census data are currently available, just 452,835 firms were launched in the United States. By contrast, during every year from the late 1970s to the mid-2000s, between five and six hundred thousand new companies were born.[7] Our shortfall in creating innovative new companies helps to explain lagging job growth, slow expansion of gross domestic product

(GDP), and stagnant individual and family incomes. In short, when entrepreneurship declines, everyone suffers.

Yet there is plenty of room for hope. An untapped reservoir of future entrepreneurial talent exists in our midst—the millions of girls who could become part of the movement, as Bri Connelly has done. Developing entrepreneurial thinking in our daughters is crucial for our country's economic future. We can't lead the world with our girls relegated to the sidelines. We need them pushing their way onto the playing fields of business, technology, and problem-solving in every arena with a growth mind-set, knowing that their creativity, hard work, and perseverance will make a difference.

TACKLING THE THREE-PART PROBLEM

PERHAPS YOU'RE BEGINNING TO SEE WHY ENTREPRENEURIAL EDUCATION can be the key to solving the three-part problem I outlined in the first chapter—the interlocking challenges of attracting more girls to study science, math, and technology; of encouraging women to pursue careers as business leaders; and of combating the syndrome of low self-esteem and lack of self-confidence on the part of girls and women.

Many good people and organizations have been working to tackle one or another of these challenges. But surprisingly few have tried to address all three prongs of the dilemma.

As I mentioned in Chapter One, the Girl Scouts is the original growth mind-set organization for girls interested in STEM. The Girl Scouts Research Institute (GSRI) is dedicated to "elevating the voices of girls on issues that matter to them and their futures" and dispelling myths. In a study titled *Generation STEM*, they report:

- Three-quarters of high school girls are interested in STEM subjects.
- African American and Hispanic girls share the widespread interest in STEM but need more support and exposure to take full advantage of their opportunities.
- Eighty-five percent of high school girls like puzzles and solving problems, while 83 percent like working on hands-on science projects.
- Ninety-two percent believe they are smart enough to have a career in STEM, and nearly 100 percent believe they can do whatever boys can do.[8]

These are encouraging data points. They suggest that today's young women are trying hard to overcome the cultural and social barriers that have discouraged past generations of girls from pursuing their interests in science, technology, and math. And there are a number of organizations working to help them—not just the Girl Scouts but others like the National Science Foundation, whose ADVANCE initiative makes "transformational grants" to help universities develop programs to support women in STEM, as well as the two groups I've already mentioned, Girls Who Code and the Grace Hopper Celebration of Women in Computing.

But as I've argued, STEM alone is not the solution to the three-pronged challenge women face. It must be combined with entrepreneurship and self-confidence to produce the change we seek.

A few groups have been working on the entrepreneurial piece of the puzzle. One example is Prepared 4 Life, a Houston-based nonprofit organization founded by entrepreneur Michael Holthouse. It's dedicated to revolutionizing the way children learn by teaching entrepreneurship, especially to at-risk youth. Holthouse has also launched National Lemonade Day, an annual event that provides step-by-step instructions for children to start, own, and operate a lemonade stand with a "third-third-third" model of "spend some, save some, share some." Dozens of cities have joined Lemonade Day, and Google for Entrepreneurs is now partnering with Lemonade Day to develop an online curriculum for children around the world to become entrepreneurs for a day, and—who knows?—maybe for life.

Other organizations with entrepreneurship training programs for students include BizWorld.org, the National Foundation for Teaching Entrepreneurship, and the Grow Your Own Business Challenge. Even the mainstream media have gotten into the act. ABC's hit television series *Shark Tank* gave ten-year-old entrepreneur Mikaila Ulmer a platform to help her market her BeeSweet Lemonade (more on Mikaila later in this book).

It's encouraging to see the work of groups and people like these. They've produced some good results that illustrate the importance of entrepreneurship for young people—including young women. But combining STEM and entrepreneurship with lessons and experiences that inculcate self-confidence is the final, crucial step in solving the three-pronged problem of the female empowerment gap.

Because entrepreneurship is about seeing opportunities and creating solutions to problems, it has a natural connection to STEM. In today's world, technology, science, and math are at the heart of many innovations—not just in business but in government, education, the nonprofit sphere, and practically every other life arena. As a result, girls (and others) who embrace the entrepreneurial approach to life often develop a powerful curiosity about science, technology, engineering, and math, even when they may have felt intimidated or bored about STEM in the past. Suddenly they realize that math formulas, scientific theories, and technological details aren't just facts to be memorized for an exam. They are also powerful tools that anyone can use to create innovations that benefit real people.

A lasting solution to the challenges facing today's girls has to be built around an approach that emphasizes the natural, creative connections among STEM, entrepreneurship, and self-confident female leadership. In the next chapter, I'll outline an approach that brings all three pieces of the puzzle together. It's one that I've personally developed and experimented with through my VentureLab program, and one that you can apply yourself—in your home, your school, your community organization, or anywhere you spend time with your own daughter or with any girl or girls you care about.

3

The Buzz at VentureLab:

Giving Girls the Tools They Need to Transform Their Lives and Our World

As I learned about the three-part problem that today's young women face, I realized that a three-part solution is necessary. My contribution to the solution was to create VentureLab—a nonprofit that provides kids with an entrepreneurial mind-set and skill set designed to help them learn and apply math and science techniques to solve real-world challenges. In the process, they achieve successes that build their self-confidence and help them develop the growth mind-set that will open the doors to achievement in every area of their lives. Our mission is to build a movement to spread the entrepreneurial mind-set around the world and to empower youth, and girls in particular, with the tools needed to become the next generation of innovators and change makers.

VentureLab was launched in 2013 in San Antonio, Texas,

with a series of Maker, Gamer, Girl Startup, Youth Startup, and High School Startup camps specifically designed to teach girls ages five to eighteen how to be inventors and entrepreneurs. Within the first summer, parents began seeing changes in their daughters' confidence and knowledge base; some began asking whether their sons could attend as well. I opened co-ed camps the following year, and I liked the idea that we would be teaching the boys that girls are equally capable.

By 2015, schoolteachers and administrators who had heard about us began asking for our style of entrepreneurial education in their schools. I worked with elementary and high school teachers to develop a suite of courses for teachers to use in schools. In 2016 and 2017, we were honored to be invited by UNESCO, the United Nations agency dedicated to educational, scientific, and cultural development, to lead courses in the TeachHer program, which centers on encouraging girls to pursue careers in science, technology, engineering, arts and design, and math (STEAM).

Since VentureLab's founding, we've taught nearly ten thousand students how to be inventors and entrepreneurs through our camps and classes. We've trained over six hundred teachers in our entrepreneurial education methods, and some thirty-five schools across Texas and California have implemented our programs. More than one-fifth of VentureLab students use the ideas they develop in our classes to start real businesses—in fact, they've already raised more than $265,000 in capital to support their fledgling companies. We've also developed free online youth entrepreneurship programs for parents to use at home and for teachers to use in school, after-school, or summer programs. Currently parents and teachers in more than forty-five countries are using our programs to teach kids.

The process of designing, building, and expanding VentureLab has been quite an adventure for me. And the most satisfying and rewarding aspect of the story has been seeing the difference that entrepreneurial training can make in the lives of girls from all kinds of backgrounds.

Imagine for a moment the life of a destitute teenage mother, still a child herself yet forced to struggle on her own against abuse, neglect, and prejudice. When a group of these young moms living at Seton Home in San Antonio attended a VentureLab camp, they began with such low self-esteem that you could see it in the way they walked—their bodies hunched over, their eyes cast down, their voices hesitant and barely audible. Asked what they wanted to do with their lives and how they hoped to support themselves and their children, they could only mention menial jobs: hotel maid, fast-food worker. So what happened in the course of their three weeks with us was remarkable.

As part of their entrepreneurial training, one team of girls identified a pet problem they all faced—having just one pair of shoes, making it impossible to match their footwear with the rest of their outfit. In a brainstorming session, they came up with a possible solution: sandals with interchange-able straps in different colors. Simply talking about their ideas infused them with an initial boost of confidence.

As the project evolved, it became increasingly apparent that Norma, one of the members of the team, was a natural leader—though neither she nor the people around her had ever realized it. During the third week of camp, the young moms had to present their work to an audience of fellow campers—their first-ever experience of speaking in public. When the education coordinator at Seton Home came unannounced to watch Norma practice her presentation—and nail every point with clarity and style—she shook her head in disbelief. "That can't be Norma," she declared. "That's a different girl."

Later that year, when Seton Home held its annual gala, Norma addressed the gathering with elegance and ease. A few months later, we weren't surprised when we got the news that Norma had won a college scholarship.

Norma's story illustrates the extraordinary power of entrepreneurial education to transform the attitudes of a young person. Research has shown that when students begin to develop entrepreneurial skills at a young age, they become accustomed to expanding their brains and forming new neural synapses in response to challenges and problems. In other words, they develop the growth mind-set that I explained in Chapter Two. They also learn to employ what's called the *curiosity cycle,* discovering how to learn about anything and everything simply by asking questions that fascinate them and then taking steps to discover the answer—building foundations of knowledge on which they can expand as they follow their curiosity. All in all, they learn what it takes to achieve mastery in any field, in the process developing the entrepreneurial traits that help to increase their chances of long-term success.

At VentureLab, we believe all girls should follow their passions, whether in music or business, art, technology, education, or science, and be brave enough to overcome obstacles no matter where they arise. The spirit of entrepreneurship is relevant in all these fields. As we've seen, entrepreneurship isn't just about founding companies. It's about devising strategies to solve problems, make connections, serve markets, and achieve great things. A musician who figures out how to connect with appreciative audiences is using entrepreneurial skills. So is a doctor who creates a successful practice providing care to an underserved community . . . an artist who builds an online gallery to market innovative works . . . a teacher who uses unconventional activities to spark curiosity in her students—all are entrepreneurs in their own way.

This is the premise that underlines everything we do at VentureLab. We are demonstrating that entrepreneurial education holds the key to sparking girls' interest in engineering, math, and technology—and, more important, that it also is the best way, bar none, of developing girls who are confident, courageous, and persistent. We want to empower girls to do anything they desire, while recognizing that, in today's world, practically everyone needs to have a basic level of comfort with technology. We help girls achieve this combination of entrepreneurial skills with technological savvy by:

- Making STEM subjects real and relevant as girls learn to think like entrepreneurs about subjects that matter to them.

- Encouraging curiosity, perseverance, and grit, important traits in entrepreneurship, science, and technology as well as in practically every other field of endeavor.
- Providing opportunities for girls to learn from failures and become wiser each time, as successful entrepreneurs do.
- Introducing career possibilities in fields that girls might not otherwise even consider, helping them picture themselves as engineers, computer scientists, technology leaders, and entrepreneurs while visualizing their own success—a crucial development practice known as *self-casting*.

Virtually every product and service our teams of budding entrepreneurs imagine involves some form of science, technology, engineering, or math, so stepping into those STEM fields is natural and necessary. From a new kind of fashion accessory to a scientist's tool, many of the product prototypes the VentureLab participants dream up are programmed and produced on a 3-D printer.

We have now taught entrepreneurial skills and concepts to thousands of VentureGirls. We help girls learn to look around their worlds and notice problems, snags, or everyday processes that could go better. We ask "What if?" questions repeatedly, pressing to break down mental silos. We encourage girls to stretch their imaginations, allowing room for their gut feelings and intuitions as well as logic.

Then we encourage brainstorming about solutions and zeroing in on promising ideas. Teams of girls learn to design and create a product or service prototype, which may be as simple as a sketch or an outline on paper, or as elaborate as a full-blown model of a usable product. They learn to conduct research by asking friends and family for their feedback on the prototype. They follow through with their best solutions to challenges raised, and they learn to make smart decisions about pricing, promotion, and distribution. They present and sell their solutions to an audience, usually of friends and parents.

These girls aren't just inspired—their transformation is inspiring!

THE SEVEN CORE BELIEFS ON WHICH VENTURELAB IS BUILT

- Entrepreneurship Is for Everyone
- Potential Is Universal
- Failure Creates Opportunity
- Diversity Powers Innovation
- Empathy Fuels Collaboration
- Impractical Is Not Impossible
- Learning Is Limitless

FROM CALMING FEATHERS TO DOGGY BOOTIES—THE VENTURELAB EXPERIENCE

AT VENTURELAB, WE BELIEVE THAT GIRLS SHOULD BE ENCOURAGED TO have an entrepreneurial mind-set—and the best way to model that attitude and to let our girls experience it is by giving them a chance to play the part of real-life entrepreneurs. Here are a handful of stories that illustrate how we make that happen.

One group of five- and six-year-olds in a weeklong VentureLab summer camp decided that their project would be to make and sell bracelets. They used Venture Bucks, our class currency, to purchase pipe cleaners, beads, and glittery trinkets from the in-class store. By noon on day three, they had made several beaded bracelets in bright colors as prototypes, and they felt proud of their work.

Now the girls realized that they would have to stand in front of an audience of parents and friends to present their bracelets. It meant they had a serious problem to solve: How could they calm their fears and anxieties enough to talk to an audience? How could they do it without succumbing to tears?

They went back to the store with their remaining ten Venture Bucks. They bought a small sack of colored feathers and incorporated them into the bracelet design. The feathers weren't just striking additions; they were "calming feathers" that they could touch to calm their fears. Each girl wore a bracelet during the final presentation. Now their prospective buyers weren't just purchasing fuchsia, cobalt, or purple bracelets. These bracelets had calming powers that the girls demonstrated right then and there, touching the feathers at their wrists in front of a roomful of incredulous parents and siblings.

Afterward, one father said he simply had no idea that his daughter had the capabilities he'd seen her exhibit in those moments.

One middle school participant—I'll call her Rhonda—loved to bake. Her group chose to work on the problem she threw into the mix, that baking leads to eating, and cakes and cupcakes are not exactly the healthiest food choices. It was weighing on her mind, since her parents—and many others—were rightly starting to focus on fitness and health. Rhonda's group wondered: Could they solve the problem by developing healthier recipes for baking? They came up with Fit Cakes, cupcakes with added protein and icing made from low-fat yogurt.

This group had the added advantage of attending the Anne Frank Inspire Academy, an unusual charter school in San Antonio with a maker architecture and approach: learning studios instead of classrooms, student-directed learning, facilitators instead of teachers, and no factory-model bell schedule. Many of the girls already had a sure-footed confidence—yet, for most, this was their first contact with the entrepreneurial process. Translating a good idea into something tangible and marketable was a new experience. They came up with prototype recipes that they could bake at home at night and deliver the next morning for taste tests. They developed ingredient labels, packaging, website marketing, and presentations they could use to sell the goods. In fact, Fit Cakes became the fastest-selling product on the final day of VentureLab.

Sometimes a VentureLab student strikes out on her or his own. A third grader named José (one of the boys who participates alongside our girls) imagined a backpack that would help him with the challenge of keeping organized. He called it the Fun Pack. Our instructor observed José with a pouty look staring out a window, his group having chosen to work on other ideas. What was the matter? "I want to do it by myself," he said. The instructor told him he had one week to pull it together and prove he could do it alone.

He made two identical prototypes, one to take home and show his mom to get her feedback. He made a drawstring bag from blue fabric and used pale blue duct tape to attach pockets and labels for such cargo as Pokemon cards. Before long, José was on cloud nine, with the other students watching his progress. On pitch day, he brought his mother and grandmother, who were proud to witness and cheer his demonstration. At its close, he displayed a poster thanking all of the teachers. From day one to that final day, José was thoroughly engaged in the process of product designing, testing, and learning from failure, and before he left that day, he straightened and cleaned the room with an abundant joyful energy. Best of all, José's classmates were as proud and supportive of him as they were of themselves.

Or take another student, a young girl named Olivia, whose problem involved her dog. His paws would get painfully burned when he walked on the blacktop in the blazing

Texas sun. Her team chose a different problem, but Olivia didn't give up on her idea. She enrolled in the next camp session so she could work on her idea.

This time, to convince her fellow team members of the urgency of the problem, she involved them in a visceral way. She led them out into the parking lot, then urged, "Kneel down and put your hands on the blacktop." After three to five seconds, they each cried out in pain.

"Now imagine how your dog feels when you take him out for a walk on a summer afternoon!" Olivia said. The passion of this calm, reserved, quiet girl ignited a drive to solve the problem for the dogs of San Antonio. She and her teammates went on to design, make, and sell little padded boots to protect dogs' feet—a new product dreamed up by a team of girls to better the lives of their pets.

Financial literacy is part of entrepreneurial learning. We don't start class with a bucket of materials. We start instead by investing in the students. It's their first-ever business loan, one they don't have to repay. Groups begin with an initial investment of one hundred Venture Bucks, a currency honored nowhere else, but that can buy a great deal in the class store. Determining how to spend their seed money can take the better part of a day as students realize their resources are limited, and they need to conserve in the event that their first prototypes are catastrophic failures—which happens. You hear, "Do we really *need* this colored paper?" If a group wants to use the 3-D printer, they'll need to allocate ten Venture Bucks for the materials fee. Sometimes they'll find items on sale that can stretch their budget. As much as possible, spending and budgeting require real-world decision-making.

Parents of VentureLab participants report that their children who once didn't like working with numbers are now doing better in math. They've realized that math is useful in real-world activities: for calculating product dimensions, managing a production budget, and figuring out how much money they will make—or lose, if they don't incorporate efficiencies into the production process. They've learned the meaning of costs, revenue, and profit margins.

Many parents call us after the VentureLab class comes to a close, saying, "I don't know what has happened, but my kid's grades have gone up!" We know what happened: Their child has gained a powerful motivation to count and calculate. While the kids think they are playing, we've effectively tricked them into learning.

Children learn that a different set of rules apply in entrepreneurial skills class. To begin with, they make the rules, whether it is not speaking when others are talking, letting ideas flow without criticism during brainstorming, or the overarching "have fun." The children are in charge, and instead of being told what to do, they have *agreed* on what to do. VentureLab offers one of the few classrooms where kids have the autonomy and responsibility of being in charge. Middle school teachers have told us that they can see a shift in their classrooms when VentureLab kids are present—fewer disruptions and faster work, with the responsibility for solutions subtly shifted to their students.

When I began VentureLab, I hadn't anticipated that students would want to repeat the class or camp—but many do, either to continue to work on their product idea or to branch out. Returning students are generally savvier, more supportive of their teammates, and likelier to build more prototypes to sell on pitch day. Some of the revenue records—more than two hundred dollars in product sales—are set by these returning students.

On the first day of class, *entrepreneur* and *entrepreneurial* are words many students have never spoken. But on the final day, they can freely say them and spell them and have proven to themselves that they *can think* like an entrepreneur—curiously, creatively, expansively, and resiliently. It just takes practicing the new mind-set they've learned.

Entrepreneurial education also exposes kids and families to a new way of thinking and to a new world of opportunities. One group of girls from Highlands High School in San Antonio came to VentureLab for a three-day intensive camp on a full scholarship. Most of the girls said they hadn't been thinking about applying for college, and when we asked about entrepreneurship as a career choice, they said it was not for them.

As we do with other groups, we then asked them about problems they'd like to solve. They began to identify everyday problems in their lives, like forgetting to brush their teeth, making it to school on time, having food to eat for lunch, or having school supplies. By the second day, the girls began to work on solutions. One girl—I'll call her Trisha—said she needed help with her homework. Trisha began to prototype and design a website and app that would match students up with other students to help with tutoring. At the end of the third day, she proudly presented her prototype to an audience—including her parents, who'd had no idea about the kind of project their daughter had embarked upon. After the presentation, Trisha's parents—practically in tears—profusely thanked the VentureLab team for helping their daughter unleash her potential. As for Trisha, she announced she was planning to apply to college.

ENTREPRENEURIAL LIFE SKILLS AS A CORE COMPETENCE

ONE OF THE MOST FAR-REACHING CHANGES WE CAN MAKE FOR OUR CHILDREN and their future is to establish entrepreneurial life skills as a core competence for all students beginning as young as kindergarten and continuing through high school.

What changes when students develop entrepreneurial skills at a young age? They learn that they can grow their brains, forming new synapses and abilities just by learning new things. They develop a mind-set that makes learning a way to strengthen and enhance their potential. They learn to employ the "curiosity cycle," building foundations of knowledge on which they can expand as they follow their curiosity. They discover what it takes to achieve mastery in any field.

Finland's tremendous success as an entrepreneurial nation emanated from the conscious decision by schools, government, and the private sector that success in the global economy demands entrepreneurial skills on the part of all citizens. Surely the United States can achieve what Finland has achieved—citizens with an entrepreneurial skill set that will help them achieve their potential in any endeavor, preparing them for a future in which the only constant may be change.

To accomplish this, schools need to teach entrepreneurial life skills. You can help to make this happen. Find fellow advocates to visit with your local school administrators to ask for courses that teach entrepreneurial skills. Use this book to help make your case. And be persistent—you are advocating a paradigm shift in the way we think about school, and that kind of change does not happen with a single attempt.

Because the most effective entrepreneurial learning is project-based, entrepreneurial lessons can also be incorporated into all kinds of classes. It's easy to imagine, for example:

- A biology class that analyzes environmental or health problems that science has the potential to solve.
- A language class that identifies translation challenges that a student armed with computer tools could tackle.
- A physical education class that uses fast-paced team activities to challenge and exercise the brain.
- An art class that includes the use of new technologies—3-D printers, for example—to create new forms of self-expression.

Why do some young women persevere and succeed?

What I see is this: The women who stick it out are different. They are more determined, more conscious of their struggles, and more inventive about getting the help they need. They cast themselves in a successful future and build the bridges to get there.

They don't opt for "easy." Like Bri Connelly, the young ballet dancer who found her way to a leadership role at Google, they seek out like-minded spirits, cultivate friendships, and address setbacks with renewed energy and determination. They can imagine themselves jumping the hurdles, feeling more confident and empowered with each step toward success.

Most important, however, a girl doesn't have to be born this way. These traits can be learned and nurtured. Entrepreneurial projects provide hands-on practice that build these strengths and prepare girls for the trials and errors that lie ahead in life. A girl who has experience bouncing back after failures and persisting in her pursuits can adapt to all kinds of challenges. She has a growth mind-set, knowing her brain and abilities can grow. She'll admit when she's in over her head and needs help—whether she turns to a mentor, her big sister, a classmate, or the inspiration of a role model.

One reason I love teaching entrepreneurship is that there are built-in opportunities to introduce role models in the curriculum, even to bring them to class. Nothing tops seeing a woman in charge for inspiring young women to imagine themselves as future technology leaders and innovators.

I encourage girls to be themselves, to find and feel their confidence, to work as teams, bolstering their strengths, to express and sell their ideas, to find their role models and mentors, to cast themselves in a future that captures their imaginations. After all, an entrepreneur is someone who believes she has a better idea, something that people will want—so she has reason to persevere.

You've seen in this chapter that entrepreneurial education, like the teaching we do at VentureLab, has the ability to transform the lives of girls, opening up doors of opportunity they can take advantage of, wherever life may lead them. But it's not necessary for a girl to attend VentureLab to get the benefit of this approach.

Next, in Part Three of this book, I'll show how you can create your own entrepreneurial curriculum at home or in your community and have fun turning the girls you love into VentureGirls!

Part Three

How to Raise a VentureGirl

4

Help Her Start Her Entrepreneurial Adventure

At VentureLab, students get to act out the stages of imagining and launching a real-life business. The goal is *not* to turn every VentureLab participant into a business founder. Instead, it's to let them all experience the creative challenge and fun of thinking about problems, devising solutions, and working out ways to turn those solutions into realities. These are skills they'll be able to use in later life no matter what kinds of careers they may choose to pursue. And they've been proven to work for countless girls and women all around the world, in practically every walk of life.

Fortunately, girls of every age can participate in their own entrepreneurial adventure whether or not they have a chance to attend a VentureLab class or camp. We've developed a curriculum that has nine universal steps—the nine steps of the entrepreneurial process. This method of teaching can be carried out wherever you may live, no matter what else you may be doing—during the school year, on weekends and evenings, over the summer holiday, or whenever. Girls can experience the fun and learning of entrepreneurship with their parents at home, with friends at school, in a community group, a scout troop, a church club, or at camp. No special equipment, supplies, or work spaces are required. All that's needed is a spirit of openness, creativity, and experimentation.

In Part Three of this book, we'll explain exactly how it's done. We'll offer instructions, advice, and tips for parents, teachers, youth leaders, mentors, coaches, and anyone else who wants to help a kid—especially a girl—get started on her own entrepreneurial adventure.

To begin the process, we'll explain how we teach the nine-step entrepreneurial process at VentureLab.

STEP 1—SET THE STAGE: CREATIVITY AND TEAMWORK

We begin with ground rules. Students need a sense of what they can expect to accomplish in the class and what is expected of them. As we follow the nine stages of entrepreneurship, students are invited to offer their ideas no matter how unusual they are, to listen when others are talking, to provide time for everyone to participate, and to refrain from criticizing or dismissing others' ideas.

Next, we talk about the importance of free-wheeling creativity. Being creative means being bold and imaginative and not limiting your thinking to what's already been done. We urge students to elevate their sights to think differently, loosening their imaginations so that they have the license—indeed the mandate—to think of products that people would buy and learn how to overcome obstacles in the way of creating them.

Teamwork is another critical piece. It's rare for someone to accomplish great things by her- or himself. Everyone has something to contribute, and teams need diverse perspectives, skills, and talents. We let our students know they'll be working like a team of scientists to develop and test product ideas, turning vague concepts into concrete realities.

We also let our budding VentureGirls know that individual team members will play different roles as the project continues, so that everyone has a chance to try on different parts. It's the best way for students to strengthen their wings, develop their weaker competencies, and find their strong suits. The *leader or facilitator* guides the project to ensure that everyone participates and that the team meets its objectives. The *materials manager* is responsible for gathering and returning supplies, ensuring that materials are used safely. The *timekeeper* keeps the group on task and on time. The *recorder* compiles and records team member ideas and writes down questions. The *reporter* shares the team's work with the class.

Even very young girls who cannot yet read, write, or count past twenty can learn and master these roles. And everyone is accountable—most importantly, to ask for help when needed.

We also talk through the question, why do people become

entrepreneurs? Surprise! Money isn't the only reason, or even the main reason. Most entrepreneurs want to pursue an idea or a passion. They think they have something people will want, or something that would help people or the planet, and to accomplish their dreams, they need to strike out on their own. Some want to provide for their families better than they feel they can as someone's employee. Some need more flexibility in their schedules. Some want to make a difference in the world. Some want to be their own bosses. Many entrepreneurs start with a small business to supplement their day job, and later find that the side business has become their passion.

Of course, the most important rule we explain is the simplest one: Have fun! When kids are having fun and playing, they are learning much more than they realize. There is no success or failure in play; it's safe to experiment and discover. Play nurtures curiosity and stimulates creativity.

STEP 2—IDENTIFY PROBLEMS AND SELECT ONE TO FOCUS ON

At VentureLab, we encourage critical thinking that leads to constructive ideas. It's often fun to start by thinking of pet peeves—little things in life that we wish we could change. We encourage students to think that their ideas have value—that they can make a real difference. Because *maybe* they *can* make a difference, if only in refining how they think about the world and their own experiences.

"Look at your world, all around you," our teachers and

counselors urge the students. "What rubs you wrong? What problems do you experience day-to-day? Visualize your home, school, travel time, sports, family, food . . . What problems do you experience? When you think, 'They should do something,' who is 'they'? Could *you* do something? Can you *imagine* a solution?"

This stage of the entrepreneurial experience is also about understanding other people and the problems they experience, which may be very different from the things that trouble you. Learning empathy is a key part of our process, and it's another trait girls can learn through practice. In the words of entrepreneur Mike McDerment, CEO of FreshBooks, empathy is "a muscle you develop over time."[1]

Thinking about problems might sound negative, but in reality this exercise is the opposite. Thinking that problems can be solved is *optimistic*. It unleashes the creative energies inside us all.

STEP 3—IDEA GENERATION: BRAINSTORM SOLUTIONS, AS MANY AS POSSIBLE

Ideation and brainstorming are high-energy group activities. We urge VentureLab students to generate ideas, imagining as many solutions as possible. We like to use the phrase "Yes, and . . ." when students come up with ideas, thereby adding to and building on ideas rather than ignoring or criticizing them. We encourage the sense that there are no silly ideas. Many times, students are concerned that they don't have good ideas, but we reassure them by pointing out that even great photographers must take thousands of photos to get that one great image.

Once fresh thinking bursts forth, it's hard even to remember the connecting sparks along the way. The more solutions students think of, the more likely it is that they will come up with a sensational idea that they want to pursue. It's also important that they use a journal to capture their ideas, not just through writing but through drawing and using colors. At VentureLab, we have students brainstorming on windows and on walls using colorful whiteboard markers. Ideas often flourish and flow when students are using all of their senses.

We also teach our students to use the language of inventors: "What if . . . ? Let's hypothesize . . . Could we . . . ? I wonder if anyone has tried . . ." These are phrases and concepts that students will later find are useful not just in a science lab but in an artist's studio, a theater workshop, an English class, an architect's office, a corporate boardroom—any place where fresh thinking is desired.

The teacher or guide may also use probing questions to deepen the students' thinking. Why is this problem so troublesome? Why is it resistant to a solution? What do we know about it and why do we think this? Are there assumptions or is there conventional wisdom clouding our thinking about it? Crazy ideas are okay, as long as students can justify what they want to create by citing relevant experiences.

Choosing the team's solution is a crucial exercise. They're going to have to select just one to pursue as a team. Can the team define in simple terms the solution they might want to focus on? For example, a team that's brainstorming solutions to the problem of environmental damage in and around the school they attend might come up with a lot of ideas. The most promising might be "Get kids involved in finding opportunities to help the environment." Not bad . . . but it needs to be defined in clear, concrete terms. One possibility: "Create a smartphone app that students can use to report whenever they spot wasted water, energy, or other resources on school property—a leaky faucet, a light left burning overnight. Award points and prizes to kids who identify the most opportunities to save." Now we have a clearly defined concept that could become the basis of a successful project.

At this stage, we will reassign a team member if she's discovered she's more interested in another team's problem or solution. In the event that several want to change out of a group, that tells us something else; the team may need to select a different problem or solution to focus on. Our team leaders adjust accordingly.

STEP 4—OPPORTUNITY ANALYSIS

Ideas are one piece of the problem-solving puzzle. Another piece is determining whether any of your creative ideas can and should be brought to life. Figuring out whether an idea represents an opportunity is not an exact process. Timing can play a key role. Entrepreneurs often talk about the "window of opportunity" for an idea, which depends on many factors, including social, technological, and economic trends, as well as the actions of competitors. Many entrepreneurs have had great ideas only to have a competitor launch a similar product first, thus closing the window of opportunity!

Other entrepreneurs find that the world is simply not ready for their ideas. For example, the idea for Airbnb was developed over ten years before its launch. The concept seemed great, but before the heyday of social media and technology, people could not imagine sleeping in a stranger's spare room. By the time Airbnb launched, social and technological changes had created a window of opportunity. Meeting people and connecting over the Internet was well established, and the technology to upload photos and write reviews was readily available. The time was then right for launch, the service was feasible, and there were customers willing to try the service and pay for it. Airbnb quickly became one of the fastest-growing entrepreneurial ventures in the world.

At VentureLab, we teach students to do research online, analyzing trends to determine whether an idea will be successful and whether now is the right time to get started. They learn to focus on ideas that:

- Can realistically be turned into a product or service using technology and resources that exist or can be created;
- Meet the needs of customers who would be willing to buy the product or service; and
- Can be priced in a way that will generate sufficient sales and profits to be attractive to the entrepreneur and any investors.

If your first idea doesn't measure up, don't worry—your second idea might . . . or your third, your fourth, or your twentieth!

STEP 5—CONDUCT MARKET RESEARCH

Opening up the world of market research is a revelation for girls. It is an immersion in learning what makes people tick. They begin by doing research online. Who else is having the same problem? Is anyone else solving that problem? Who might my competition be? How much are they charging? Then they move to in-person interviews and research. What do people need and desire? What would they expect to pay for a solution to their problem? How many prospective customers or users are there?

Our students learn to begin by defining the market. That means a group of people who share certain characteristics and who might be interested in using your product or service. The market for a particular product might be students at a single school (a small market), young women attending high schools anywhere in the United States (a large market), or people around the world who own a phone (a very large market).

It's fun to slice and dissect the characteristics of a market. Our curriculum includes playful exercises on learning how to think about markets in terms of age, gender, grade level, education, location, and geography. For example, what do people in cold climates need that warm-weather residents do not? What are the characteristics of girls who are more likely to play Minecraft or Survivalcraft? We'll even think about whether characteristics like people's political leanings make a difference in their consumer attitudes.

Then we cast students as social scientists, brewing questions that can be answered only through careful research. Students learn the importance of defining research objectives at the outset. We prompt them to ask other people if they experience the same problem. Are they "in the market" for a solution? What can you learn from prospective customers? What do customers think such a product would cost?

It's very important for students to develop the confidence needed to go out and talk to customers—lots of them. We ask our older students to shoot for a hundred. The students will feel uncomfortable at first, but over time, they gain confidence. We have our younger students interview other students in their own class or in another class. Sometimes they will interview their teachers or friends' parents.

VentureLab students discover that *listening* is one of the most important traits of entrepreneurs. What are prospective customers really saying, and how can girls factor that into product design?

Girls often find it fascinating that they can learn about the needs and desires of prospective customers in any number of ways, including conversations with friends and family members, surveys (online or not), interviews, focus groups, observations, traffic counts, and data from the US Census or private research companies. If a prospective solution seems right intuitively, but the market research isn't supporting it, what do students do? Students are fascinated to discover that even Fortune 500 companies face this very dilemma.

The lesson: No matter how brilliant the entrepreneur, it is the customer who chooses what product they purchase. That is why market research is critical.

STEP 6—BUILD A PROTOTYPE

Designing, testing, and redesigning prototypes is a crucial phase of the VentureLab experience. We provide the settings, tools, and materials needed for students to translate the inventions in their imaginations into products or viable services. It's a chance for girls who like inventing, designing, and making things or conceptualizing services to shine.

Prototyping involves designing and developing sample versions of your product that are used to test and to sell your concept before it is fully developed. It's important for several reasons:

- Prototyping lets you share your ideas with teammates, ensuring everyone knows what you're trying to create and preventing confusion once the building process starts.
- Prototyping helps you determine whether customers will want your product. You can save money by drawing pictures of your product or building a sample out of cardboard before you waste the material you have creating stuff people might not want.

- Prototyping lets customers see your product so you can gather feedback that will help you make improvements.

Part of the process is prototyping for look and feel: What does the product look like? What is it made of? And part is prototyping for functionality: What does the product do? How do people use it?

Students test the prototype, conduct additional market research by having prospective customers try the prototype, and rework and retest the design, likely with multiple attempts and iterations. Observing and interviewing prospective customers as they try out the prototype, seeing how they use it, students are sure to catch things that can be improved. Prototyping is a repetitive cycle, and sometimes there's no clear finish line.

Aspiring technologists get in gear in the prototype phase. We encourage students to use whatever technology assists they can imagine, which can include 3-D modeling, filmmaking, website creation, coding, or game design. Depending on the nature of their product, they may learn about fields they didn't know existed, like hydroponics, the science of growing plants in water without soil.

Part of the challenge is finding sources of information about relevant technologies. An expert willing to give advice might be found at the local school or at a company in your town. A nearby science museum or community college might offer a helpful course or a link to an instructor. And, of course, libraries and the Internet offer articles, reference materials, and instructional videos on almost every topic imaginable. In planning your project, build in time for research and learning. It's part of the challenge of entrepreneurship—and a big part of the fun.

A product is finally ready when its design reflects a team's best thinking, from conception through redesign, taking into account cost, price, sustainability, and whatever factors matter to the market.

STEP 7—DEFINE YOUR BUSINESS MODEL: HOW WILL YOU MAKE MONEY?

In this stage of the process, we help students work their way through a series of questions:

- What is the product? Why might someone feel they have to have it?
- What is the product's most important benefit to customers—otherwise known as its "unique selling proposition"?
- Who would buy the product—that is, who is your customer/market?
- What do you know about your customers? How large is the market?
- What will it cost to produce your product and get it to your customers?
- How will you get your product to your customers?
- What price must you charge to make a profit?

- Based on your knowledge of the market, how many products do you think you can sell at that price?
- Are there ways to reduce the cost of production, either to reduce the price or to increase the profit margin?

The answers to these questions define a business model—and the business model, in turn, defines how your problem-solving enterprise will work.

As an example, one of our student groups decided to sell glitter slime, which is all the rage with girls and the subject of many YouTube videos and channels. They determined the cost to purchase the materials to make the slime. They determined the cost to package the slime, and determined the cost for a table, poster, and materials to market their slime.

Based on their market research they calculated what their customers would pay, compared that with what the slime cost to produce, and determined how much profit they would make based on selling a certain quantity. Then they created a free website, and set up a poster and table outside one girl's house to sell their slime. They were in business!

STEP 8—DEVELOP MARKETING AND ADVERTISING

The advertising, marketing, and promotion phase of the VentureLab system allows students to visually promote what they've created. Many students love this phase of the entrepreneurial process. It involves visuals, graphics, sometimes music, and many other creative arts.

Marketing and advertising can be done by simply creating posters to display their products, benefits, and pricing. It may also involve creating an online presence. VentureLab teams often create a web page to market their product or services. For young students, this is usually the first web page they've ever created. They learn to use free and simple website creation tools. They write the content, upload photos of their product, and use a plug-in to create a cart to sell their products. The goal is, always, to build girls' confidence, creativity, and technology competence.

Creating a video advertisement is the culmination of the marketing stage at VentureLab. The video commercial is the thirty-second crucible of all product development. A lot rides on it. It is the on-air, online pitch to prospective customers, and all of the systems must be ready to handle the demand if it materializes—which makes it rousingly fun to film and produce. Having been targeted by a lifetime of television and Internet commercials, our students love having the chance to strike back with their own best ideas. At VentureLab, they get a close-up look at how advertisements are made and targeted to their audiences. Many older students will create videos to put on crowd-funding pages in order to get their projects funded.

STEP 9—PITCH TO PROSPECTIVE USERS AND INVESTORS

Pitching happens in the final segment of the class, when students present their product to parents and possible investors. It's one of the most intense, challenging, and exciting experiences in the entire VentureLab journey.

In a team, it isn't about who can deliver the best pitch. Every member needs the experience of standing before a group. Every member learns the challenge of making a problem and a solution understandable to an audience. That's the essence of pitching, and a vital skill that practically everyone needs to use at some point in their lives.

We use warm-up games along the way to help students become comfortable with presenting their ideas in public. A favorite among girls is the Pitch Card Challenge. On a table are three piles of cards: Nouns, Adjectives, and Verbs. A student draws one of each and uses the three words as inspiration for a product and to make a sales pitch for it. It's a fast-paced game that helps girls discover the fun of thinking on their feet. The more girls practice this fun, silly, no-pressure game, the more comfortable they are speaking to a group and advocating that you, yes *you*, buy and try their product.

On the final day of class, when girls invite parents and family members to attend the pitches, we also invite role models from the community. The newly formed pride and professionalism of the VentureLab participants are evident to all. By then, students have developed an air of confidence. They have practiced communicating and learned a wide array of life skills. They are optimistic, energized, and engaged.

Students know that not everyone who attends VentureLab will start a million-dollar company. Most won't. But all have learned positive, empowering entrepreneurial skills they'll be able to use every day and throughout their lives.

HELP HER SCAMPER HER WAY TO SUCCESS

Mastering entrepreneurship is about learning to use ways of thinking that can help you address challenges and discover fresh approaches to problems that might seem impossible to solve. When girls discover these tools, they become empowered in an extraordinary way—one that often leads to remarkable achievements in school, in their careers, and in life.

At a summer VentureLab camp, one group of nine- and ten-year-old animal lovers was determined to use their entrepreneurial skills to help protect endangered species. After much brainstorming, they decided to focus on a method for protecting leopards living in wildlife parks and nature sanctuaries from sport hunters. (Statistics show that hundreds of these beautiful and rare animals are killed by poachers every year—for example, more than a thousand just in India between 2010 and early 2017.)[2] They came up with an idea they called Metal Leopard—a life-size model of a real animal designed to fool and trap hunters. It would be equipped with a GPS tracking device and a camera to snap a picture of the hunters as they fired their rifles, making it possible for wildlife authorities to identify and prosecute them.

So far, so good. But creating a prototype of their product and developing a realistic business plan proved to be a significant challenge. The team members set to work doing research on the Internet. They came up with price points for the computer devices and the camera equipment they would need, as well as for the materials from which the bulletproof shell of the Metal Leopard would be forged.

As the financials took shape and the selling price mounted, a debate erupted among the girls over whether the market prospects for the device were realistic. "Who's going to buy it if we have to charge three hundred dollars?" one of the team members demanded. As a result of the give-and-take, the team embarked on a quest to find more affordable components and materials, eventually developing an alternative, more affordable design they believed could attract buyers at game parks in Africa, Asia, and other regions where leopards roam.

This team of young conservationists was getting a taste of the kinds of real-life challenges faced by engineers, designers, and entrepreneurs in every field who must use their creativity and ingenuity to strike an effective balance among product characteristics like quality, durability, weight, flexibility, and price. Their ability to solve such knotty equations often spells the difference between success and failure.

One of the tools we give them to master those problems is the SCAMPER system. It's a mnemonic we teach our VentureLab participants for remembering the entrepreneurial strategy that stimulates new, often better ideas:

- *Substitute*—What materials or resources can you substitute or swap to improve the product? What other product or process could you use? Can you use this product somewhere else, or as a substitute for something else?

- *Combine*—What would happen if you combined this product with another, to create something new?
- *Adapt*—How could you adapt or readjust this product? What else is the product like? What other context could you put the product into? What part of the product could you exchange for something else?
- *Modify*—How could you change the shape, look, or feel of your product? What could you add to modify the product? What could you emphasize or lessen to create something new? What if you change all or part of the product? What if you enlarge the product or a part of it? What if you shrink the product or a part of it?
- *Put to another use*—Can you use this product somewhere else, perhaps in another industry? Who else could use this product? How would this product behave differently in another setting? How can you use the product for a different purpose?
- *Eliminate*—What features, parts, or rules could you eliminate? What elements could you understate or tone down? How could you make the product smaller, faster, lighter? What would happen if you took away part of this product?
- *Reverse/rearrange*—How could you reorganize or rearrange this product? What would happen if you reversed the way the product is used? For example, if the product is designed to speed something up, what if you

deliberately tried to slow things down instead? What if a product you designed to be small and portable instead were enlarged? What would be gained? What would be lost? Sometimes a great new idea emerges when you think about reversing your concept.

One of the cardinal rules of creativity is that your first idea is rarely your best. Investing time in rethinking, re-imagining, and rediscovering often produces breakthroughs that transform so-so concepts into works of genius. SCAMPER perfectly enables this process of reinvention.

TRY THIS AT HOME—AN ACTIVITY GIRLS WILL LOVE: SCAMPER WITH OREOS*

In this activity, parent(s) and kid(s) SCAMPER their way to brainstorming creative ways to change Oreos (or any cream-filled sandwich-style cookie) or to create an entirely new cookie product.

TIME: 15–45 MINUTES

You Need

Something to write and draw with (pens, pencils, crayons, or markers)

---

* For more detailed instructions with pictures and videos for this activity and all the others in this book, please visit www.venturelab.org/curriculum.

Paper to write on

Optional: A box of sandwich-style cookies, as well as food items you may have in your house, such as ice cream, yogurt, fruit jelly, peanut butter, graham crackers, Ritz crackers, chocolate chip or sugar cookies, food coloring

Directions

- Think about a sandwich-style cookie. Look at a picture of one. If you have some cookies, take them in your hand and examine them. Maybe even eat a few.
- Now start brainstorming how you could create something new using the cookies. Write down or draw as many ideas as possible.
- When you are stuck, start using SCAMPER.
- Substitute: What could you substitute in the cookie? (Examples: For the cream filling, substitute peanut butter, or strawberry jelly; for the chocolate cookie wafers, substitute graham crackers or Ritz crackers.)
- Combine: What could you combine with the cookie to make something new? (Examples: Combine cookies with ice cream to make cookie ice cream; combine with a coating of yogurt to make yogurt-covered cookies.)
- Adapt: How could you adapt or readjust this product? (Example: Make a large round stack of cookies, "glued" together with filling, to use as a birthday cake.)
- Modify: How could you change the shape, look, or feel of your product? (Examples: Make the cookies smaller

to create mini-cookies; enlarge them to create super-cookies; double the amount of cream filling to create a double-stuffed cookie; dye the cream filling green to create a St. Patrick's Day cookie.)

- Put to another use: How can you use the product for a different purpose? (Example: Crush the cookies and use the resulting mixture as the crust or the crumb topping for a fruit pie.)
- Eliminate: What parts could you remove? (Examples: Eliminate the cream filling; eliminate the chocolate wafers; eliminate one chocolate wafer; make reduced-fat cookies using a lighter cream filling.)
- Reverse/rearrange: How could you rearrange or reverse the design of this product? (Example: Put the cream filling on the outside of the cookie.)
- If you have cookies and the food items you need, you can actually create the products you are brainstorming and try them.
- Once you have written down, drawn, and even created your new products, write down your thoughts on which of the new products you like best, and why.

Later, you can use this same technique on any problem you are trying to brainstorm a solution for.

TRY THIS AT HOME—AN ACTIVITY GIRLS WILL LOVE: START A BUSINESS SELLING REPURPOSED LEGOS

Most families have Lego bricks and other parts lying around the house. (I refer to them all simply as "Legos.") After you're finished building something with them, you're left with boxes of Legos sitting around without a purpose. What if girls could repurpose Legos and sell them?

TIME: 2–4 HOURS

You Need

A supply of leftover Legos
Something to write and draw with (pens, pencils, crayons, or markers)
Paper to write on
Cardboard box
Ziplock bag

Directions

- Use your imagination to think about a cool product you can build out of Legos. Draw a design of the product you want to build. For example, you might want to build a large Lego horse.
- Gather and organize the Lego pieces you have to build your product. Experiment with the best colors, sizes, and shapes.
- Create step-by-step instructions with pictures showing how you built your product, so that someone else

could build the same product—just like the instructions you get when you buy a Lego set.

- Develop your product package. If you can find or buy a cardboard box, you can decorate it with a picture and description of your Lego product. Put all of the required Legos in a ziplock bag and place them inside the box. Include your instruction guide.
- Promote, market, and sell your product. You can make a poster to advertise your product or create flyers to distribute. You may want to set up a stand outside your house or in some other convenient location where you can sell your product.
- Sell your product, and watch customers have fun building your Lego creation!

5

Start Her Young

How old must girls be before they're ready to learn entrepreneurial skills? Ten? Eight?

Try as early as age *five*.

Don't let their size fool you—little girls can develop an entrepreneurial mind-set even before they can read. Anyone who's recently spent time with a five-year-old will recognize how sharply observant she can be. During one VentureLab camp, I asked a group of five-year-olds to tell me about problems that they were experiencing and wanted to solve. One five-year-old had a problem at home that kept landing her in time-out. She shared it with the other pint-size participants in her group: "I get in trouble for eating my play dough," she said. "My mommy says it's bad for my tummy and I'll get sick." Others chimed in, saying yes, eating play dough could be a problem. (For the record, the popular Play-Doh product sold commercially by the Hasbro company is nontoxic.

However, it does contain salt, which can pose a health hazard when eaten in large quantities.)[1]

This prompted a spirited discussion among the kids: If play dough is bad to eat, what makes it bad? And what can we do about it? Even children who had never been so daring as to taste play dough had seen other children do it. Could they think of possible solutions that could keep their classmates out of trouble?

Out of the fertile minds of five-year-olds sprang the idea of "edible play dough." If you make play dough out of food, then you shouldn't get in trouble, right? So the group developed their own edible dough.

VentureLab counselors guided them through market research as they surveyed other kids in different camp groups—girls and boys—about their favorite colors and flavors. They tallied their findings and came up with chocolate chip and pink strawberry as the two most popular flavor options. The students then went home and surveyed parents and relatives as to how much they would pay for an edible play dough product. A counselor bought ingredients, helped the girls create a tasty recipe through trial and error, and packaged it according to five-year-olds' specifications. They named it "Tasty Doh." Counselors helped them create a website and post their photos and pricing online. Because the authors of the contents were five years old, there were quite a few misspelled words, grammar lapses, and nonsensical sentences, but it made the website even more endearing. On the last afternoon of camp week, the kids pitched their product and website to their parents, and watched as sales orders began to flow. And once the girls ran out of product, they became even more entrepreneurial and began to sell copies of their recipes. At the end of the day, the kids in the group left with profits of more than ten dollars each—a windfall they'd proudly earned.

KINDERGARTEN DREAMS: ENCOURAGING AND CHANNELING A GIRL'S IMAGINATION

At five, girls are natural explorers. Every day is a new adventure filled with first-time experiences, discovering opportunities and boundaries along the way. Girls discover that it can be tempting to try new things, even at the risk of getting in trouble.

The entrepreneurial twist is to encourage girls to identify their problems and think about *solutions* to frustrations, focusing on developing creative ideas and then improving them, with just enough guidance and assistance from grown-ups.

Whenever I work with five-year-olds, I'm continually struck by their imaginative take on the world, with free associations few adults could predict. Here are a few random samples:

- "I wish I could invent a candy magnet. You would just hold it up, and all of the candy in the world would come straight at you!"

- "I wish we had 'Happy Squirrel.' Like 'Happy Meals,' but for squirrels, so they would come close and I could touch them."
- "I wish there was no gravity. Then everything would float in the air, and when we lost something, we could see it floating and could find it."
- After a five-year-old spilled Cream of Wheat on her seat belt, she remarked, "I am trying to get it with my tongue, but my tongue is not the right size . . . A frog's tongue is the right size."
- "I wish everything in the store cost one leaf. Then fall would be the best season."
- Watching her mother struggle to cut open a package: "They should make a laser for cutting open packages. A laser would cut right through this."
- After a rainstorm, a girl goes out in a rain jacket and her pants get soaked, prompting, "Why don't they make 'pants raincoats'?"

Why not? Who knew that not having enough candy, not being able to touch skittish squirrels, and having rain-soaked pants were frustrations in the lives of five-year-olds? When we encourage young girls to explore the needs *that they themselves express,* we make entrepreneurial learning relevant and accessible to them. In addition, we teach girls that their needs are important and powerful, and that exploring them is a step toward success.

Entrepreneurial education values a child's perspective.

As adult supporters, we have to learn not to critique their off-the-wall project ideas or their sometimes simplistic approaches. We need to trust the process and stop hovering so that girls have the space and freedom to develop their ideas.

Once we adopt this mind-set, we find that entrepreneurial classes for girls ages five to seven work best when they are not very different from classes for older kids. The emphasis is on creative problem-solving, following a scientific process that they can practice and master over time:

- Identifying a problem or frustration
- Brainstorming solutions and selecting one to focus on
- Analyzing the opportunity
- Conducting market research—that is, asking friends and parents for reactions
- Building and testing prototypes
- Perfecting a business model
- Developing marketing and advertising
- Pitching their product to prospective users, customers, or investors

The process begins when you encourage girls to let their imaginations run free. Edward de Bono, a pioneer in brain training, coined the term *lateral thinking*. When a person gets stuck trying to devise the solution to a problem, the challenge is often that they persist in thinking about the problem repeatedly in the same way. Lateral thinking is about changing directions, perhaps by thinking in ways that might seem impractical. One of de Bono's techniques, called *wishful thinking*, encourages people to imagine ideal solutions without constraints and without censorship.[2]

At VentureLab, we've developed a number of activities designed to promote lateral thinking and the unfettered creativity it sparks. You can easily adopt these activities for use at home. One of my favorites is called "When Pigs Fly." The phrase is a funny way of describing something that will never happen. But what if it could?

With that challenge in mind, we encourage girls to imagine as many ways as they can that pigs *could* fly. Within moments, the ideas start to flow:

- Catapult the pig!
- Tie a rocket to it.
- Drop it from a diving board.
- Put it on a roller coaster.
- Send it up in a plane.
- Drop it with a parachute.
- Attach helium balloons.
- Send it to the moon.

Often, one kid's idea will build on another's:

- Fuse it with a bird . . .
- And then splice their genes!

In a matter of fifteen minutes, a typical group of kids may come up with thirty, forty, even sixty or more ideas—each one crazier and funnier than the last. The key is that there are no constraints! The pig doesn't have to be alive. The "pig that flies" could be a pig-shaped dirigible, a food fight with bacon, a pig drinking Red Bull energy drink (because, according to the commercials, it "gives you wings"), or a pink football with a curly tail at the back—a real "pigskin"!

It doesn't matter whether the ideas are impractical—at VentureLab, we constantly teach that "impractical" doesn't mean "impossible." After all, every breakthrough idea, from the Apollo moon project to the first digital computer, was originally considered impractical. The exercise is about generating ideas, and having fun doing it. It helps girls learn how to brainstorm without judging or criticizing, how to listen to others' ideas and piggyback on ideas, how to think creatively, how to approach the "impossible" with a sense of possibilities, and how to collaborate as a team.

Are young girls innately interested in acquiring entrepreneurial skills? I think so. They are curious and receptive. Hundreds of observations tell me that, at age five, they are ready for age-appropriate lessons in the fun and creativity of entrepreneurial problem-solving.

In some ways, five-year-olds are *better* equipped to embrace the entrepreneurial mind-set than their older brothers and sisters. Most five-year-olds have not yet been to school. They have not yet been educated out of their creativity. They don't yet understand what it means to earn a failing grade. What better time to reinforce creativity and introduce them to the entrepreneurial skill of learning from successive failures?

Testing, trying, failing, rethinking, adjusting, failing again, and learning—this cycle that is essential to entrepreneurship comes naturally to five- to seven-year-olds. They don't experience failure as something to fear or avoid. So when they try to use duct tape to attach a wheel to their prototype product—a mobile dog food bowl—they laugh when it falls off, and a minute later they are working on a new way to make it stick.

By contrast, many twelve-year-olds are perfectionists who have spent years being conditioned to choose low-risk projects with less chance of failure and who stress out when things don't work. Teaching these older kids the joy of entrepreneurship starts with breaking this fixed mind-set. It can be done. But why should we have to "break" anything? All the more reason to start them young!

NEURAL PATHWAYS AND THE GROWTH MIND-SET

Our brains are filled with neural pathways, connections made of bundles of neurons that receive and pass on information to different parts of the nervous system. New habits, experiences, practice, and any kind of learning, cause neural pathways to rearrange and change. And this ability of the brain to constantly develop, grow, and evolve—the trait known as plasticity—is one of the most powerful traits we enjoy as humans. Throughout our lives, because of our brains' plasticity, our intelligence and skill can grow when we put our minds to the task.

So when it comes to brainpower, the old slogan "Use it or

lose it" isn't quite right. A truer statement is "Use it, or work harder to develop it later on."

Young children have twice as many synaptic connections as adults. As we grow, the brain actually reduces the number of connections because as functioning adults, set in our path, our brain doesn't need as many. What happens in the early years of a girl's life affects the formation of her brain. Every day, specific neural pathways are being generated and strengthened—or not. A girl who is encouraged to explore, hypothesize, observe, and discover patterns is going to develop the brain of a creative problem-solver. She will develop more acute powers of observation, an ability to concentrate, and a gift for generating ideas. Her brain will be calibrated to succeed in a world of rapid, continual change.

Conversely, unused neural pathways may atrophy or fail to activate. A girl whose curiosity is suppressed, whose mind seldom ventures into uncharted environs, who accepts the conventional role she's been assigned, and who is disadvantaged by the fear of looking stupid may get good grades, but her brain will not be rich with neural pathways. It's as if there is a blockade in her brain that reduces her aptitude for creative problem-solving.

Brain development in the first six to seven years sets the stage for the rest of a child's life. Early experiences matter in ways that neuroscientists are still discovering. Genes and experiences are intertwined in determining capacities and talents.

Even more important—and surprising—is the fact that understanding how our brains can expand and change actually seems to *enhance* our ability to develop new skills. It's an insight we owe to Carol Dweck and her concept of the growth mind-set. What Dweck has proven in study after study is that children who understand that their brains can grow tend to develop a growth mind-set. This knowledge can catapult learning in fields like entrepreneurship and the STEM subjects. Teach a girl that, with effort, she can become smarter, and she becomes more likely to make the effort to grow her mind and increase her knowledge and intelligence. And the sooner this process starts, the more likely that a girl will get this life-altering message and make the effort that will make her smarter.

At VentureLab, we incorporate this message into our work with the very youngest children, ages four and five. We let them know that they have the power to stretch their brains, sharpen their minds, and become smarter. Once they get this, they develop a level of self-confidence and fearlessness that helps them reach their full potential as creative, competent individuals. They absorb the message *I have good ideas. People are interested in my ideas. My ideas matter.* And for most five-year-old girls, that's a remarkable message—one they don't hear often enough in mainstream society.

Yes, there are wonderful parents who impart this message of encouragement and empowerment to their daughters and sons. But all of us can do a better job of spreading the word about the growth mind-set—starting with the girls (and boys) whose lives we touch.

GIRLS AND BOYS—HOW THEY DIFFER, WHY IT MATTERS

THE CONCEPTS OF PLASTICITY AND GROWTH MIND-SET APPLY EQUALLY TO boys and girls. But there are some differences between the sexes that are helpful to understand if you're particularly interested in nurturing the mind of a young girl. In the words of Dr. Lise Eliot, neuroscientist and author of *Pink Brain, Blue Brain,* "Boys and girls are different." But Dr. Eliot also notes that at one time, the sensational reporting of boy-girl differences exaggerated the extremes:

> *[The] reality is that the brains of boys and girls are more similar than their well-described behavioral differences would indicate. . . . Just as boys' and girls' bodies start out more androgynous than they end up in adulthood, their brains appear to be less sexually differentiated than adult men's and women's. This doesn't mean, however, that neuroscience can't teach us something about sex differences in children.*

Dr. Eliot notes that during the first few months of life, infants experience "what endocrinologists refer to as a 'mini-puberty.' . . . Boys experience a surge of testosterone. . . . Girls undergo an estrogen rise within a similar time frame. . . . Clearly, sex hormones are flowing early in life. Though there is little evidence of it in newborns' behavior, boys and girls are undergoing their separate mini-puberties, which may have lasting consequences for how their brains and bodies develop further."[3]

Leonard Sax, who has written extensively on "why gender matters," offers further detail. Sax, who has a PhD in psychology and an MD, spent two decades as a family physician, often seeing parents seeking prescription medication for their sons to treat attention deficit disorder (ADD), a diagnosis often first made by teachers. Troubled by how frequently boys were medicated, Sax began studying differences for clues to their attention difficulties in class. His curiosity led him to study gender differences and their origins, and to present evidence in terms that parents and teachers can understand.

Sax explains that, from birth, girls seem wired for mutual gazing. They study faces, notice changes in expressions, and respond to emotional tones of voice. By contrast, many mothers of boys feel as if they must be doing something wrong, because their baby boys don't gaze with rapture at their faces. This gender difference doesn't result from socialization. Studies show that these behavior patterns are innate and universal. It makes sense when you consider the human experience in the millennia leading up to the twenty-first century. Evolutionarily speaking, preserving social harmony, calming conflict, and keeping peace were once matters of life and death for females of primate clans.[4]

Social differences between the sexes persist as children grow. For example, girl toddlers are more likely to seek signs of approval or disapproval before they act. In one study comparing twelve-month-olds, girls glanced at their mothers' faces ten to twenty times more than boys to check for clues on whether to touch a forbidden object. The boys rarely glanced at their mothers' faces and touched the object despite being told "No!"

Neurological differences between the genders also appear at an early age. Girls generally have stronger neural connectors in their temporal lobes than do boys, leading to more detailed memory storage, better listening skills, and sharper discrimination among tones of voice. The brains of girls usually have a larger hippocampus, strengthening their learning advantage in the language arts. And the prefrontal cortex in girls is generally more active and develops at an earlier age, reducing the tendency to make impulsive decisions.

Other experts have studied additional aspects of the differences between the sexes. Linguistics professor Deborah Tannen describes "genderlects" of young children—differences in communication style that are widespread among girls and boys. Tannen reports that studies of children ages two to five show that girls propose play using collaborative language—for instance, "let's," as in "let's play house"—more than boys that age. Tannen is not claiming that girls are always innately communicative and cooperative—she calls that a "misguided stereotype born out of the contrast with boys." There are plenty of outspoken girls, even aggressive ones. But Tannen's genderlects reflect persistent differences between girls and boys that parents, teachers, and others who work with kids find useful.[5]

The differences between girls and boys don't limit what either gender can achieve. But improving their chance to achieve requires that we make an informed effort to find the most effective teaching methods for each.

ENGAGING YOUNG GIRLS IN STEM

UNDERSTANDING THE DIFFERENCES BETWEEN GIRLS AND BOYS CAN provide us with tools we can use to encourage young girls to retain and develop their innate interest in science and math rather than allowing social influences to discourage that interest.

For example, Leonard Sax studied how kids learn math in three hundred schools in seven countries from the United States to Australia, the United Kingdom to Mexico. He observes:

> *Many middle-school boys seem to learn algebra better when you start with numbers, whereas many same-age girls seem to be more engaged if you start with a word problem. For example, if you are teaching equations in multiple variables, the typical 7th-grade boy will do better if you begin by asking, "If $x + 2y = 60$, and $2x + y = 90$, how do we solve for x and y?" But the typical 7th-grade girl will be more engaged if you begin by asking, "If a sweater and two blouses cost $60, and two sweaters and a blouse cost $90, how much does each blouse and each sweater cost?" . . . Many girls are more engaged if you begin with the word problem and then work your way back to the equation.*[6]

Those of us who have become sensitized to the ways stereotypes can reinforce gender discrimination may cringe a little at Dr. Sax's example: "Blouses and sweaters—that's so . . . feminine!" But *it's okay*! Lots of girls are interested in fashion. If they find a problem related to fashion an intriguing gateway to math, why not use it?

Bella was a VentureLab student who was intrigued with female characters in mystery and detective books—especially the legendary Carmen Sandiego, the clever female protagonist of a series of computer games. Bella loved to imagine herself as an international woman of mystery with a cool repertoire of spy gear. In a VentureLab camp, she realized she could invent a product that expressed her interests. She sold her teammates on the idea of making trendy headbands, each containing a secret compartment in the form of a specially designed plastic cylinder, in which to hide notes, keys, computer chips, or other miniature items a detective might need. This could be a fun way to combine two of her passions—mystery sleuthing and fashion!

The challenge was that the best way to produce the plastic cylinders was by using a 3-D printer. Bella had never been exposed to 3-D printing before. Now she had to absorb the math required to perform 3-D modeling in order to design and print the cylinder. She was a bit daunted—but she was energized by her product idea. Once she set to work, she found herself mastering math techniques she'd once assumed would be too hard for her to learn. On pitch day, the stylish spy headbands designed and made by Bella's group sold out faster than any other products on offer.

Bella's story illustrates one of the secrets of VentureLab: Rather than fighting the differences in the ways boys and girls learn, we use those differences to our advantage. If you're a parent or teacher, you can easily use the same technique to help the kids in your life discover the power and fascination of science and math.

The "sauce" that makes the math tastier doesn't have to be fashion, of course—it can be any topic that a team of girls decides to tackle. Here is the same math problem rephrased in other terms—examples that an entrepreneurial class of girls might hit upon while testing how a nutrition idea might work with mice:

> *If the lab's one white mouse and two gray mice weigh 60 grams, and two white mice and one gray mouse weigh 90 grams, how much does each white and gray mouse weigh?*

Or if a team is thinking of solutions for global humanitarian needs:

> *For a village, if one farm tool and two books cost $60, and two farm tools and one book cost $90, how much does each farm tool and book cost?*

Research also suggests that female students are more interested in developing and using technical skills when they recognize them as elements of a career dedicated to helping people—as tools for improving the world. By contrast, most boys find it more appealing to think of computer and other technological devices as toys that are fun in their own right.

This difference has an impact on the most effective ways to encourage entrepreneurial learning. Girls tend to understand math better when the problems are cast in real-world contexts. For many girls, applying what they learn to help people and the planet inspires them to pursue difficult subjects as a way to make the world a better place.

Yet another difference between girls and boys has to do with spatial relations—the ability to understand, interpret, and use information about the ways things fit together in space. Spatial relations have to do with the relative size, shape, weight, and positioning of things. And studies have shown that a strong sense of spatial relations is associated with success in mathematics, science, and engineering. In fact, a child's spatial relations skills in second grade are a better predictor of whether that child will pursue STEM studies than that child's math skills in seventh grade, according to Dr. Sheryl Sorby, an engineer whose pioneering research has been largely funded by the National Science Foundation.[7] And, according to the results from a Vanderbilt University longitudinal study, spatial ability at age thirteen predicts creative and scholarly achievements more than thirty years later.[8]

Unfortunately, many girls' spatial relations skills lag significantly behind boys'. And it's not just girls who start at a spatial disadvantage. Also lagging are kids of low socioeconomic status. Impoverished minority girls often fall at the far losing end of the spatial skills spectrum. Without a concerted intervention, the gap will follow them throughout their schooling.

However, there are plenty of things we can do to help close this gap. A strong intuitive sense of spatial relations can be developed or enhanced by opportunities to play with toys like building blocks, Tinkertoys, boxes, cars, trains, and wagons. This helps to explain the gender gap in regard to spatial relations: Many girls' homes are devoid of toys like Legos and Hot Wheels tracks, or are stocked with "girl versions" that are less challenging. Parents can address the problem by giving their daughters challenging toys that will let them manipulate and use physical objects just the way boys have traditionally done.

You can also refrain from steering girls mainly toward typically "girly" playthings like dolls, kitchen sets, and dress-up supplies. Not that there is anything wrong with behaving like a girl! If your daughter gravitates toward traditional female play, let her enjoy it. And along the way, provide her with opportunities to discover the STEM connections to the games she favors. For example, you can work with her to make a custom-built dollhouse using cardboard boxes and other simple materials—and in the process, show her how she can use a ruler, a pencil, and basic math to design her project. If she likes to play at cooking, introduce her to the metric and English systems for measuring ingredients.

FROM KINDERGARTEN TO THE CEO SUITE

Do the activities of five-year-old girls really have any relationship to the women they will grow up to become? The answer seems to be yes. One of the striking characteristics of women entrepreneurs is how early their experimental ventures began.

Randa Milliron started her first business when she was just six years old. "I taught myself to draw flowers and bugs and developed a talent for it," she recalls. "Some of the neighbors asked how to do it, so I decided to start an art school. I had five students, girls and boys, and charged five cents for lessons. Everyone needs to learn how to draw, right? I taught them, and the more a drawing looked like an iris, the better. I felt the pride of accomplishment, and that was the start of it."[9] *It* was her entrepreneurial drive. Not only did Milliron have a growth mind-set, but her students, too, could see their work paying off. Years later, Milliron cofounded a rocket company, Interorbital Systems, and became its CEO.

Catherine Crago was five when a bright idea drove her to climb onto the kitchen counter to get a bag of lemon cookies hidden in the top cabinet:

> *While my mom was napping, I went door-to-door rounding up kids in the neighborhood. I told them it cost twenty-five cents to come to my party, and a bunch of them came and paid. The problem started when I ran out of cookies. Then their mothers heard about the party, and they were mad. Their kids were in trouble for stealing coins out of their purses.*

By then, my mom was awake. I had to return all the money I'd made—three dollars and fifty cents. After everyone left, I asked my mother if she was mad at me, too. She smiled and surprised me, saying, "No, I'm proud of you."[10]

At that moment, five-year-old Catherine Crago knew she wanted to create things that people would buy—and she knew that her mother believed in her and would support her in pursuit of her dream. Years later, Crago would climb her way into the semiconductor industry.

Childhood is our universal shared experience. It is a crucible for character and capabilities. It's when girls learn language, confidence, and social behavior. It is when they first experience the joy of curiosity, learning, and trial and error—or not. It is when they learn concepts like justice, inequality, ethics, trust, sacrifice, and the value of hard work. Girlhood is when girls learn what they *can* do—and are socialized to learn what they can't do and shouldn't try. Girlhood is when girls learn to listen to their inner voice—or to suppress it. Girlhood is when girls learn to be helpless or resourceful.

Virtually every trait of what women will become is evidenced somewhere in girlhood. So if we want to engage more females in becoming scientists, engineers, physicists, tech entrepreneurs, and change agents—all fields in which women are desperately underrepresented—then we must begin early in the lives of girls.

TRY THIS AT HOME—AN ACTIVITY GIRLS WILL LOVE: REDESIGN ME!

In this activity, kids use their imaginations to redesign familiar objects in a variety of surprising ways—the more unusual the better.

TIME: 15—45 MINUTES

You Need

Something to write and draw with (pens, pencils, crayons, or markers)
Paper to write on
Index cards

Directions

- Create a pack of index cards on which the names of various familiar objects are written—umbrella, necklace, footstool, flowerpot, three-ring binder, broom, and so on.
- Invite a girl to pick a card from the pack. Then challenge her, first, to imagine how she would redesign the object chosen to make it *more fun*. Provide plenty of drawing paper and pencils or crayons to let her sketch her new design ideas. Encourage her to let her imagination run free.
- Second, ask her to redesign the object for *an entirely different purpose,* which she should specify. (Examples: Redesign the umbrella to serve as the frame of a decorative mobile to hang over a baby's crib; redesign

the footstool to serve as a rotating lazy Susan stand for snacks or hors d'oeuvres in the middle of a table.)

This exercise is mainly intended to stimulate a girl's creativity, encouraging her to think freely (even wildly!) about the possibilities in a simple object.

TRY THIS AT HOME—AN ACTIVITY GIRLS WILL LOVE: YES, AND . . .

This is a great improvisational game for brainstorming and storytelling.

TIME: 15–30 MINUTES

You Need

A group of friends

Directions

- The members of the group, or one designated leader, should suggest a topic or a challenge for the whole group to tackle together. For example, the topic could be "a new way to travel."
- Go around the group, with each member responding to the topic in a few words. For example, the first member might say, "I am going to build a rocket ship."
- The second member agrees and adds a few words of her own. For example, the second member might say,

"Yes, and the rocket ship is going to travel to the planet Mars."

- Continue in this way through the whole group. For example, the third member might say, "Yes, and the rocket ship will be made out of a bouncy material." The fourth member might say, "Yes, and the rocket ship will be carrying lots of people who are going on vacation to Mars."
- Keep going, giving members additional turns as needed. Stop when the game "feels" complete or when everyone is laughing too hard to continue!

TRY THIS AT HOME—AN ACTIVITY GIRLS WILL LOVE: MARKERBOTS

In this activity, parent(s) and kid(s) build one or more Markerbots that will create colorful art on their own. You can experiment with colors, number of markers, and number of Markerbots to create a variety of different styles and designs.

TIME: 30–45 MINUTES

You Need

An electric toothbrush—one for each Markerbot you want to make

Batteries for the toothbrush

A foam pool tube or noodle

3 to 6 thin markers of different colors per pool tube/noodle
Scissors or knife (adult use)
Rubber bands
White printer paper or butcher paper
Optional: Googly eyes, pipe cleaners, and/or stickers to decorate your Markerbots

Directions

- Take the toothbrush out of its packaging. Insert batteries as needed. Test the toothbrush to ensure it works.
- Cut a length of pool tube about the same length as the toothbrush.
- Push the toothbrush into the center opening of the tube. The bottom of the toothbrush should be even with the bottom of the tube. Make sure the on/off switch is within reach.
- Using rubber bands, attach 3 to 6 markers with rubber bands on the outside bottom part of the pool tube. The marker tips should be pointing down and protruding equal lengths beyond the bottom of the tube (see illustration). The Markerbot will balance best with 4 markers, but using other numbers will allow you to create and experiment with different designs. Leave the caps on the markers until you are ready to use the Markerbot.
- If desired, decorate your Markerbot with googly eyes, pipe cleaners, and/or stickers.
- Roll out a sheet of printer paper or butcher paper on a solid flat surface.

- Remove the marker caps, turn on the toothbrush, and place the Markerbot with the marker tips touching the paper. Then watch the Markerbot draw!
- Be ready to grab the Markerbot when it moves off the paper, to avoid staining your table or floor.
- Improve on your design through experimentation. Try different colors and different numbers of markers to see the change in spin speed and picture form. Test each variation on a separate piece of paper so you can see a clear change.

Two Markerbots in action
Photo © VentureLab

Building and using a Markerbot brings together STEM and art. The process allows you to practice brainstorming, designing, experimenting, and prototyping.

6

Make Playtime Curiosity Time

ONE OF THE MOST VITAL INSTINCTS IN EVERY HUMAN BEING IS CURIOSITY—the desire to learn more about our surroundings and to understand the world we live in. Following our curiosity nurtures crucial underlying strengths like resilience, adaptation, and problem-solving. In evolutionary terms, it is not the strongest species that survives, but the one that is best able to adapt to the changing environment—and curiosity plays a key role in generating that adaptive capability.

In my work with VentureLab, I've had many opportunities to watch kids following their curiosity instinct, often with magical results.

Nine-year-old Emma worried that her pet mice were not sufficiently entertained by the toys in their cage. She often added extra sticks and toys in an effort to keep them engaged and happy, but she still believed they needed more excitement and stimulation in their little lives. Her curiosity instinct kicked in. Emma wondered: Could she design a more interesting environment that her mice would really respond to? How would she know whether the mice liked it?

Emma decided to design a maze that would challenge the mice. Emma's mom recognized that Emma's maze-building idea was, in effect, a miniature engineering project, and she provided Emma with the tools needed to make it possible. When Emma followed up with an analysis of how the mice handled the maze—recording the directions in which they turned when they came to a T-shaped intersection with no clues as to the way out—the project morphed into a statistical study, and Emma's mom helped her with the math.

Now Emma is planning a bioscience project to see whether genetics plays a role in rodent behavior. She is already collecting samples of mouse fur and blood, to be analyzed when DNA testing comes down in price to meet a nine-year-old's budget.

NURTURING THE CURIOSITY CYCLE

A girl who is in touch with her natural curiosity can entertain herself without requiring external stimulation like television and video games. Instead of drifting toward disengagement, she sharpens her ability to formulate questions, imagine possible answers, create predictive models, test them, and then repeat the process with more information and new insights. A curious girl who is filled with questions about the world around her is less likely to sink into passivity. She is more likely to define herself as an *active creator.*

Jonathan Mugan is a "robot guy," a computer scientist who is working at the cutting edge of disciplines like artificial intelligence. When he's not working on software coding, he spends a lot of his time studying how children learn. It's not just a hobby for Mugan: understanding the minds of children, especially preschoolers, makes it possible for humans to create robots that can learn in similar ways.

Mugan explains that children learn, in part, by building *mental models*. Children absorb concepts from their environment and use these concepts to build models that explain what is likely to happen in the world around them. Consciously or unconsciously, they then test their models, refining their knowledge, improving their adaptive behaviors, and often developing new models along the way. It's a process that begins at a very early age. For example, a toddler who has discovered that doorknobs open doors might then try to open a particular door and find that it doesn't budge. This leads to a new mental model, the locked door, calling for new forms of adaptive behavior. Mugan calls this iterative process *the curiosity cycle*. He says,

> *Using models to predict the environment is crucial to the curiosity cycle because testing improves models. The mind-set of seeing the world through prediction has the benefit of allowing your child to view knowledge as*

> *tentative. Knowing you might be wrong is the first step toward undoing an assumption and finding the right solution to a problem. Children must always be aware that some of what they know could be wrong—and probably is. They learn that even an* incorrect *model is better than no model.*[1]

Thanks to the curiosity cycle, the more your child knows, the more curious she becomes. The experiential learning fostered by the curiosity cycle means that your child doesn't just know facts by rote; she has models for why things are true and sees how they relate to everything else that she knows. For this reason, Mugan has concluded that *deep learning begins with curiosity*.

In entrepreneurial education, we bring curiosity to the forefront of the class. The curiosity cycle is set in motion—if necessary, through gentle nudging. When stimulated by curiosity, learning doesn't feel like work because it is play—that is, in Mugan's words, it is activity that is "internally directed and intrinsically motivated. . . . A child feels like a free and natural human being doing what she wants to do."

STARTING WITH A FEATHER: FREE-RANGE CURIOSITY

A curious girl can be comfortable and confident in environments of uncertainty. She has a lifelong strength that must come from within and cannot be bestowed from outside.

Curiosity enables her to embrace her sense of wonder and to become a critical thinker, unafraid of posing questions and primed to take calculated risks.

During my childhood, my mother would take my sisters and me on nature walks to a local creek to look for fossils, or to a field in South Austin to look for meteorites. Sometimes at night we would just lie in the driveway and look up at the stars. All of these unstructured activities developed my curiosity. A curious mind can find things to explore almost anywhere, especially outdoors. I call it *free-range curiosity*.

Take something as simple as feathers that have fallen from a passing bird. If you walk through a neighborhood where lawns aren't cultivated like crops, and where nature's "irregularities and imperfections" haven't been blasted away by leaf blowers, chances are you'll spot a few stray feathers.

Simply by beginning to look closely at feathers, a girl can become more observant. I've observed this effect ever since my daughters, Maribel and Cate, were in preschool. When they would pick up feathers from the ground, we'd examine them together and notice small differences: perhaps one feather might be iridescent in the sunlight, while another is tipped in white. The girls would notice textures—downy fluff, or an unusually rigid quill. By smoothing a ruffled feather, they could make its vanes flatten out and adhere, forming a classic feather shape. They were curious about how the parts fit together. "Is there a special glue?" they wondered. Later, inside the house, they could use a magnifying glass or microscope to detect the rows of tiny barbs that help form a feather's structure.

How can something as simple as a feather be such a powerful stimulant for exploration and thinking? Because it prompts a girl to ask *questions* and to care about the answers. Further research in books or on the Internet can open up new doors of discovery. Curiosity about feathers can lead to questions about aeronautic design, evolutionary adaptation, mechanical engineering, fractals, and materials science. She may wonder whether the leading edge of feathers in flight is the narrower side, and why. A question like this can lead a girl to explore the websites of the Cornell Lab of Ornithology and the National Audubon Society, rich with images and information. She can listen to their recorded bird calls. She might watch a PBS *Nature* documentary about birds around the world.

As a child's mind map of feathers grows more complex, her brain's neural pathways multiply. Following her curiosity where it leads is an essential step toward mental growth.

Now overlay entrepreneurial learning. When encouraged to think like an entrepreneur, a girl whose curiosity has been stimulated by studying feathers may begin to wonder how the world could be made safer for threatened bird species. What can she do to improve the world for birds? With this shift, she may explore becoming a social or environmental entrepreneur. The problem of preserving our endangered bird species might become her life's work. Or she may begin to wonder whether the incredible properties of feathers could be applied to "maker" projects. Could the remarkable lightness and strength of feathers, which make flight possible, be adapted to some new kind of product? It is the beginning of envisioning a career that could in some way improve the world—all beginning with a few windswept feathers.

This is the essence of entrepreneurial education: stimulating learning, finding questions to be explored and problems to be creatively solved. It's not about coming up with the one and only "correct" answer to a question. There are no bubbles to fill in with number two pencils and no essays to be structured just so and graded on their faithfulness to a rigid template. Free-range curiosity leads to discovery, as demonstrated in this account by single mother Sue Kolbly:

> *My friend salvaged a flat-panel television that someone had left beside a Dumpster and brought it over to me, thinking my kids might enjoy having a larger monitor for TV and computer games. They tested it and decided it was beyond repair. "Let's take it apart!" my oldest son said, grabbing a screwdriver and safety glasses. My other children, including my thirteen-year-old daughter, helped take apart the layers of the television. They enjoyed the polarizing layers especially—and puzzled over how it is that when you turn one of the layers sideways you somehow block light going through it. We even extracted a large white sheet of plastic that I now use to diffuse light when I photograph stuff to sell on eBay.*[2]

A WORLD FULL OF QUESTIONS

You may not run across an abandoned flat-panel TV set very often. But in our daily lives we have many opportunities to encourage play that stimulates and satisfies curiosity. We simply need to open our minds to recognize the endless questions that surround us, waiting to be explored and answered. Parents and teachers who are trying to nurture their kids' curiosity don't need to have all of the answers—and even if they have the answers, it's often best to keep them to themselves to make room for exploration and surprises. You just need to be able to raise questions, challenge the logic behind ideas, and discuss what resources might be useful—say, a 3-D printer or a computer program—even if those items are not immediately available to you.

Once girls are in the curiosity cycle, they can generate fascinating questions, big and small, on topics that are doctorate-worthy. Here are some samples from VentureGirls I've known:

- Our dog ate a toad and foamed at the mouth. Why was it so yucky? How can I keep my dog from eating another toad? Would it happen with a frog? What's the difference between a toad and a frog? Can the two mate? Would a toad-frog have useful properties? (Questions from a girl, age ten.)
- Was the mother of the first human a monkey? (Age five.)

- I'm always wondering about early humans. How can we use fossilized DNA to try to re-create one? (Age nine.)
- How do nocturnal animals see? (Age eight.)
- Can we use the wind on the sides of moving cars to generate wind power? Is it possible to build a wind-powered hybrid car? (Age sixteen.)
- When I grow up, I want to drive an electric car. Do they have to be so expensive? What if you could plug it in anywhere? (Age ten.)
- Could we make a hybrid animal to ride instead of a car? (Age six.)
- I want to make white paint. But when I mix colors, they get muddy. How can I make white? (Age eight.)
- For bottled water, can we make a plastic that isn't bad for you? (Age ten.)
- If we only had a small amount of farmland—say our front yard—could we raise enough food for our household, like the astronaut in *The Martian* did? (Age ten.)
- How do you know if it's a good spider or a bad spider that bites? (Age six.)
- Can we use less metal to make a fence? Could we make a superstrong fiber the size of a single hair? (Age eleven.)

Questions like these lead naturally into topics ranging from genetics and physiology to agronomy, chemical engineering, and entomology. From there, with encouragement, it is possible to help girls follow their curious thinking into problems they'll want to solve—problems that spark exploration, innovation, discoveries, and inventions.

Don't worry if you don't know enough to quickly answer your child's questions. At age sixty-two, scientist Richard Feynman described a childhood experience that shaped his entire life. He and his dad were walking along a road. Young Richard was pulling a red wagon with a ball in it when he felt moved to ask his father a question: "Say, Pop, I noticed something. When I pull the wagon, the ball rolls to the back of the wagon. And when I'm pulling it along and I suddenly stop, the ball rolls to the front of the wagon. Why is that?"

"That, nobody knows," his dad responded. "The general principle is that things which are moving tend to keep on moving. And things which are standing still tend to stand still, unless you push them hard. This general tendency is called 'inertia'—but nobody knows why it's true."[3]

And that was the answer that would stick with Richard Feynman for life. He realized something that he would rediscover countless times during his career as a scientist—that the world is full of wondrous mysteries waiting to be solved. Feynman became a theoretical physicist who did pioneering work in subatomic particles, quantum computing, and nanotechnology, becoming what some have called the greatest scientist since Einstein.

What I love about this story is that it shows that the frontier of knowledge is within a child's grasp. By telling his son "No one knows," Feynman's father confessed his own vulnerability. He conveyed that the world has many unknowns, questions with incomplete models. Instead of quenching his son's curiosity, he sparked it. The question his father couldn't answer made Feynman even more eager to learn.

To lead, teachers don't need the answers, but rather to raise questions, probe their students' logic, and discuss what resources might be useful—a ruler, a magnifying glass, a camera, a computer program, or even just a pencil and notebook. Children who follow their curiosity are demonstrating the natural human instinct to learn and discover for themselves. No amount of cramming facts or formulas into their brains will ever be as enjoyable and meaningful as when a child learns by herself, armed only with a curious mind and a willingness to explore.

THE POWER OF PLAY

One of the most natural outlets for curiosity—as well as a stimulant to it—is play. For growing humans, play is a biological imperative. Often what looks like simple play can be deep experiential learning of the kind that is best suited for a young mind.

The quality that distinguishes play from other activities is that it is open-ended. Unstructured play expresses freewheeling creativity—wherever it goes, no eye on the clock—and thereby encourages exploration, independence, and confidence. It's an important corrective to our tendency to impose too much structure on the lives of our kids. "The trouble with over-structuring is that it discourages exploration," explains neuroscientist Jay Giedd, who has spent his career studying the development of the young human brain.[4] It's not natural for a young child to be required to sit in a chair and draw letters. Children need to move about and play to follow their curiosity.

Playing is also one of the cornerstones of creativity and innovation. When you play, you aren't seeking a specific goal or following a carefully shaped plan. Play is for the fun of it. In playing, you can make and build, create new worlds and personas, invent new games and even break the rules without fear of consequences. Play helps develop potential entrepreneurs and innovators because it's risk-free. Play gives kids a fresh perspective; it transcends disciplines and reveals new patterns and connections, which is often critical in solving problems and being innovative.

For all these reasons, play is a common denominator in every entrepreneurial class or camp we offer at VentureLab. Fortunately, in our daily lives, we have many opportunities to encourage play that builds confidence. We simply need to open our minds to recognize them.

In the words of Robert S. Root-Bernstein and Michèle M. Root-Bernstein, authors of *Sparks of Genius: The Thirteen Thinking Tools of the World's Most Creative People*, "We can think what cannot be said, and we can invent new ways of saying previously unsayable things—if we do it as a game."[5]

EMBRACE THE SPIRIT OF MISCHIEF

I've said that curiosity is an instinctive human trait that can't be imposed from outside. That's true—but the environment we create for our kids does a lot to determine whether their natural curiosity will be stimulated or squelched. That's where parents, family friends, teachers, and youth leaders have an important role to play.

Fostering curiosity is an important element of the Bill and Melinda Gates Foundation's work in education. Bill Gates has thought a lot about how social surroundings can impact a child's attitude and behavior. "Every kid starts out with a lot of curiosity, and thinks that 'Boy, maybe I could invent something. [But] if you don't get a chance to play around, experiment, and put things together . . . then probably you start to think, 'Hmm, maybe I can't . . . Maybe this is too hard. Maybe there were supersmart people who already invented everything.' So you get kind of discouraged. So it takes a conscious effort on the part of teachers and parents to imbue someone with the sense of 'No, you can.' "[6]

One reason many adults subtly discourage curiosity is that from time to time, it can lead to what looks like mischief. A mother I know took her nine-year-old daughter Jessie to a kid-friendly museum exhibit called "Androids and Aliens." One interactive element let kids create their own little parachutes to see whether an airstream would lift their designs out of a Plexiglas tube. After an hour of this, Jessie's curiosity took hold. She cut a piece of paper into tiny bits, shoved them into the launch opening, and *eureka*! The entire room was blasted with her confetti, which drifted down over the children to their delight. Other kids started creating their own confetti showers. Within a few minutes it had become a "situation." Mom slipped out of the exhibit, Jessie in tow, just in time to avoid the museum staff members who had come to shut down the attraction and clean up the paper bits that had wafted into every corner of the room.

It's too bad Jessie was discouraged here. If the museum staff had been open to this kind of play, they might have gotten some ideas for wonderful new interactive exhibits that even more kids would love, and learn from.

When your daughter's eyes start to glitter with mischief, don't get scared! Instead, stand back and take note. She may be on the brink of a creative idea. Explore it with her and help her discover a safe way to turn her inspiration into reality.

VentureLab is special, in part, because it provides a wide-open, encouraging environment for children to explore where their curiosity leads. There are no penalties, no criticism, no embarrassment, and no right or wrong answers—only ideas, information, and discovery that feeds the curiosity cycle. On the first day, many girls arrive at VentureLab feeling nervous and hesitant. They're wondering, "Is it *really* okay for me to try whatever comes into my mind?" As they gradually realize that the spirit of open-ended exploration is for real, the tension vanishes, replaced by a spirit of exuberance and joy in which they discover the sheer fun of science, math, and entrepreneurship. You can nurture the same spirit of curiosity in your own family.

SIMPLE WAYS TO ENCOURAGE CURIOSITY

In our daily lives, we have many opportunities to encourage kids to experience the excitement of the curiosity cycle. In most cases, little or no special equipment, materials, or space is required. You simply need to open your mind to recognize an interesting question when it pops up. One mother of four describes the kind of curiosity-based play she fosters at home:

> *Our income is so low that we qualify for the free lunch program, and a good cheap education is hard to come by. So we're resourceful. We explore the world of science all the time, often at the spur of the moment. Just the other day, we built a small spectrometer out of a cheap pair of novelty glasses and went around the house exploring what made up the "white" in different types of light bulbs.* Other projects have included the classic Mentos and Diet Coke, match rockets, rock candy, baking soda and vinegar, and any number of experiments involving light (my oldest son goes to college, and has taken a good number of experimental physics classes). All of these are good ways to learn science at home. If you don't have an enterprising teenager, there exist any number of good websites and science-experiments books you can check out from the library for free.*

---

* Easy instructions on making a homemade spectrometer are widely available on the Internet. If you don't have a pair of novelty glasses, you can use an old CD, as described here: http://www.livescience.com/41548-spectroscopy-science-fair-project.html.

Here are some ideas for easy ways you can stimulate and nurture the curiosity cycle at home and in your own neighborhood.

When something mechanical breaks, consider its teaching value. One dad recalls how he explored science as a kid using junk—discarded and fascinating: "My grandfather, who worked for a moving company, would bring home all sorts of discarded mechanical and electronic gizmos. Armed with only a screwdriver and a hammer (and no goggles), we would dissect these marvels to see what made them work. Try taking apart a modern cellphone or a laptop computer. Assuming you can even figure out how to pry it open, the inside is as mysterious and inscrutable as the outside."[7]

Look for older appliances to take apart, just as I did with our family's rotary phone when I was a little girl. Unlike me, however, I suggest you *not* take apart a perfectly good appliance. Wait until it breaks, and unplug it before you start tinkering! And when you're experimenting with items that could crack, break, and splinter, wear goggles to protect the eyes.

Outfit a "maker space" at home. With today's tight school budgets, getting access to a real science lab isn't easy for many kids. It doesn't matter. If you have a spare corner at home and a few bucks to spend on simple, basic items, you can create a "maker space" where curiosity can run wild. Collect tools and gadgets like gears, ball bearings, screwdrivers, nuts and bolts, pliers, paints, and other miscellaneous hardware. If possible, hang up a pegboard where all the goodies can be displayed within easy reach. Spread out old newspapers or a painter's drop cloth to protect the floor and tabletops. Then turn your daughter and her friends loose to construct and deconstruct whatever they can imagine. And be there yourself to help problem-solve and provide whatever additional materials may be needed.

Visit the nearest kids' museum or hands-on science museum. One of the great trends of the last few decades is the proliferation of hands-on museums of science, technology, and math, many of them geared specifically to kids. At last count, there were more than 250 such museums, all featuring marvelous hands-on exhibits where children can play with gadgets, tools, experiments, and demonstrations that foster curiosity and stimulate exploration. Some museums have low or no admission fees; others have special days or evenings when entry is without charge; and still others offer special discounts or "scholarships" for families in need.

Embrace nature. The outdoors offers endless opportunities to ask fascinating questions about how the world works. Plant life in all its variations—grasses and shrubs; trees of many kinds; seeds, leaves, bark, fruits, and roots; mosses, ferns, mushrooms—all provide countless opportunities to collect, examine, study, and analyze. Any local brook, stream, river, or seashore is an extraordinary ecosystem that reflects thousands of years' worth of geological change and biological adaptation. Even the sky overhead, with its clouds of many varieties and its nighttime array of moon, stars, and planets, is a source of beauty, mystery, and inspiration. Natural attractions like these are available to almost everyone, whether you live in the countryside or in the midst of a big city; a bit of online exploration or a call to the local government office can tell you where the closest park or undeveloped land can be found and enjoyed.

Here's a specific suggestion you and your daughter may love: Look into bird-watching activities with your local Audubon Society—there are more than four hundred chapters in the United States. Consider participating in the society's Christmas bird count between mid-December and early January, conducted each year for more than a century. It's a great way of learning about local bird life in your community and actually contributing to scientific knowledge about avian habits and travel patterns. Participation is free, and beginning bird watchers are teamed with at least one experienced "birder." Fair warning: You might need to arise long before dawn. But what a way to sharpen your powers of observation, stimulate your curiosity about and insight into the world of nature, and form new neural pathways as you make discoveries about the world around you.

Let children cook. The home kitchen is a great place to conduct simple experiments driven by curiosity and based on "What if?" questions. Let your kids learn what their mistakes produce: misshapen pancakes, scrambled eggs that are way too salty, rice turned emerald green with food coloring (no, that does not make it a vegetable), and a loaf of bread that could double as a doorstop. Don't bemoan the waste of a few ingredients—regard them as teaching props and the pennies they cost as an investment in your child, one with a priceless return. Cooking failures are some of the funniest moments you will have. And there's a lifelong bonus: Children learn the joy of cooking.

Choose toys that stimulate curiosity. I've emphasized how easy it is to enjoy question-and-exploration activities while spending little or no money. But when you have the opportunity to choose gifts for your daughter—at holiday time or for her birthday—look for toys, books, and other items that will help her discover the world of curiosity.

You can find plenty of great options by asking your child's teacher or any science-oriented friend, or by visiting any of the many websites dedicated to reviewing kids' toys. One favorite of mine is Snap Circuits, a series of electronics activity kits that have won a raft of awards from parenting magazines, organizations, and rating agencies. Snap Circuits kits range in price from twenty to fifty dollars and up, and each one creates the possibility for your daughter to try dozens, even hundreds, of technology-based projects.

One ten-year-old girl and her kid brother devised an application that has more than repaid the cost of their Snap Circuits kit. Their mother was always finding batteries around the house and could never tell whether they could be reused or should be discarded. These entrepreneurial kids realized they could build a simple circuit attached to a tiny fan. Insert the mystery battery and voilà! An instant test for battery power. Last I heard, the two kids were working to solve a new problem—how to measure the precise amount of energy left in a battery.

THE CURIOSITY PAYOFF

The curiosity cycle is its own reward. Girls driven by curiosity are never bored. They see the world as an endless string of mysteries waiting to be explored; one question leads to another and another, with knowledge and discovery waiting around every corner. Young women who have been raised with this attitude toward life are likely to develop careers they find continually stimulating; they are self-starters, brimming with creativity, drive, and passion. And because they've been encouraged from an early age to dabble fearlessly in the unknown, they're not afraid to tackle tough challenges, whether at work or in life. They'll become the great problem-solvers of the future.

The greatest scientific minds have been ceaselessly curious. Polish scientist Marie Curie was the first woman to be awarded a Nobel Prize. She and her husband, Pierre, along with another scientist, Henri Becquerel, won the prize in physics in 1903, based largely on Marie's daring and dangerous research on radioactivity (a word that she herself coined). How was a woman positioned to perform that groundbreaking research in an era when women were rarely afforded such opportunities? Originally, the project that led to her discoveries was handed to her in the belief it wouldn't lead to much—and in the hands of someone else, it might not have. But Marie Curie developed the theory of radioactivity, devised methods for isolating radioactive isotopes, and discovered two elements, polonium and radium.

Unfortunately, as a female scientist, she still had obstacles to overcome. The Nobel Committee originally intended to award the prize to Pierre Curie and Becquerel. But one member of the committee—Magnus Goesta Mittag-Leffler, a Swedish mathematician who advocated for women scientists—objected and notified Pierre, who registered his own objection with the committee. This prompted them to award the prize she'd earned to Marie Curie as well. Far from hanging up her lab coat, Curie won a second Nobel Prize eight years later, this one in chemistry, becoming the first person to win two Nobels.

Marie Curie kept coming up with marvelous questions and discoveries throughout her life. It was pure science, driven by her innate curiosity. Her advice resonates a century later in our celebrity-obsessed culture: "Be less curious about people and more curious about ideas."

Science is not the only field in which curiosity plays a critical role. When CEO Lori Senecal interviews job candidates, she asks, "What have you invented?" Senecal explains that she isn't looking to hire *inventors* in the most common use of the term: "That doesn't mean you have to have created a robot that can get a beer from a fridge. It could be anything. It's to see whether they have the mind-set of creating something. That shows a desire to find fresh solutions."[8]

Senecal led a company that employs scientists, engineers, technologists—but it is an advertising agency. CP+B Global Network also employs "app makers, rule breakers, artists, anthropologists, snowboarders, problem-solvers, heavy metal drummers, and everything in between." What does this varied assortment of smart, creative people have in common? All have the gift of insatiable curiosity.

For some, the doors that swing open with a push from the curiosity instinct can be truly remarkable. Consider Lalita Srisai, a thirteen-year-old girl from the Koraput district in eastern India, one of the poorest agricultural regions in the country. From an early age, Lalita earned a reputation at her local public school as one of the most curiosity-driven kids in her village. She was forever taking long walks in the neighborhood, observing the activities on the nearby farms, and asking questions about what she saw. When she learned in class about Mankombu Swaminathan, the genetic scientist who helped launch India's Green Revolution, which helped feed millions of poor people, she decided she would be a scientist one day.

Lalita got a chance to test her prowess earlier than expected. When she noticed heaps of corncobs drying and decaying in the sun during her neighborhood walks, she began asking farmers to explain. She learned that after harvesting the corn, they would cut off the kernels to feed their animals, then discard the useless cobs by the side of the road.

Lalita got an idea. She wondered whether there might be a way to use the dried-up corncobs to help solve one of rural India's endemic problems—a lack of clean water. A simple experiment in her family kitchen convinced her she was on to something. She placed a bunch of dehydrated corncobs in a bowl of dirty water and, after several hours, observed that the water looked cleaner. The absorbent cobs, it seemed, had soaked up most of the impurities in the water.

Many hours of experimentation later, Lalita had developed a low-cost filtration system made with plastic bottles and straws that could be used by farmers to remove contaminants from groundwater and rain tanks. The key ingredient: dried-up corncobs, which serve the same purpose as more-expensive ingredients in commercially manufactured filtration systems.

In September 2015, Lalita's invention carried her all the way to Mountain View, California, where it won the Community Impact Award at the Google Science Fair, a global competition for science-loving kids ages thirteen to eighteen. The ten-thousand-dollar prize Lalita received will go a long way toward funding her future education. Even more important, in Lalita's own words, winning the award has played "a big role to boost my curious bend of mind and [encourage me to] pursue scientific research for the mass benefit of society."[9]

TRY THIS AT HOME—AN ACTIVITY GIRLS WILL LOVE: THE ENTREPRENEURIAL EGG DROP CHALLENGE

In this activity, parent(s) and kid(s) will try to meet the challenge of creating an egg protection device that will enable an egg to fall from a high place without breaking. Here's the catch: Your egg is not really an egg, but rather a fragile product of your choosing that you are trying to deliver safely to a customer. Will your product survive its journey?

TIME: 60—90 MINUTES

You Need

Something to write and draw with (pens, pencils, crayons, or markers)

Paper to sketch on

Poster board

Raw eggs

Various craft items or recycled supplies: boxes, plastic bottles, foam, straws, strings, tape, glue, stickers, and so on

Directions

- Brainstorm and sketch various ways to build an egg safety device that will protect an egg from breaking when being dropped from a high place. You get to choose the height from which the egg will be dropped: from five feet, or from the top of a one-story or two-story building. Think about ways to use the materials you have in your design.
- Build a prototype for your device. Test it and modify the design as needed until you find a design that keeps the egg safe when it is dropped.
- Now, think like an entrepreneur: Imagine that your egg safety device is a package developed to protect a fragile product that you are creating to solve a problem. The egg represents the product you would like to deliver safely. Brainstorm a problem and a product that you would like to deliver. Think about who your

customer is and how much you would sell your product for. For example, you could be trying to safely air-drop vaccines from a plane in the midst of a zombie infestation, or you could be a delivery person who wants to use an air cannon to shoot a package safely to a customer's front door.

- Design a poster that includes the name of your product, the problem it is solving, the price, who your customer is, and a sketch of the product.
- Decorate and make any needed adjustments to your egg safety device/product package, and do a final test drop.
- Before an audience of your choosing, present the name of your product, the problem it is solving, the price, who your customer is, and a sketch of what your product would look like. Conclude the presentation by demonstrating your product package making its trip to its customer.

This fun entrepreneurial spin on a popular classroom project can be done by anyone from preschool kids to high school students. If you use it with older kids, you can include an explanation of Newton's laws and the nature of gravity. The exercise lets you practice applying STEM concepts through an entrepreneurial lens, solving a real-world problem (or an imaginary one) using creative thinking.

TRY THIS AT HOME—AN ACTIVITY GIRLS WILL LOVE: SPACE FARMING WITH HYDROPONICS

In this activity, parent(s) and kid(s) will learn about plants and hydroponics, using recycled materials to grow food in the same way that space explorers might grow it during an expedition to colonize the planet Mars. You'll build a wick system, which is one of the simplest hydroponic systems to build. It works best with plants, like herbs and lettuce, that are small and require modest amounts of water.

TIME: 1–2 HOURS

You Need

Plastic soda bottle (at least 1.2 liters)
Scissors or box cutter
String or fabric to make a water-carrying wick
Potting soil
Hydroponic nutrient solution
Seeds of your choosing (such as sunflower, snap pea, or herbs)
Optional: Duct tape, drill, fertilizer, seed-starting grow plugs

Directions

- Imagine that you are an astronaut, tasked with helping colonize Mars by growing plants to feed people. The climate on Mars is harsh, with an average temperature of –80 degrees Fahrenheit and a dusty atmosphere, about a hundred times thinner than the atmosphere of Earth and made up of 95 percent carbon dioxide. The environment doesn't support plant growth, but you can use hydroponics to grow plants in a climate-controlled indoor setting.

- Cut the plastic bottle in two parts, seven inches from the bottom. The top part of the bottle will sit within the bottom part of the bottle, with the screwed-on cap facing downward like a funnel. The top part is where you will put your soil and seeds, and the bottom part is the reservoir where you will put your water and nutrients.
- Cut or drill a hole near the top of the bottle or through the bottle cap. The wick that will deliver water and nutrients to the plant will pass through this hole.
- If you like, you can cover the cut edges of the bottle with duct tape and decorate the bottle.
- Now choose materials to make a wick that will carry water and nutrients to the plant. Some commonly used materials are wool felt, nylon rope, fabric from cotton clothing such as a T-shirt, and yarn. Choose three materials to test and cut a three-inch strip of each. (Tip: washing the material first can help improve its wicking ability.)
- One at a time, touch the end of each material to the surface of a bowl of water and hold it there for a set amount of time—for example, one minute. Notice how far up the strip the water rises, and mark the high point. Which material allows water to travel the far-

thest? Why do you think that is? Choose the material that wicks the best.

- To make a wick, cut the chosen fabric into a strip one inch wide by six inches long. Then place the wicking material through the hole in the top of the bottle, letting it hang down into the bottom of the reservoir.
- Now assemble the hydroponic system. Fill the bottom part of the bottle (the reservoir) one-third full of water and put in a teaspoon of hydroponic nutrient solution. Then put potting soil in the top part of the bottle (mixed with fertilizer if you like). Put at least two seeds of the same kind into the soil and cover them.
- Optional: To maximize the chances that your seeds will germinate, put them into a seed-starter grow plug. Then lightly bury the grow plug into the potting soil.
- The completed plant system should look like the ones in the illustration.

Photo © Luz Cristal Glanchai

- Lightly water the soil. Then place the plant system in front of a window with access to full sunlight. At a temperature of 70 to 75 degrees Fahrenheit, it can take anywhere from seven to fifteen days for sunflowers, snap peas, basil, or mint to sprout. Rosemary or thyme may take fifteen to thirty days.

What do plants need to grow? Plants need water, nutrients, structure, sunlight, oxygen, and CO_2 (carbon dioxide). Thinking about these requirements helps to explain why various plants grow best in different climates—shady versus sunny, warm versus cold, wet versus dry. The great thing about hydroponics is that it lets humans grow varieties of plants in areas whose climate might otherwise be inhospitable. By controlling all of the plant inputs, hydroponic farmers can grow plants out of season. In urban environments, hydroponics is an optimal choice because it can be operated within existing structures or outside, regardless of soil quality or external environment. And someday, when humans colonize Mars or other extraterrestrial locations, hydroponics may be the key to their survival.

TRY THIS AT HOME—AN ACTIVITY GIRLS WILL LOVE: ROBOTIC HAND

Imagine that you don't have hands, or that the hands you have won't let you do something you need to do—to reach something on a very high shelf or to safely grasp something that is really hot or cold. In this activity, parent(s) and kid(s) will become robotics engineers. They'll gain an understanding of how human hands and fingers work, and they'll design and create their own "robotic hand" like one that could be used to solve real-world problems.

TIME: 45—90 MINUTES

You Need

Something to write and draw with (pens, pencils, crayons, or markers)
Paper to sketch on
Cardboard, card stock, or a sturdy paper plate
String
5 to 7 straws and (optional) a large-diameter straw
Tape or hot glue (for older kids)
Optional: Stickers or colorful tape

Directions

- Imagine that you are a robotics engineer. Start by brainstorming problems that you think a robotic hand could help solve. Pick a task for which a robotic hand could be used.
- Now think about what the robotic hand needs to do to accomplish the task. Think about who would use this robotic hand, how it would be used, and what materials it would need to be made of. For example, if you are trying to reach something really high, you may need to design a really long arm attached to the robotic hand. Your robotic hand will need fingers—but depending on its purpose, you might want to include fewer than five fingers, or more than five. Sketch your design idea

and modify it until you have come up with the best design.

- Now draw your robotic hand on a piece of cardboard and cut it out. If needed, include moveable joints in the fingers. Draw lines on the cardboard fingers where the joints would be. (Human hands have two joints on the thumb and three on each of the other fingers, but the joints in your robotic hand may be different.) Next, fold the fingers toward you along each of the lines. Then unfold. You will now have fingers that bend at the joints.
- Follow these steps to mechanize your hand:
  - Cut a piece of string, 18 to 24 inches long, for each finger on your hand. Tape or glue one piece of string to the tip of each finger.
  - Cut pieces of straws to fit in between each joint of the robotic fingers. Thread these straws onto your string and tape or glue these straws to the hand, in between the joints.
  - Cut out one more small straw piece for each finger of the robotic hand. Thread one straw piece onto each string, and tape or glue these straws on the palm of the hand in a fan shape. They should be taped close together at the bottom of the palm, and fan outward toward each finger.
  - Finally, cut out a last piece of straw (preferably using a larger-diameter straw). Thread all of the finger strings through this straw, and tape or glue it vertically at the very base of the hand.

- You can decorate the hand with stickers or colorful tape if you like.

Experiment with your hand. When you pull on the strings together, you can watch the fingers move. Using the straws and strings mimics the way that tendons and muscles work to bend the fingers of your own hand. Experiment with grabbing things, watching what happens when you pull on different strings. Have fun!

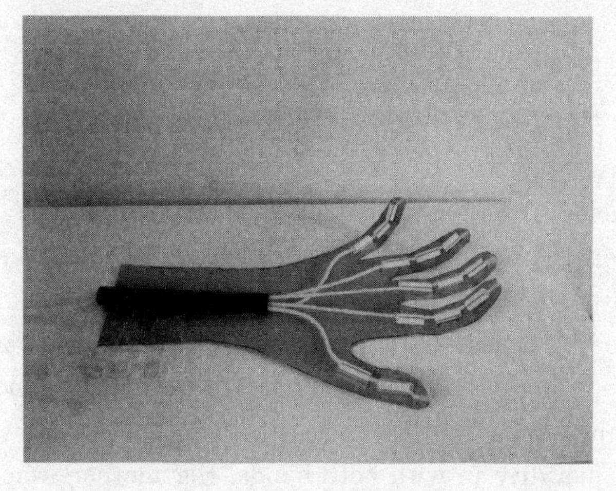

Photo © Luz Cristal Glangchai

7

Please Get Messy!

A COMMON MEMORY THAT COMES UP WHENEVER WOMEN IN SCIENCE OR technology reminisce about girlhood is getting dirty. A lot of us spent more time in jeans than dresses. Many of us recall the fascination of playing with mud.

Today's VentureGirls are no different. Nine-year-old Jessie loves to get a large plastic box, fill it with dirt, and add water just for fun. Stir with a stick? Sometimes, but usually she'll just dive in with both hands. Her mother—who also loved mud as a child—has learned to repress her impulse to say, "Clean up!" She understands that Jessie is learning by touch and observation. Concepts like viscosity, textures, and adherence will have experiential references for her as Jessie advances in science. Oh, and mud is fun!

Messiness is one of the keys to developing the kind of open-ended, creative mind that entrepreneurship demands. That means that one of our natural instincts as parents—the desire to keep our kids clean and neat—can be harmful, especially when carried to extremes.

THINKING CREATIVELY—AND MESSILY

WHEN IT COMES TO BEING MESSY, AS WITH SO MANY ISSUES, WE ARE TORN between conflicting impulses. On the one hand, we value creativity in business, technology, the visual and performing arts, and media. We encourage self-expression in our kids, make superstars out of singers and filmmakers who invent new artistic styles, and put the faces of high-tech innovators on the covers of magazines. Based on this evidence, it would seem as if the value we prize above all others is creativity—the wilder the better.

On the other hand, as parents and educators, we often send our children the opposite message. Our elementary and high school education systems are heavily focused on student "outputs," measured primarily by how kids perform on standardized tests. Kids who are too boisterous, talkative, or active in the classroom often earn poor grades for "conduct" or "behavior," and sometimes get diagnosed with attention deficit/hyperactivity disorder (ADHD)—as if the enthusiastic liveliness that comes naturally to so many kids is a sickness for which they need to be medicated. And parents too often communicate to their children—directly or indirectly—that the ultimate success of their high school years will be measured by their ability to win admission to a prestigious, competitive college . . . which usually means ticking off a set of unvarying boxes (grade point average, test scores, extra-curricular activities) on an application form.

In short, we praise creativity, yet we tend to penalize children who express it through their unconventional, outside-the-box behavior. Result: the preemptive loss of a national resource, the true value of which we will never know.

The fact is that there's a strong connection between creativity and messiness. Both involve violating conventional expectations, bending or breaking the rules that generally constrain our thinking and behavior, and being willing to risk the possible negative consequences—a ruined dress, the teasing of peers, the disapproval of parents or teachers. And both creativity and messiness reflect the natural impulses to play, experiment, and take chances that most people are born with—impulses they gradually learn to suppress through years of training that emphasizes neatness, orderliness, rule-following, and always providing the "right answer"—that is, the expected answer.

In the words of Sir Ken Robinson, an influential voice for transforming schools to encourage creativity and to develop more fully our human potential, "All children start their school careers with sparkling imaginations, fertile minds, and a willingness to take risks with what they think." Unfortunately, as the years pass, this natural aptitude for creative behavior tends to be stifled. As a result, Robinson says, "Many highly talented, brilliant creative people think they're not—because the thing they were good at in school wasn't valued, or was actually stigmatized."[1]

Expressing creativity in school can result in a poor grade.

Even activities that are ostensibly focused on encouraging creative thinking can lead to criticisms that crush the creators' spirit. Art classes that emphasize sophisticated technique at the expense of imaginative self-expression have discouraged countless aspiring artists. Writing classes focused on grammar, spelling, and punctuation rather than fresh thinking or emotional honesty have caused many would-be novelists, poets, and essayists to abandon their keyboards.

A former English teacher describes her frustration serving on a committee chosen to award writing prizes to middle school students. The problem began with the contest rules, which forced the students to write about "assigned topics that would make anyone snooze." Still, a few students managed to transcend the boring assignment. "There was one essay on 'my summer vacation' that was delightful, warm, with an intelligent twist. I'd have given it first prize. But it didn't even place because it didn't follow writing conventions. I wish I'd been able to find that girl and say, 'Loved it, keep it up! Stay different!' "[2]

Unfortunately, too many teachers find it easier to follow the path of conventional thinking rather than daring to recognize, reward, and encourage the "messy" minds they encounter. The best thing that can happen to some budding young geniuses is to somehow fall between the cracks of our all-too-orderly educational system. As journalist Malcolm Gladwell says, "Let's be thankful that Cezanne didn't have a guidance counselor in high school who looked at his primitive sketches and told him to try accounting."[3]

Dr. dt ogilvie—yes, that's how she prefers to spell her name—is a professor of urban entrepreneurship and design thinking at Rochester Institute of Technology. She observes that our tendency to systematically discourage creativity in schools is mirrored in grown-up society:

> *I was with the CEO of a major multimedia conglomerate who was bragging about his "creativity group," and yet said, "We don't tolerate failure here." That's a big disconnect. Creativity is messy. Imagine if Edison worked for a modern company and hadn't gotten the light bulb right yet.*
>
> *"Tom, what's going on? Is there a problem?"*
>
> *"I'm working on the light bulb."*
>
> *"You've been at it now for what, twenty tries?"*
>
> *"Nine thousand, nine hundred and one. I'm not there yet. But I'm learning—"*
>
> *"I think you need a new job."*[4]

Experts in innovation agree that a "no-failure-tolerated" organizational culture is unlikely to provide space for a creative mind like that of Thomas Edison—and as a result is almost guaranteed not to produce breakthroughs like the light bulb, the phonograph, or the motion picture. As Dr. ogilvie says:

> *People expect ideas to come out full-blown and perfect. If you come up with a crazy idea you may never get pro-*

moted. But great ideas start messy and are seldom the product of one person. It takes a team to bounce an idea around, piggyback, ask questions that help. It's not just about creative product design; there are opportunities for creativity up and down the value chain—technology, materials, marketing, customer service, packaging, distribution.

The link between messiness and creativity may extend even to the desks we work at. A study at the University of Minnesota examined the behaviors of experimental subjects in neat and messy environments. People given tasks to work on in neat rooms were slightly more likely to engage in socially approved behaviors—for example, to make a small donation to charity or to choose an apple over a candy bar as a snack. But those asked to work in rooms strewn with papers and office supplies produced more interesting results when challenged with a creative task, such as coming up with imaginative new uses for Ping-Pong balls. "Disorderly environments seem to inspire breaking free of tradition, which can produce fresh insights," researcher Kathleen Vohs concluded. "Orderly environments, in contrast, encourage convention and playing it safe."[5]

It seems that Dr. ogilvie is right—the tendency of teachers and parents to overvalue neatness, order, and conventional behavior, and to penalize messiness, disorder, and rule-breaking, sets kids off in a direction that may limit their creative possibilities . . . not just in school, but in work and in life.

WANT KIDS TO LEARN? LET THEM GET MESSY!

Messiness isn't only an essential ingredient in the creative process. It's also vital to learning—beginning at a very early age.

This is true in the most literal sense you can imagine. Researchers at the University of Iowa made headlines in 2013 when they released the results of a study that found that toddlers given the opportunity to get messy in their high chairs were better able to learn words and concepts than others. Kids who explored a variety of nonsolid objects—stuff like applesauce, pudding, soup, and milk—by touching them, squeezing them, licking them, and even throwing them did the best at mastering information about those substances. In fact, "[t]he toddlers who interacted the most with the foods—parents, interpret as you want—were more likely to correctly identify them by their texture and name them," the study determined.[6]

"It may look like your child is playing in the high chair, throwing things on the ground," researcher Larissa K. Samuelson commented. "But they are getting information."[7]

Learning is also deeply related to "messiness" in the sense of boundary-crossing—"coloring outside the lines" rather than believing in rigid rules that define activities, spheres of knowledge, and even personality traits.

In his book *A Whole New Mind,* writer Daniel Pink describes people he calls "boundary-crossers" who are not afraid to dabble in many areas of activity, without worrying about whether they are violating any unspoken rules about what is and isn't acceptable. Pink believes that boundary-crossers understand one of the keys to success in today's ever-changing, complex world: "They develop expertise in multiple spheres, they speak different languages, and they find joy in the rich variety of human experience. They live *multilives*—because that's more interesting and, nowadays, more effective."[8]

To encourage this kind of creative, open-minded boundary-crossing in our kids, we need to develop our own willingness to accept "messy," non-rule-bound thinking about the kids themselves. That means refusing to label them in ways that define, and therefore limit, their potential. As author Lisa Rivero explains,

> *Our temptation to label and pigeonhole others is often for reasons of our own comfort and efficiency. If we know Johnny is an extrovert, we know, or we think we know, what to expect from him and what his needs are. However, to encourage children to give themselves more options for how to feel, think, and act, we can refrain from typecasting them as either/or and, instead, give them permission to be both/and: Both extroverted and introverted, both playful and disciplined, both feminine and masculine.*[9]

Thankfully, human beings are more complicated, varied, and "messy" than our simplistic stereotypes suggest—and that's what makes them much more interesting, creative, and fun. Resist the temptation to apply clear, rigid, logical labels to your kids and their behavior. Let them color outside the lines—and enjoy the adventure with them.

THE INTRIGUE OF "DANGEROUS" THINGS

THE SAME PRINCIPLE APPLIES TO THE NATURAL DESIRE THAT PRACTICALLY every parent feels to keep our kids safe. Many parents are diligent about childproofing their house—adding gates, latches, furniture anchors, padding, and all kinds of devices to keep their children from falling down stairs, getting hold of a knife, bumping into a sharp corner, or getting electrocuted.

Of course, it's important to protect our kids from serious harm. But balancing the need for safety with the need to encourage exploration and discovery is crucial to raising tomorrow's entrepreneurs, scientists, innovators, and creators. It's about shielding kids from dangerous conditions in their homes while still allowing them access to age-appropriate tools and activities they can use for playing, experimenting, and testing the limits of their own creativity.

That might mean crayons and blunt-ended scissors for a toddler, a hammer and a glue gun for a third grader, and a soldering iron or a power drill (along with protective eyewear) for a middle-schooler. Items like these can be used safely by kids as long as you provide them with the necessary training and supervision. Most kids find it exciting to get the chance to try using "dangerous" tools like these—and that sense of excitement can fuel their creativity and the sense of pride they'll feel when they complete a project. This applies especially to girls, who are often needlessly excluded from workshop-style activities and instead are often shunted toward the kitchen. The fact is that kids of both sexes can have enormous fun and learn a lot from *all* forms of hands-on creativity—from making a soufflé to building and racing a go-cart.

Letting your kids enjoy adventures that overprotective parents might consider "dangerous" also involves getting outside the house to explore nearby parks, meadows, forests, streams, and beaches. Many women entrepreneurs attribute their success in part to childhoods spent outdoors, doing whatever boys would do, their love of STEM sparked by their experience of nature. By contrast, girls who are overprotected may never get to experience the natural world.

In our VentureLab camps and classes, we try to build outdoor activities into our weekly routine. When we can't get outside, we bring the woods and outdoors in. Sticks and bark, pebbles, leaves, bottles of water from a nearby pond, samples of soil or sand from a local beach . . . these are all natural materials that can be incorporated into projects and fuel early learning about science, the earth, living things, and the materials that shape life on this planet.

John Medina, author of *Brain Rules: 12 Principles for Surviving and Thriving at Work, Home, and School,* is a molecular biologist focused on the genes involved in human brain development. He tells this story about his "little professor"—his son at age two:

Noah and I were walking down the street on our way to preschool when he suddenly noticed a shiny pebble embedded in the concrete. Stopping midstride, the little guy considered it for a second, found it thoroughly delightful, and let out a laugh. He spied a small plant an inch farther, a weed valiantly struggling through a crack in the asphalt. He touched it gently, then laughed again. He noticed a platoon of ants marching in single file, which he bent down to examine closely. They were carrying a dead bug, and Noah clapped his hands in wonder. There were dust particles, a rusted screw, a shiny spot of oil . . . I tried to move him along, having the audacity to act like an adult with a schedule. He was having none of it. And I stopped, watching my little teacher, wondering how long it had been since I had taken 15 minutes to walk 20 feet. The greatest Brain Rule of all is something I cannot prove or characterize, but I believe in it with all my heart. As my son was trying to tell me, it is the importance of curiosity.[10]

It's easy to imagine another parent responding differently to Noah's curiosity: "Ugh! A dead bug! Stay away—it might make you sick! A rusty screw—don't touch, you could get tetanus!" Noah's sprouting fascination with nature might have been crushed. The only lesson he would have learned: that the world is dangerous, and the only way to be safe is to hide from it.

One safety-compliant mother I'll call Sandra was so petrified that her four-year-old daughter could get hurt that she signed up for an evening seminar called "Dangerous Things Your Kid Could Do." When Sandra arrived, the other parents milling around seemed to be happy and relaxed. She wondered why. Weren't they there to learn about dangers in their homes and neighborhood? Why weren't they as anxious as she was?

Moments after Gever Tulley began his talk, Sandra was startled to realize that Tulley was promoting *letting* children do dangerous things. He was encouraging parents to let their kids climb trees, build campfires, play with mud, and own a pocket knife—and to learn to do so safely. Tulley is the author of *50 Dangerous Things (You Should Let Your Children Do)*, and an advocate for parental openness to adventure, experimentation—and messiness.

As Sandra listened to Tulley's presentation, she began to realize that maybe she'd had the wrong approach to parenting. Maybe she had become *over*protective. She eased up and relaxed.

Tulley's talk was a turning point for Sandra. She didn't exactly become a free-range parent, but instead of squelching her daughter's curiosity, she began to encourage it. When her daughter brought a dead honeybee into the kitchen to show her mom, instead of shrieking, Sandra handed her daughter a magnifying glass and helped her safely study it.

When they walked along a trail, she let her daughter wander into the woods a bit instead of stopping her out of a vague fear of poison ivy. She used this as an opportunity to teach her child to avoid thick brush and to recognize poison ivy and poisonous snakes. Little surprises, like tripping over a root, turning over a rock and finding bugs, or getting prickly burrs stuck to her clothes, became experiences, not setbacks or occasions for hand-wringing.

As Sandra later told me, "I realize I've been an anxious mother. I've kept my daughter away from the woods and made her an 'indoor girl.' It turns out she loves nature. She sees things I miss—like praying mantises and tiny tadpoles, the vertebrae from a dead bird. Who knew?" And instead of a stern "Be careful" when saying goodbye to her child, Sandra has picked up positive language. Her new mantra is "Be safe, have fun learning!"[11]

FREEDOM OF IMPROV: LETTING OUR BRAINS GET MESSY

If we as parents and teachers want to give our kids the freedom to be creatively messy, we need to develop our own tolerance for messiness in all its forms. One great way to do this—and to have a load of fun along the way—is to get involved in the art of improvisational theater, often called simply *improv*.

If you've ever been to an improv show, you've seen performers who are quick on their feet, creating characters, speaking styles, and complete story lines on the spot in collaboration with their fellow performers. A particular skit may be sparked by an idea shouted out from the audience or a concept drawn at random from a hat; a prop or two might be provided (a saxophone? a bouquet of flowers? a locked treasure chest?) to stimulate an off-the-wall reaction. Sometimes the miniplays that the improv artists come up with are brilliant, hilarious, surprising, and moving. In other cases, they are silly, awkward, and confusing. You never know in advance what you are going to get—and that's part of what makes improv so addictive, both for performers and for audiences.

It fact, improv and the entrepreneurial process have a lot in common. Both are about creatively interacting with the resources available, playing off individual strengths, stretching beyond comfort zones, changing course when an opportunity appears, withholding judgment, taking risks, turning "mistakes" on their heads, and working at a rapid pace. If necessity is the mother of invention, then building on an idea is the mother of improv. At their best, both processes are capable of producing results far more memorable and extraordinary than anything a single individual could have planned or imagined.

Gail Papermaster is an attorney for young technology companies—by day, that is. At night, you may find her practicing improv at the Hideout on Austin's Congress Avenue, a small theater on the walk between Austin's famed Sixth Street and the state capitol. Papermaster began taking improv lessons as a fun way to relieve stress. She stuck with them when she discovered how they enriched her life. Improv has made her more observant, nimbler, more willing to step into unfamiliar territory, and closer in sync with the startup entrepreneurs she advises.[12]

"Improv makes you an amazing listener," says Kevin Benson of Spokane-based Bold Move Consulting & Coaching, who coaches entrepreneurs. "Listening involves more than just speaking and hearing. Listening is a deeper level of awareness for the communication and messages being sent by others."[13] Improv performers learn to pay attention to details and nuances in the language used by their colleagues, which can open up a scene to entirely new creative territory. In the same way, entrepreneurs who learn to listen carefully can discover unimagined opportunities. As entrepreneurial magnate Sir Richard Branson puts it, "Listen more than you talk . . . I am endlessly surprised by what new and useful information I can gather just by keeping my ears open."[14]

The spirit of improv is the spirit of messy, uninhibited, free-range curiosity. That's why I recommend it to aspiring entrepreneurs and to those who want to teach and inspire them—including our counselors at VentureLab. Try checking out the local improv theater in your own town. If you find it fun, you may want to join an improv group, club, or class at the nearest community center or college theater department. You can also use improv-inspired exercises with the girl or girls in your lives. Playing collaboratively with characters, situations, props, stories, and language is a great way to feed the sense of open-ended creativity that great scientists, technology makers, and business founders all seem to have in common.

THE LIMITS OF NICE

If reading this chapter about the joys of getting messy has made you just a little uncomfortable, you might want to think about why. It's possible that you are—consciously or unconsciously—being influenced by powerful social stereotypes about what's appropriate for a girl or woman . . . stereotypes that, unfortunately, can severely limit what females are permitted to achieve in our society.

It doesn't take much to evoke these stereotypes. Often a single word can conjure them up. Take the word *ladylike,* for example. It brings to mind a whole array of behaviors—ways of dressing, speaking style, social attitudes—that countless young women have been trained to practice, and to use in judging the behavior of others. Maybe this word was used in your own family as a way of guiding and controlling the behavior of girls. Or maybe other words were deployed in the same fashion—words like *polite, proper, decent, appropriate, well-behaved,* or, simply, *nice*.

The problem with words like these—and the stereotypes they evoke—is that they tend to block girls and women from behaviors and activities that are essential to success in today's competitive world. When you devote a lot of time and energy to being *ladylike, polite,* and *nice,* it can be very difficult to be recognized as a powerful, smart, energetic leader in the classroom, the science lab, the workshop, or the boardroom.

Sometimes, the best way to break free from the constraints that these stereotypes impose is to deliberately defy them. That's a common theme in the stories I hear from women leaders.

"I grew up in Canada, the second of four girls," says Maria Klawe, president of Harvey Mudd College. "When I came along, I was supposed to be a boy," she explains with a laugh:

> *I thought of myself as a boy, and my father definitely thought of me as a boy. If something was "for boys," by definition I was going to do it. Math, science, engineering—I took for granted that I could do them. The fact that girls didn't usually do these things in those days was an incentive, not a challenge. My father thought I was one of the most talented humans on the face of the earth, and one of the most obnoxious people on the face of the earth.*[15]

The word *obnoxious* captures an attitude that is the polar opposite of *nice*. And Dr. Klawe isn't the only impressive woman I know who has embraced it. Eileen Pollack, who was the second woman physics major to graduate from Yale University and later became a professor of creative writing at the University of Michigan, tells the story of an elementary school teacher who got so impatient with her that she said, "Eileen, has anyone ever told you how obnoxious you are?" The word triggered a moment of discovery for the young rebel: "Obnoxious, I repeated, delighted and appalled by the toxicity of the word. Obnoxious, was I? Fine. I shunned the company of other girls and hung around with the roughest boys who were even more obnoxious than I was."[16]

Dr. dt ogilvie talks about the limitations of being nice in a slightly different fashion. "We are trained in school to be good little girls," she says, "sitting at our desks, coloring within the lines, and smiling, unlike Johnny, who is standing on his head and screaming. But coloring within the lines will only get you so far. If the kid who is standing on her head can get her act together, she has a shot at being an entrepreneur." Dr. ogilvie's recommendation: Little girls need to develop "disagreeableness" if they hope to succeed later on as entrepreneurs.[17]

Obnoxious, disagreeable, pushy, aggressive, tough, dangerous—whatever word you like, it describes an attitude toward life that is decidedly *not* ladylike. It involves accepting the unknown, the unplanned, the uncontrolled, the risky—all the things that make life messy, rewarding, and fun. You'll do the girls in your life a huge favor if you teach them from an early age not to fear these things, but rather to embrace them!

TRY THIS AT HOME—AN ACTIVITY GIRLS WILL LOVE: SCAMPER WITH PIZZA

In this activity, parent(s) and kid(s) SCAMPER their way to brainstorming creative ways to change pizzas to create a new product or new type of pizza.

TIME: 15—45 MINUTES

You Need

Something to write and draw with (pens, pencils, crayons, or markers)

Paper to write on

Optional pizza items—for example, different crusts (plain, whole wheat, gluten-free); different toppings (cheeses, pepperoni, bacon, mushrooms, basil); different sauces (tomato, Alfredo)

Alternative: A play pizza set with crust, toppings, and sauces made of paper, felt, wood, or other materials

Directions

- Think about a pizza; if you like, look at pictures of different pizzas.
- Now start brainstorming how you could create something new using the basic features of a pizza. Write down and draw as many ideas as possible!
- When you are stuck, start using SCAMPER.
- Substitute: What can you substitute in pizza? (Examples: Substitute different toppings, substitute different kinds of crust, substitute different sauces, substitute different cheeses.)
- Combine: What can you combine with a pizza to make something new? (Examples: Combine pizza seasonings, toppings, and cheese with bread to make pizza bread; combine different toppings all at once on top of the pizza.)
- Adapt: How could you adapt or readjust this product? (Examples: Use gluten-free crust; use the pizza crust as sandwich bread.)
- Modify: How could you change the shape, look, or feel of your product? (Examples: Create a mini-pizza

or large pizza; create a pizza that is square-shaped or shaped like an animal; create a pizza folded over in half like a sandwich; create a thin- or thick-crust pizza.)

- Put to another use: How can you use the product for a different purpose? (Examples: Use pizza to feed animals; use a frozen pizza on a bruise to reduce the swelling; put the pizza in a blender and drink it.)
- Eliminate: What parts could you remove? (Examples: Eliminate the sauce, eliminate the cheese, eliminate the crust.)
- Reverse/rearrange: How could you rearrange or change the order of this product? (Examples: Put the cheese inside the crust; put the toppings inside the crust; make a pizza with crust on top and bottom.)
- If you have the food items you need, you can actually create the products you are brainstorming and try them.
- Once you have written down, drawn, and even created your new products, write down your thoughts on which new products you like best.

Later, you can use this same technique on any problem you are trying to brainstorm a solution for.

TRY THIS AT HOME—AN ACTIVITY GIRLS WILL LOVE: SLIME TIME

Most everyone loves to play with slime. It's fun to make and experiment with. Here are a couple of great slime recipes to try. You can experiment with slime, then package and sell it as a fun entrepreneurial project.

Classic Slime

TIME: 30—60 MINUTES

You Need

Glass bowl
Spoon
Clear glue or glitter glue
Liquid laundry detergent
Ziplock bags
Optional: Food coloring, glitter

Directions

- Squeeze ¼ cup of glue or glitter glue into a glass bowl.
- Mix in 1–2 tablespoons of laundry detergent. The more you add, the harder your slime will get.
- Add food coloring or glitter, if desired.
- Stir the solution with a spoon until the slime starts to come together.
- Knead the slime with your hands until it is smooth.

Color-Changing Slime

You Need

Glass bowl
Spoon
Clear glue or glitter glue
Baking soda
Saline contact lens solution (must have boric acid as an ingredient)
Thermochromic temperature-activated pigment (available on Amazon)
Ziplock bags

Directions

- Squeeze 5 ounces of clear glue into a glass bowl.
- Mix in 1 tablespoon of baking soda. The more you add, the harder your slime will get.
- Mix in ½ teaspoon of thermochromic pigment.
- Stir the solution well with a spoon.
- Add the saline contact lens solution a teaspoon at a time and continue mixing until the slime starts to come together.
- Knead the slime with your hands until it is smooth.
- To see the color change, put some ice on your slime or put it under some hot water.

When you're done experimenting with your slime, package it neatly in ziplock bags or plastic containers so that you can sell it to people. People like things that look nice and clean, so make sure your packages are not messy.

TRY THIS AT HOME—AN ACTIVITY GIRLS WILL LOVE: SUPERHERO IMPROV

SuperHeroes is a fun improv game that gets you up and active and playing different characters.

TIME: 15—45 MINUTES

You Need

A group of friends

Directions

- A leader or a designated member of the group announces a silly problem to be solved; for example, "Help—I can't open the cap of my toothpaste tube!"
- The leader or member also names a list of random objects—as many as there are members of the group. For example, if the group includes six members, the objects might be a shoe, a toothpick, a potato, a stick of dynamite, a Hula-Hoop, and an ice cream cone.
- The leader picks a second member to be a superhero armed with the first object—for example, Super Shoe Woman. The second member acts out her attempt to solve the problem—but she fails, and maybe even makes the problem worse.

- The second member picks a third member to be a superhero armed with the second object—for example, Super Toothpick Woman. The third member acts out her attempt to solve the problem, which may or may not be solved.
- The game ends when the last superhero acts out a clever way to finally solve the problem.
- Repeat as many times as desired.

8

Encourage Failure

WHEN SARA BLAKELY WAS GROWING UP BACK IN THE 1970S AND '80S, dinner conversations at her house had an unusual twist. Each night, Sara's father would ask her, "What have you failed at today?" He was teaching Sara the value of failure as a tool for discovery—a way of figuring out new skills that can make you more competent, more insightful, and more powerful tomorrow than you are today.

By the time she entered college, Blakely was steeped in failure and experienced at rebounding. After she scored poorly on the Law School Admissions Test, ruling out her dreamed-of law career, Sara decided to become an entrepreneur instead. Her quest began with a problem—the visible panty lines that spoil the smooth, shapely lines most women want to achieve. Sara set about solving that problem.

It wasn't easy. With no investors, Blakely spent five thousand dollars of her personal savings on researching and developing ideas. It took a year for her to come up with a satisfactory prototype for a new kind of line-smoothing undergarment. When she tried to interest the established, male-dominated undergarment manufacturers based in North Carolina, she struck out everywhere—until one mill operator got back in touch with her because his daughters liked the idea. Unable to afford a patent attorney, Sara wrote the first patent application herself. Improvising a demo, Blakely invited a Neiman Marcus representative into the restroom to demonstrate her product. She made the sale. Until she could pay employees, she enlisted her mother and friends to help fill orders.

Today, Sara's invention is the cornerstone product of one of the world's fastest-growing apparel brands—Spanx. And Sara is the first self-made female billionaire in US history.[1]

Toward the end of our entrepreneurial classes, we often ask students the question that Sara Blakely faced each evening: "What have you failed at today?" This simple question, which can be asked in every home and classroom, sets in motion a paradigm change, and a new way of thinking—that failure is essential to learning.

THE BENEFITS OF FAILURE—AND THE COSTS OF AVOIDING IT

I REMEMBER BEING A JUNIOR HIGH SCHOOL STUDENT CRYING IN A BATHroom stall after failing my first geometry test. I remember telling my dad, "I can't do it!" Calculating angles of a polygon was just too hard.

My dad responded in the right way. Instead of consoling me by saying, "Maybe math just isn't for you," he figured out how to help me understand math in my own way. He also told me I could be anything I wanted to—but I had to work hard for it. And his message stuck. Years later, my parents watched proudly as I became an engineer.

I pass on the same message whenever I have the opportunity. When my university students walk in nervous and excited on the first day of class, I always tell them, "I expect you to fail. But that doesn't mean you won't pass my class. Failure is a temporary state. You overcome it by believing that you have the potential to overcome challenges and being persistent in achieving your goals."

The same message is also crucial for the elementary-grade children at VentureLab. One of the exercises we always do with them is to brainstorm ways to talk about failure. Failure has a vocabulary all its own, and each expression has its own connotations: *setback . . . messed up . . . lesson . . . challenge . . . one more down . . . now we know . . . opportunity . . . hit a wall . . . time to redesign . . . epic fail . . . experience . . . teachable moment . . . blunder . . . goof . . . screw up . . .* Maybe you can think of a few more.

You can see that some of the expressions in this list are harshly negative, while others are much more positive. They represent two ways of looking at failure—as the closing of a door that represents a vanished opportunity, or as the opening of a door to the possibility of learning, growth, and ultimate success. If we want to help young people achieve their dreams, it's vital that we adopt the second view of failure and teach it to our kids. Being able and willing to learn from failure is one of the crucial characteristics that marks successful high achievers.

In his book *How We Decide,* author Jonah Lehrer describes the science of learning from mistakes. He explains how researchers at the University of Iowa and the California Institute of Technology studied the physiological reactions of a person playing a gambling game. When the player made a wrong choice, the neurons in the brain that produce the chemical dopamine immediately stopped firing, causing the player to experience a negative emotion. As a result, he learned not to make the same mistake again. By contrast, when the player made a correct choice, his brain was flooded with dopamine, producing a positive emotion and encouraging him to repeat that choice. In other words, our nervous system is designed to help us learn from our mistakes—undoubtedly an evolutionary advantage for humans competing for survival.

"Mistakes aren't to be discouraged," Lehrer concludes. "On the contrary, they should be cultivated and carefully investigated." He goes on to observe:

> *[I]n general, shouldn't we try to avoid blunders? It depends. Yes, we don't want to make the same error over and over. But that is different from thinking that we not only can but must do everything perfectly, and if we don't, we are failures. Such a mind-set creates marriages and relationships where people exert enormous amounts of energy blaming each other when*

> *something goes wrong rather than finding a solution. Where defensiveness and accusations take the place of apologies and forgiveness. It creates workplaces where taking chances and being creative while risking failure is subsumed by an ethos of mistake-prevention at the cost of daring and innovation. Or conversely, workplaces where superstars are never challenged; rather they are rewarded for making really bad decisions. And we end up with a culture where people feel shame at making mistakes—big or little—and pass this on to their children.*[2]

Jonah Lehrer is right. Everyone needs the skills to deal objectively with failure, learn from it, perhaps laugh at it, and move forward, smarter and undeterred. Yet our schools, and sometimes our homes, tend to be oriented in just the opposite way. Rather than learning from failure, we stigmatize it, branding students who experience temporary setbacks with a permanent capital F.

We don't necessarily engage in this behavior deliberately or even consciously. People, including teachers, like to repeat comforting platitudes about failure—mottos like "Learn from your mistakes" and the cheerful "If at first you don't succeed, try, try again." But as Alina Tugend points out in her book *Better by Mistake: The Unexpected Benefits of Being Wrong,* these positive maxims are contradicted by "the reality that we often get punished for making mistakes and therefore try to avoid them—or cover them up—as much as possible."

Tugend has researched "how parents and teachers often

unwittingly encourage such an error-avoidance mind-set and how such children grow into adults who fear and dread making mistakes." And she quotes social psychologists Carol Tavris and Elliot Aronson, authors of the book *Mistakes Were Made (But Not by Me)*, saying, "Most Americans know they are supposed to say 'we learn from our mistakes,' but deep down, they don't believe it for a minute. They think mistakes mean you are stupid."[3]

Our tendency to stigmatize failure hampers kids' ability to learn. Everyone makes mistakes, especially when tackling an unfamiliar subject. Experts agree that one of the best ways to master a new skill is to try it, get it wrong, recognize the error, and then try again, gradually correcting your own mistakes and developing an intuitive sense of how to avoid them in the future. But how can children improve if they are ashamed to admit their mistakes? In a failure-averse classroom, kids often become so fearful they simply stop trying, unwilling to risk making a mistake. Students paralyzed by these constraints aren't likely to pursue challenging subjects where learning is cumulative and where students' errors need to be used as teachable moments. That includes STEM fields like advanced math, computer science, and engineering.

The spread of standardized testing, and the increasing influence of such tests in the design of school curricula, has helped to exacerbate the problem of failure-aversion. The impact of standardized tests on student and teacher attitudes can be subtle, yet it is pervasive—especially since the advent of Common Core teaching standards, which are often linked to high-stakes standardized tests by which students, teachers, and entire school systems may be judged.

By their nature, standardized tests, which rely on short-answer, usually multiple-choice questions with a single, predetermined right answer, reward speed, cleverness, conventional thinking, and rigid, black/white reasoning. In all these ways, the tests are fundamentally different from most of the challenges humans face in real life, where patience, thoughtful analysis, creative thinking, and flexibility are most likely to be successful. The more we encourage schools to "teach to the test," the more we are promoting anxiety-provoking, failure-averse attitudes toward learning . . . to the long-term detriment of our children.

Furthermore, evidence suggests that, in our society, females suffer most from the fear of failure—and not just in school, but throughout their careers. Tugend cites research findings showing that "women tend to agonize more about their mistakes, at least in the workplace; women often speak more hesitantly to men than to other women . . . So there is less room for women who speak up, who demonstrate their expertise, who are willing to disturb the status quo, who take more risks and therefore make more mistakes. And women, fearing their mistakes may be judged more harshly than men's, are far more reluctant to risk them." Furthermore, Tugend says, women "tend to be more dejected by negative feedback than buoyed up by positive responses"—which means that they are likely to perceive a "balanced" mixture of praise and criticism as being overloaded with condemnation, leading to a deeper sense of failure and a greater tendency to avoid challenging situations.[4]

All of this illustrates the importance of reframing girls' attitudes so that they are more willing to risk failure. We need to condition girls not to internalize failure as a sign of their own unworthiness, but rather to view mistakes dispassionately and learn from them.

PERFECTION PRESSURE AND THE IMPOSTOR SYNDROME

AMBITIOUS, HIGH-ACHIEVING GIRLS ARE PARTICULARLY PRONE TO TAKE failure too much to heart. Many have been raised to judge themselves by unrealistic standards, regarding anything short of perfection as inadequate and shameful.

Ironically, the more successful some young women seem to be—as measured by high test scores, good grades, an attractive appearance, athletic skill, popularity—the more dangerous the drive for perfection can be. It can lead to the *impostor syndrome* that I described in Chapter Two—a pervasive feeling that, no matter how much you may have achieved, you are really a fraud and a failure whose shortcomings are sure to be exposed someday.

"Almost to a woman, Ivy League students experience the 'impostor syndrome,'" says Dr. Kimberly Wright Cassidy, president of Bryn Mawr, a legendary college for women. "It's not possible to live up to their perfect personas."[5]

In recent years, social media have elevated girls' expectations for perfection. Young women in high school and college may sift through dozens of selfies to find the one in which they look loveliest and happiest for Facebook. Eager to depict themselves as "having it all," many girls hide behind a false online front that only increases the pressure on other girls to strive for the same apparent level of perfection. The *New York Times* described how the intimidating facades of other women deepened the social pressures experienced by a student at one prestigious university:

> *Classmates seemed to have it all together. Every morning, the administration sent out an email blast highlighting faculty and student accomplishments. Some women attended class wearing full makeup. . . . They talked about their fantastic internships. . . . Friends' lives, as told through selfies, showed them having more fun, making more friends and going to better parties. Even the meals they posted to Instagram looked more delicious.*[6]

College is stressful enough without the perceived need to compete against the perfect images projected by other students. No wonder even a smart young woman may drift toward abandoning the STEM courses and entrepreneurial projects she once found enticing. After all, if you believe that only a summa cum laude and a perfect GPA are acceptable, why not restrict yourself to easier, less challenging classes?

Even some of the world's most successful women continue

to grapple with the impostor syndrome. Sheryl Sandberg, bestselling author and Facebook COO, told *Womenomics* authors Katty Kay and Claire Shipman, "There are still days when I wake up feeling like a fraud, not sure I should be where I am."[7]

I've suffered from this problem myself. A few years ago, I went to an entrepreneurship conference with a male student. At the registration desk, we were asked to choose name tags indicating whether we were novices, average, or experts in entrepreneurship. I remarked to my student, "You know, I don't really think I'm an expert. Maybe I should just take average." He immediately replied, "No way, we are experts!"

This floored me. After one year in class with me, this student felt comfortable calling himself an expert, while I was hesitant after teaching entrepreneurship for five years!

We both took "expert" tags, and I haven't looked back since.

Of course, many men experience the same kind of self-doubt. Jason Seats, a Techstars Ventures partner, observes, "Most founders I know have this deep-seated anxiety that they don't really know what they are doing." However, our culture encourages men to ignore their inner feelings of unworthiness and keep pushing their way to the top. Seats goes on to say, "The truth is that none of us really do [know what we are doing], but the people that end up doing the best are the ones that get really used to operating with that feeling of uncertainty in the pit of their stomach every day."[8] In other words, men are trained to "fake it till they make it," while women learn instead to listen to the whispering voice of doubt . . . which leads them, all too often, to withdraw from the competitive battle.

I observed the effects of female perfectionism and the impostor syndrome while teaching an undergraduate course in entrepreneurship at Trinity University in San Antonio. The course drew nearly equal numbers of male and female students, but the most vocal participants were the men. The women typically had to be called upon before they would speak up. They also tended to judge their own performance in class very harshly. All of these students were very bright; the simple fact that they'd been accepted at a competitive college like Trinity meant they'd been standouts in high school, consistently earning As and Bs. But when the male students earned an occasional C at Trinity, they quickly bounced back, while the females were devastated. In their eyes, a grade of C branded them as failures, unworthy even of a seat in class. It was the first time that I truly recognized how girls can be cowed and immobilized by gender stereotypes.

Of course, I did what I could to encourage the women in class. I called on them more, intervened when the men interrupted them (as they often did), and reassured them when they had trouble with a particular topic (as practically every student, male or female, sometimes did).

In the end, the cure for perfectionism is simple enough. It's *imperfection*. It's getting it *wrong*. For a student, it's learning how to fail; and for a teacher or parent, it's learning to value and appreciate failure rather than responding to it with criticism or disdain, and modeling how to use mistakes as stepping stones to deeper understanding.

At VentureLab, we've taken this principle to heart. In every entrepreneurial class or camp we run, instructors ensure that there will be plenty of frustrating, laughable, "What was I thinking!?" failures. And how do we ensure this? It's easy. We encourage girls to try new ideas, test them, stretch beyond their skill set, and take a shot at things that no one thinks will work. And they usually *don't* work. That's the beauty of it. We need only create an environment where failure is anticipated, welcomed, analyzed, and celebrated. When mistakes get made, we've been known to shake a can of carbonated water and spray the team, or break out New Year's Eve noisemakers. When I say that we *celebrate* failures, I really mean it.

Girls who pass through our classes are often surprised and delighted to realize that while their ideas or experiments failed, often repeatedly, *they succeeded*. They realize that the goal of the course is not to earn a perfect score or a top grade, but rather to learn to think like an entrepreneur. And that means embracing failure. As a scientist, I see failure as part of the scientific method. In any sort of project or new endeavor, you develop a hypothesis and test it, and it either works or doesn't work. A failure yields information—whether it's questions missed or a hypothesis disproved. Failure means learning what doesn't work, trying again a different way, and getting closer to a solution.

Entrepreneurs aren't discouraged by failures—at least not for long. They learn from failures. Look at history: There are many well-known entrepreneurs who failed their way to success—J. K. Rowling, Henry Ford, Walt Disney. And Thomas Edison always said, "I have not failed. I've just found ten thousand ways that won't work." When entrepreneurs are knocked down, they pick themselves up, dust themselves off, and incorporate what they've learned into their next moves. They refrain from casting blame.

Doesn't that sound like someone you'd like to spend time with?

GIRLS, GRIT, AND THE ENTREPRENEURIAL MIND-SET

GRIT IS AN ESSENTIAL ELEMENT OF THE ENTREPRENEURIAL MIND-SET. IT has two component parts, according to Angela Duckworth, a research psychologist and MacArthur "genius" grant winner whose lifework has been dedicated to grit. Duckworth came up with the term based on the 1960s Western movie *True Grit,* in which a young girl named Mattie (played by Kim Darby) seeks to avenge the murder of her father with help from John Wayne, playing an aging US marshal. (The film was remade by the Coen Brothers in a 2010 version that starred Hailee Steinfeld and Jeff Bridges.) Mattie hires the marshal for his grit, but what the story reveals is a girl whose grit matches his.

Duckworth says that one aspect of grit is *resilience,* a term with several overlapping meanings. It can mean *optimism,* a positive way of thinking about life and the improvements we can make in our lives. It can mean *buoyancy,* a readiness to bounce back from failures and difficulties. It can also mean *toughness,* the ability to thrive despite threats like poverty and abuse. "What all those definitions of resilience have in common is the idea of a positive response to failure or adversity," Duckworth says.

The second aspect of grit is *perseverance,* a willingness to maintain focus and stay on task in the face of obstacles—or, as Duckworth puts it, "not being a dilettante, not being a flake."[9] The person with perseverance doesn't fall into a behavior pattern of abandoning tasks just for the sake of change or because they've gotten tiresome. She is determined to see things through and develop mastery, even when the path is uncomfortable, frustrating, difficult, discouraging, or boring.

Entrepreneurial education infuses failure with positive meaning. It gives girls what I call "practice at failure." They learn that *everyone* fails, and that how you deal with it makes all the difference.

Because successive failures are built into the curriculum at VentureLab, our classes become safe environments for girls to examine the role of failure in real time, surrounded by supportive groups of peers. For a lot of girls, it's the first time that they have seen failure as a valuable, vital part of the learning process. There is something transformative about learning that you have within yourself the ability to create an idea and make it grow—that you actually have the tools needed to overcome obstacles and achieve long-term success in the face of short-term setbacks.

GRADUATES OF THE SCHOOL OF HARD KNOCKS

Stephanie Sullivan grew up in one of Boston's toughest neighborhoods. She now says that she put her foster family "through hell," but they stuck with her. And Stephanie got tougher in the process. Rather than give in to her surroundings—teen pregnancy, drugs, and death—she changed them:

> *I won a neat-sounding city award, Participant of the Year, and parlayed it to convince the owner of a local McDonald's to hire me even though I was just fourteen. One day at sixteen, I made the choice: "I want more out of life, and I want all of the things that I wish I could have had, and I want to provide that to other kids. Life is too short to be unhappy." I signed myself into an all-girls convent, where I went to high school for two years and accelerated my education.*[10]

It turned out that the best predictor of Sullivan's future success was the difficulty of her early years. She refused to succumb to her dismal circumstances. "My entrepreneurial brain wouldn't shut off," she now says. "In college, I needed to make money, so I made soup and sold it, then hummus and tabouli. I wanted to be self-sufficient and independent."

Sullivan went on to found several successful technology startups. The challenges didn't stop then. "Early in my career, I worked with an arrogant man as my business partner. But I'd dealt with a lot worse. Employees stayed because I was nurturing. I learned to *engage* and *lead* employees, not just manage them. Discovering this can open doors for women."

By the time she was in her thirties, Sullivan had turned her life around. She went back to her old neighborhood to thank the foster family who'd endured her and a social worker who'd been one of her few supporters. She also decided to pass along the benefits she'd received to others. Even while working in her own demanding companies, she became a foster mother to thirty-seven babies, some drug-addicted, and she adopted one foster child, now grown. "Becoming a foster mother was a challenge, not so different from starting a company. Could I take this tiny person with such potential and help her reach the next stage of life? What could I learn in the process?"[11]

It's safe to say that Stephanie Sullivan has learned, grown, and overcome at every stage in her remarkable story . . . and shows no sign of slowing down.

I met Diane Hessan through Springboard Enterprises, an organization for women entrepreneurs. She is a Harvard MBA who has built three successful startups over the span of fifteen years. Hessan has never been more at home than she is now as CEO of Startup Institute, based in Boston and expanding into Chicago and New York. Startup Institute is best known for the boot camp it offers several times each year for entrepreneurs and students who want to find jobs in the world of startups. Startup Institute also offers intensive hands-on projects, lectures, and labs for aspiring entrepreneurs—women and men—where they can acquire the technical skills, cultural skills, and professional networks they'll need to succeed in bringing their innovative ideas to markets. It's practical, passionate, professional, and transformative—just like Hessan herself.

Hessan knows the value of grit better than most. "As a little girl," she says, "I grew up on the wrong side of the tracks."

> *Most kids from my high school didn't go to college. But I was lucky. My father had a sewing machine repair business. I loved being in his shop. I must have seemed awfully precocious, telling him how to get more customers while I was still in elementary school. . . . I loved leading. I took on leadership challenges just to see if I could do it. I would organize groups and set goals. I was fearless and undaunted by failure. I saw myself as learning, not failing. Of course, these turned out to be exactly the skills I would need to start and build companies.*[12]

Hessan could not have achieved what she has in a male-dominated business sector without support from male mentors. "There are at least forty men in the city of Boston who think my success is due to their coaching. And all of them are right. One taught me how to understand a cap table [a tool for analyzing the ownership shares in a company]. Another taught me how to manage a board of directors. And so on. I just started accumulating mentors."[13]

Hessan is utterly in tune with the Startup Institute's commitment to technology culture, networking, and mentorship. She knows how fulfilling it is to make money doing what you love, because that has been her own story.

Hessan began her career as an engineer and went on to develop and deploy wireless technology. She is passionate about helping women in STEM fields develop the courage, confidence, and camaraderie they need to get past obstacles. She characterizes herself as "stubborn and strong-willed": "I didn't pay any attention to what people said. My attitude was, 'I can do this.' "

Along the way, like most women in technology, Hessan experienced her share of discouraging encounters:

> *There was an instance that was so blatant, I still can't get over the fact that it happened. In electrical engineering, when I was getting my bachelor's, it was incredibly competitive. I was going to make the cut, I had fabulous grades, and I wasn't worried about it at all. Then I had a professor call me into his office and he told me, "You really should drop out and pick another major. There are men and they have wives and children, and they really need that spot." It made me so mad. But now I really have to thank him, because it just made me determined to show him that was the wrong thing to tell me.*[14]

One sure sign of a budding entrepreneur is the readiness to turn failures and obstacles into fuel for renewed determination. That, too, is an aspect of grit.

HOW ENTREPRENEURIAL EDUCATION GIVES GIRLS THE CHALLENGES THEY NEED

President Dwight D. Eisenhower wrote a prayer for his son that included this wish: "Lead him, I pray, not in the path of ease and comfort, but under the stress and spur of difficulties and challenge. Here let him learn to stand up in the storm." This is beautifully said. Eisenhower knew that boys need experiences that build grit—stress, difficulties, and challenge.

But what about girls? Would a father have written these lines for a daughter? In our culture, it seems almost instinctive for fathers to want to protect their daughters from adversity. The quintessentially "perfect" American girlhood is that of an indulged princess, with a beautiful home, a trendy wardrobe, and an adoring father, as imagined in the classic coming-of-age comedy *Clueless*.

The problem is that no girl ever developed grit in a protective bubble. No girl develops grit without failure. And the truth is that we are *not* princesses. Chances are, no one is going to rescue us from the adversity life brings. We need to "stand up to the storm" as much as boys.

The best way for parents to guide their daughters is not to protect them, but to prepare them with grit-building experiences, equip them with entrepreneurial skills, and condition them to learn from failures.

There's even evidence that young people who face daunting challenges may have a greater capacity to achieve than those who are fortunate enough to never face serious difficulties in their lives.

Kelly Fitzsimmons is a female CEO who has personally grappled with the problem of attention deficit/hyperactivity disorder (ADHD), which makes learning in a traditional classroom more difficult and often leads to painful setbacks in school. She overcame this challenge and has noticed the prevalence of the same condition among her fellow entrepreneurs. How does she explain this unlikely phenomenon? "We are unhirable. We have to go this direction [that is, launching companies] because nobody wants us."[15] In other words, the serious learning problems associated with ADHD can be, and often are, transmuted into an opportunity to excel.

Author Malcolm Gladwell identified a similar pattern when he studied the lives of people with the reading disability known as dyslexia. Most dyslexics struggle all of their lives, especially if undiagnosed until age eight or nine, when dyslexia can lead to serious psychological issues like low self-esteem. But in many cases, dyslexia causes people to compensate in other areas than reading. Gladwell asks, "Can dyslexia turn out to be a desirable difficulty? It is hard to believe that it can, given how many people struggle with the disorder throughout their lives—except for a strange fact. An extraordinarily high number of successful entrepreneurs are dyslexic."[16]

Nan McRaven experienced undiagnosed dyslexia as a child. She just knew it meant she had to work harder than other kids: "I loved reading then and now, but it was always a struggle."[17] Because giving up was not an option, McRaven became an exceptional listener, analyst, and strategic thinker. Today she is a vice president at a global technology company—an example of how the "stress, difficulty, and challenge" Eisenhower spoke about can be transformed into strength.

Girls need challenges growing up to learn resilience. A "perfect" upbringing—if there were such a thing—would be missing the stress and the obstacles that young people need.

This is where entrepreneurial education begins. It allows students to get healthy, multiple doses of failure. With entrepreneurial experience, girls come to see failures and mistakes as steps in learning, enabling them to apply this thinking to any challenge in life—academics, relationships, family, sports, service, and career. Girls can benefit from this new mind-set throughout life, regardless of the paths they ultimately take, since everything that's worth doing involves challenges and failures along the way.

Think of how empowered girls become when they:

- Discover that the math calculations on the market research they did for their entrepreneurial project were wrong . . . and then spend an afternoon reworking the numbers until they finally get them right.
- Build a prototype project that falls apart the first time, the second time, and third time . . . and then cobble together a fourth version that works perfectly.
- Brainstorm ten different advertising slogans for their fledgling business, test them all with homemade posters . . . and discover, to their amazement and de-

light, that the one slogan they thought was the worst actually causes sales to triple.

- Practice presenting the idea for their project to a live audience, pressing ahead even when nervousness makes them tongue-tied . . . and then perform better on their second and third opportunities.

Entrepreneurial education teaches students that the mistakes that count are the ones they use as stepping stones to success.

UNLOCKING INTUITION THROUGH FREEDOM FROM FEAR

Fear is a vital biological reaction. When it's appropriate and necessary, fear stops us from doing things that put our bodies and our futures at grave risk. But entrepreneurship is about learning the right kind of fearlessness—a freedom from fear that is not to be confused with crazy, irresponsible risk-taking. It's about taking calculated risks, knowing that you might fail and having decided that the rewards of success are worth the risk.

In entrepreneurial education, we guide girls to calculate risks with a frank assessment. "What's the worst that can happen?" we encourage them to ask. Since VentureLab participants don't receive any grade that depends on the absence of failure, they are free to take risks that ordinary classroom practices don't encourage. But, of course, there are other kinds of risks that are just as real, some of which are worth taking. A project that doesn't work? The embarrassment of launching a product that no one buys? Having a few people laugh at your presentation? These are risks worth taking. Blowing up the basement? A risk *not* worth taking. Talking through risks and what it means to calculate risk is an important aspect of the VentureLab experience.

Something breaks free in girls who internalize what failure can do *for* them, that it is not to be dreaded, and that there is no inherent shame in failure. They buckle down and lighten up.

Fear of failure inhibits the metalogic of feelings and intuition, which is essential to an entrepreneur's ingenuity. Girls who are burdened with excessive self-doubt are unwilling or unable to trust their instincts and their emotions. Instead, they look for validation from external sources or from hard, numerical data—which are not always available. When those outside sources of certainty can't be found, girls who are afraid to rely on their feelings may be paralyzed, unable to act decisively.

And, unfortunately, our educational system tends to encourage this self-doubting attitude. Dr. John Burnside, former chief of internal medicine at the Hershey Medical Center in Pennsylvania, put it this way: "One of our educational failures is a lack of serious recognition and attention towards the 'gut feeling' or inclination of common sense. Perhaps because this inclination is nonnumerical it is glossed over. . . . But I believe it can be defined and taught."[18]

Lifting the fear of failure can allow girls to be in touch with their senses by encouraging them to trust themselves on the deepest, most instinctive level. Muscular feeling, physical sensations, intuitive sensations, kinesthetic responses, and mental imaging—all these modes of knowledge play important roles in creative and scientific thinking. Instead of being disembodied, scientific learning becomes real; physics becomes physical. Robert and Michèle Root-Bernstein call this "body thinking," and they describe it in their book *Sparks of Genius*. "We are taught and tested with words and numbers," the authors say, "and it is assumed we think in words and numbers. No schooling could be more misconceived. . . . Feeling as thinking must become part of the educational curriculum. Students must learn how to pay attention to what they feel in their bones, to develop and use it."[19]

It can be taught—that is, if girls are untethered from the harsh academic consequences of failure that cause young minds to clench up. Entrepreneurial teaching can help to free their minds and give natural intuition an opportunity to flow.

LESSONS IN FAILURE: A DIFFERENT KIND OF FIELD TRIP

Living and working in both San Antonio and Austin, Texas, I am part of a regional economy that welcomes business and entrepreneurship. Recently, at VentureLab, we've begun taking advantage of the vibrant entrepreneurial communities in both cities by bringing our classes to maker spaces and coworking venues, where they can observe early-stage business startups in action. We've taken field trips and held Girl

Startup and High School Startup camps at Geekdom in San Antonio and at Capital Factory in Austin. It's mind-opening for girls to see businesses without walls, people working intensely often without pay, camaraderie that transcends industries, and women and men stretching their creativity to build companies on lean budgets. Virtually all of our students are witnessing tech entrepreneurs in action for the first time, an opportunity to meet adults who are smart, articulate, sometimes brusque but usually warm and welcoming, and always incredibly energized.

We use these field trips as opportunities to discuss the odds for success and failure and the constant adaptation that's involved in trying to turn mistakes into triumphs. Our students learn that most early startups won't make it, and that often the outcome has less to do with whether their ideas are viable than other factors—whether they can find the financial backing to develop their concepts and get them to the market, or whether the founders persevered or gave up. They also understand that, just as in class, failure is not the end. It's a repetitive factor in the learning process. Many entrepreneurs have applied the lessons from one failed business to make the next one succeed. I love the look in girls' eyes when they realize that it's not only okay to fail; it's *expected* of entrepreneurs.

Not every girl will become an entrepreneur, of course. But every single girl in our class benefits from this visceral experience. They gain an understanding of the endurance required to build a company. With that insight comes respect for the entrepreneurs who take big risks to build companies that invest in technology, deliver innovations to markets, and create jobs that keep the US economy growing.

TRY THIS AT HOME—AN ACTIVITY GIRLS WILL LOVE: THE MARSHMALLOW CHALLENGE

In this activity, parent(s) and a group of kids will complete a challenge in which teams compete to build the tallest free-standing structure. Here's the catch: The materials you get to build with are dry spaghetti noodles. And did we mention, the spaghetti tower must also support the weight of a marshmallow?

TIME: 20—25 MINUTES

You Need

Something to write and draw with (pens, pencils, crayons, or markers)
Paper to sketch on
Building materials for each team:
- 20 dry spaghetti noodles
- 1 yard of masking tape
- 1 yard of string
- 1 regular size marshmallow (not mini)

Measuring tape/yardstick
Optional: Timer

Directions

- Divide the kids in your group into teams, each with two or more members. Each team has 18 minutes in which to plan and build the tallest tower that can hold a marshmallow on the top. Teams can use only the materials they have been supplied (20 spaghetti noodles, masking tape, string, and one marshmallow), but they do not have to use all the materials.
- Teams can use the materials in any way they'd like—for example, they can break the spaghetti into smaller pieces. However, towers must be free-standing: They cannot be stuck down, taped to the floor or a wall, or suspended from above. The tower must hold the marshmallow on top and still stay standing. The marshmallow has to stay in one piece. The winning team is the one with the tallest tower that holds the marshmallow on the top.
- An adult or group leader should time the challenge, allowing 18 minutes for the groups to work.
- When the challenge is up, make sure the towers have been built according to the rules. Then measure the height of each tower. The tallest tower wins!
- Afterward, discuss the challenge:
  - What did you do in the first five minutes, and how did that affect your success?
  - How quickly did you start building the tower, and how did that affect your success?
  - How many times did you test the tower by putting the marshmallow on top?

- What choices along the way helped you be successful? How did you respond to any challenges or failures?

On average, kids do better at this activity than adults. They typically build taller and more creative structures because they play and prototype on the fly, while adults spend most of their time in planning. Also, kids often start with the marshmallow stuck on a piece of spaghetti, while adults are left struggling to put the marshmallow on at the end. An important takeaway from this activity is that entrepreneurs start making their product—prototyping, testing, and improving it—as soon as possible. This lets them identify problems sooner rather than later. Also, entrepreneurs are resilient in the face of failure. They expect to fail on the way to success, and they see failure as an opportunity to learn. The best entrepreneurs will fail small, but fail quickly!

TRY THIS AT HOME—AN ACTIVITY GIRLS WILL LOVE: ZIP ZAP ZOP

Zip Zap Zop is a fun improv exercise that focuses you and warms you up to creativity and communication.

TIME: 5—10 MINUTES

You Need

A group of friends

Directions

- Form a circle.
- One member pretends to throw an imaginary "ball of energy" to anyone else in the group. The ball of energy can be the size and weight of a baseball, a basketball, a heavy medicine ball, or any other kind of ball. It can be thrown using a one-handed throw, a two-handed heave, an underhand toss, or a bounce. As the member throws the ball, she makes eye contact with the member catching the ball, and says, "Zip!"
- The second member throws the ball of energy to a third member, making eye contact and saying, "Zap!"
- The third member throws the ball of energy to a fourth member, making eye contact and saying, "Zop!"
- The ball continues around the circle, with members repeating "Zip!" "Zap!" "Zop!" as it travels. The challenge is to do this as quickly, rhythmically, and smoothly as possible. If you get really good at it, you can also add "Boing!" whenever the ball goes back to the original thrower.
- Repeat until pleasantly exhausted.

9

Channel Her Idealism

Too often, we associate entrepreneurship solely with business success, and particularly with the drive to generate wealth. There's nothing wrong with wanting to build a big, profitable company. But not all entrepreneurs are motivated by money. Many are passionate about making the world a better place—and research shows that this is especially true of women and girls.

Thirteen-year-old Estrella Hernandez learned about the dangers of childhood obesity from her father, a volunteer with the mayor's fitness council in San Antonio, Texas. With nearly a third of its residents obese, San Antonio is one of the top five most overweight cities in the United States. Estrella learned that obesity could lead to diabetes and cause sufferers to become even more sedentary. She had family members whose health was compromised by weight, and Estrella didn't want to see her whole generation follow that path. Her outsize wish: to end childhood obesity.

A high-energy teenager, Estrella wasn't one to sit idly when she could take action. She thought, "What if I could come up with a solution to the problem of childhood obesity?" Recognizing her potential, her father enrolled Estrella in VentureLab's weeklong Youth Startup camp. Estrella and four team members recast the problem of obesity as a game. They wondered: What if they could create a phone app that would reward kids with points for walking? What if the points could be redeemed for things kids want, like video games? The more kids walked, the more they would be rewarded.

Estrella and her team experimented, tested, and pitched their idea, and when the week ended, Estrella kept working on it. She refined and advanced it—then won a scholarship to a program that helped her with the nuts and bolts of taking it to the next stage. Fluent in English and Spanish, she now learned a different kind of language: coding. She wrote the programming code for the app, developed a working prototype, and took her project all the way through pitching it to investors. Estrella ended up raising more than $200,000 in funding for her startup.

Estrella's story illustrates how teaching entrepreneurial skills can unlock girls' interest in applying science and technology to meaningful real-world problems.

FROM PROBLEM TO PURPOSE

IN OUR CAPITALIST SOCIETY, CONVENTIONAL WISDOM SAYS THAT IF YOU want to get someone to do a better job, you incentivize them with pay or profit. Money is the key to unlocking people's commitment and energy.

But the conventional wisdom isn't always true. In fact, it's not even mostly true. For routine tasks—mowing lawns, grilling burgers, washing cars—pay-for-performance may generate more output. But for jobs that involve creative problem-solving, conventional incentives often produce the opposite result. Author Daniel Pink explains the psychological phenomenon that defies conventional business management logic in his book *Drive: The Surprising Truth About What Motivates Us*.

Pink's jumping-off point is a classic behavioral experiment from the 1940s, called the "candle problem." People who were told that they would be rewarded with five dollars depending on how quickly they solved a puzzle *took longer* to solve it than people who were told simply that their time would be used to estimate typical times for puzzle solving. Paradoxically, the offer of money seemed to hinder rather than improve performance.[1]

The paradox is explained by the concept of *intrinsic interest*. Routine work can be motivated by external rewards such as money. But creative tasks need to be intrinsically interesting—that is, motivating and compelling in themselves—in order to engage the minds of workers. When external rewards are emphasized, people make the unconscious assumption that the work itself is not very interesting . . . and their level of engagement falls.

Since the 1940s, study after study has supported the finding that when money is used as reward for an activity, people lose intrinsic interest. Yet most businesses haven't gotten the message. Company after company offers conventional incentives for performance—even when they demonstrably don't work.

What *does* work is understanding what truly motivates people: The drive to solve problems and do work that contributes something of interest and value to society transcends money.

Today's smartest educators are using this insight to attract more women to STEM studies. Maria Klawe explains how this works for Harvey Mudd College: "Whether it's engineering, chemistry, math, or computer science, students want to work on problems that matter to humanity. We are making a lot of effort toward presenting them with intrinsically interesting problems that matter."[2]

What's more, it appears that women in particular are especially motivated to work on problems that affect the well-being of their fellow humans. Girls are more inclined toward math, science, technology, and entrepreneurship when they can envision real-world applications, especially ones that benefit people and the planet.[3] Time and again, I've seen the entrepreneurial spirit catch fire when girls see that they can accomplish something meaningful. A problem doesn't have to be earthshaking to be fodder for a great entrepreneurial breakthrough that will excite and motivate kids. Focusing on one problem a girl can solve is empowering.

In entrepreneurial class, girls discover that problems can lead to a sense of purpose. This realization can help girls identify the opportunities lurking in problems. This may require a mental and emotional adjustment. Girls are often raised to stifle or ignore feelings like frustration and anger that are generated by the awareness of unsolved problems. Many women spend their entire lives as "good girls" who restrain their voices, submitting and deferring to men. Women are often idealized as the nurturers, soothers, and peacemakers of the world. The taboo against girls' feeling and expressing anger is so powerful that, in the words of psychologist Harriet Lerner, "even knowing when we are angry is not a simple matter."[4]

For girls to be true to themselves, or to develop as leaders—at companies, in classrooms, in their professions, in science and technology, in the world—they cannot simply accept things that are wrong and try to play a comforting or placating role. Instead, they need to get in touch with their inner sense of outrage and anger—and allow those negative emotions to motivate their pursuit of positive change.

At VentureLab, we invite girls to think of problems that need solutions. Rather than thinking about things that are going swimmingly, we challenge them to think of things that make them frustrated or angry. Here's a sampling of some of the problems girls have mentioned, some mighty, others miniature:

- War, fighting, and shooting
- Not enough butterflies
- Not-so-good Halloween candy
- Having to go to bed so early
- Difficulty waking up in the morning
- Soap in my eyes
- Needing money
- Mean adults
- People who don't recycle
- Impossible-to-understand homework
- Children in the world being poor and hungry
- People who hurt children
- Parents who don't listen to children
- Not being thought of by adults as smart
- Having to get up early for school
- Getting grounded
- Not wanting to brush teeth
- Movie trailers that give away too much of the story
- Disappearance of species
- Loss of woods and habitats

Problems like these begin to seem less overwhelming when children cast themselves as creative problem-solvers. In entrepreneurial education, girls learn that there is more than one way to approach almost every problem—including every problem on this list. They become doers and change agents.

When girls realize that they have the power to invent a product or create a company that could make a difference to someone, they light up. The ideas begin to pour out:

- An easy-to-use website to explain homework
- Setting aside part of the woods for conservation
- Inventing a toothbrush that isn't so "pokey"
- An alarm clock that turns over your mattress so you tumble out of bed
- A social media site where parents and kids can listen to each other
- Planting city gardens with flowers that butterflies like
- Letting kids and families choose their own school schedules

"Well-behaved women seldom make history," says historian Laurel Thatcher Ulrich. There are dire needs all over the globe crying out for a solution by history-makers. In our entrepreneurial classes, we encourage the rebel inside the girl, the frustration that erupts, the anger that leads to inspiration, the logic that leads to clarity, and the crazy ideas that smash conventional thinking. We encourage girls to roar.

SOCIAL ENTREPRENEURSHIP—CHANGING THE WORLD THROUGH CREATIVE THINKING

MANY GIRLS AND WOMEN HAVE BEEN EMBRACING THE CONCEPT OF *SOCIAL entrepreneurship,* creating enterprises to solve problems that are harming or threatening our global fellow denizens.

Pamela Ryan applied entrepreneurial thinking to a heartbreaking tragedy that impacts many women—the problem of fistula, a childbirth injury that kills the baby and destroys the mother's soft tissue, causing her urine and feces to leak through her vagina. An estimated two million women, primarily in Africa, suffer with fistula, most of them village outcasts because of the stench of their bodies. Ryan and her teenage daughters became aware of the problem of fistula, and the more they learned about it, the angrier they became. They decided to do something about it. They educated themselves about medical science and obstetrics and developed an intense passion for research and innovation to solve the problem. As a family, they now invest in an Ethiopian hospital dedicated to fistula repair. Their dedication is helping teenage mothers regain their lives, one by one.[5]

Another example of social entrepreneurship is Kenguru (pronounced "kangaroo"), a startup that designed a little electric hatchback car that is wheelchair accessible. Its cofounder Istvan Kissaroslaki was a German-raised salesman in the medical device industry with an education in finance. He brought back to life an old prototype that had been shelved for a vehicle that would function as a moped for teenagers who used wheelchairs in Europe. Kissaroslaki had started reengineering and sourcing parts, had exhausted his funds, and had gotten stuck—until he found Stacy Zoern, a Texas lawyer disabled by spinal muscular atrophy who had been looking for a transportation solution for herself.

Kissaroslaki and Zoern joined forces to make this low-speed, wheelchair-accessible vehicle a reality. They teamed up as cofounders, he moved to Texas, and they obtained the financing needed to design and build the next prototype. Kenguru is a road-ready little car with an unusual kangaroo-inspired feature: The hatchback lifts and a ramp pops out, enabling a driver in a wheelchair to roll right into it without assistance. The wheelchair becomes the car seat.

Being an entrepreneur is not without its frustrations. The most recent setback in this story occurred when a company acquired Kenguru and filed for Chapter 11 bankruptcy protection less than a year later. While the future of the Kenguru is uncertain, the cofounders' entrepreneurial mind-set is hard to stifle, and hope remains.[6]

It has been heartening to see the growing interest in social entrepreneurship in recent years, especially among some of the youngest women in business. Kerstin Forsberg is one of the amazing twentysomething women on the global front lines. Forsberg works with the people of Peru to change practices such as unsustainable fishing and waste management in order to preserve the coastal environment for more than five hundred marine and coastal species.[7]

Another deeply impressive young woman, Sejal Hathi, a molecular biologist, started Girls Helping Girls while she was still in college. Her venture capital fund connects girls around the globe and invests in young entrepreneurs in countries with few resources.[8]

And then there's Ridhi Tariyal, an engineer at Harvard who came up with an ingenious method for obtaining blood samples from women without causing pain, a problem that baffled many engineers before her. For Tariyal, the solution came naturally: "I was thinking about women and blood. When you put those words together, it becomes obvious. We have an opportunity every single month to collect blood from women, without needles. There's lots of information in there, but right now it's all going in the trash." She and her business partner, Stephen Gire, have patented a tampon device for capturing menstrual flow and transforming it into medical samples: simple, creative, and brilliant.[9]

KIDS WHO WANT TO CHANGE THE WORLD

EVEN MORE REMARKABLE ARE THE GIRLS WHO HAVE LAUNCHED SOCIAL entrepreneurship projects while still in grade school.

If you ever had the pleasure of sitting through one of Mikaila Ulmer's project pitches, you'd find that her introduction sounds like any other fifth grader's. "My name is Mikaila, I'm ten, and I'm in the fifth grade. I live in Austin, Texas."[10]

But soon Mikaila puts on her business face and pushes past ordinary: "I'm a founder and CEO of BeeSweet Lemonade. I'm also a bee advisor, student, and social entrepreneur. Today I'm going to tell you about my business and some interesting facts and lessons that I have learned about being an entrepreneur."

In a matter of seconds, the girl with a flowery headband, yellow polka-dotted shirt, and matching yellow pants takes control of the room. With flashcards in one hand and PowerPoint slides flashing on the screen behind her, Mikaila tells how BeeSweet Lemonade got its start when she was four and a half years old. "I started BeeSweet Lemonade when I signed up for two kids' entrepreneurial events, the Acton Children's Business Fair and Austin Lemonade Day. While I was trying to come up with a product, two things happened.

I got stung by two bees in one week and my great-granny Helen sent me a 1940s cookbook with her favorite recipe for flaxseed lemonade."

Mikaila was determined to learn more about the bees that she had become deathly afraid of. She soon realized how important they are to the world—how they pollinate one-third of all the food produced in the United States while contributing $14 billion to the agricultural economy. She also learned that environmental changes have threatened the well-being of bees, putting the future of farming at risk.

Mikaila's fear morphed into interest, and then into inspiration and passion. She decided to start a lemonade business that would donate a portion of its profits to organizations like Heifer International, the Texas Beekeepers Association, and the Sustainable Food Center of Austin that are helping to save the bees.

Mikaila goes on to list the four flavors she's come up with and the names of retailers that have stocked her product on their shelves in the American Southwest. By the time Mikaila was ten, her BeeSweet Lemonade was generating annual sales of $25,000, and she's gotten a $60,000 investment from presenting her business on the television show *Shark Tank*. She concludes her presentation by sharing the wisdom she has gathered from her five years of entrepreneurial experience:

> *The first lesson is that working hard is a must. In order to start and grow my business I had to work really hard. Some people would say that I had to wear a lot of hats. I had to wear a marketing hat, a finance hat.*

I developed a passion for the bees, learning about the bees . . . I think that passion helped me create my business, a growing, successful, and thriving business.

The last lesson is that you can be sweet and still be profitable. As a social entrepreneur, my business is giving back. I donate my time and money to saving the bees. BeeSweet Lemonade is proud to say that we're making a measurable impact on saving the bees, and we're profitable at the same time.

Today, Mikaila's business has been renamed Me & the Bees Lemonade, and her product is available at Whole Foods stores and a growing number of other outlets.

Of course, not every girl will end up launching a business as successful as Mikaila's. Just as important are the everyday opportunities for parents to introduce girls to social entrepreneurship thinking on a small scale.

Take Anne Boysen, a futurist who studies Homelanders, her term for the generation born after 9/11. She advocates teaching entrepreneurial skills to children to prepare them for whatever the future holds.

One day, Boysen heard her nine-year-old daughter suddenly screaming and crying while she was working on the computer. Anne rushed in and saw that her daughter had been looking for *cute elephant* photos. Instead she was seeing horrific, sickening photos of dead elephants mutilated and beheaded, killed for their ivory tusks. Anne realized that her daughter had left off the *e* at the end of *cute*, typing "*cut* elephants" by mistake.

Anne's first impulse was to turn off the computer and try to erase the images from her daughter's mind—to pretend what they'd seen doesn't exist. But what would be the message to her daughter? Anne decided on a different course—a grit-building, empowering, entrepreneurial course. They stayed online, and Anne guided her daughter through research about the problem of elephant poaching. They learned how many African elephants have been killed for their tusks, and they discovered that Africa has lost two-thirds of its elephants. They identified organizations working to stop elephant poachers, and they chose one that seemed effective. They sent a message of support along with a small donation.[11]

Instead of letting her daughter suffer a horrific experience and believe there was no solution, Anne helped her learn to think like a social entrepreneur. Anne's story reminds us that parents are in a prime role to help daughters approach the world's problems with constructive, empowered, entrepreneurial thinking.

ALTRUISM ON AND OFF CAMPUS

You might assume that the idealistic spirit I've identified in the students who attend VentureLab is a special characteristic of young girls. Maybe the desire to use entrepreneurial skills and STEM subjects to make the world a better place gradually dies out as kids get older, replaced by more cynical and self-serving urges for money, power, or fame.

But that's simply not the case. Lots of young men and

women of college age and beyond are eager to use their talents to solve pressing human problems.

Dr. Lina Nilsson, a biomedical engineer, is the innovation director at the Blum Center for Developing Economies at the University of California, Berkeley. In 2015, Nilsson created a stir by proposing a solution to the deficit of women engineers. She said that her experience at UC Berkeley suggests that making "the content of the work itself . . . more societally meaningful" will attract women in large numbers. To test the theory, the Blum Center created a new PhD minor in development engineering for students who are designing solutions for low-income communities. The topics span clean drinking water, medical diagnostics for tropical diseases, and local manufacturing in remote regions. Result: Without any targeted outreach, the Blum Center achieved equal male and female enrollments in the new program.

Curious as to whether this experience was true elsewhere, Nilsson and her colleagues reached out to Pennsylvania State University, the University of Michigan, Arizona State University, the University of Minnesota, MIT, and dozens of other universities from coast to coast. What they found was "consistent and remarkable":

> *Women seem to be drawn to engineering projects that attempt to achieve societal good. None of the programs, clubs and classes were designed with the main goal of appealing to female engineers, and perhaps this is exactly why they are drawing us in. At the core of each of*

the programs is a focus on engineering that is cutting edge, with an explicit social context and mission.

The key to increasing the number of female engineers may not just be mentorship programs or child care centers, although those are important. It may be about reframing the goals of engineering research and curriculums to be more relevant to societal needs. It is not just about gender equity—it is about doing better engineering for us all.[12]

Sigmund Freud candidly admitted that one question he was never able to answer was, "What does a woman want?" Of course, women are so diverse that there can be no single answer. But I believe that Lina Nilsson has identified a broadly shared desire, one that women share with most men: *for our lives to have meaning.*

In my case, after graduating from the University of Texas at Austin with a degree in mechanical engineering, I worked at 3M designing copper connectors for automated test equipment. While it was fun, I always had a nagging desire to do more to help people. During that time, the terrible events of 9/11 occurred. That tragedy made me question the value of my work. I decided to follow my passion by switching careers to biomedical engineering, where I set out to find a way to reduce side effects for cancer patients. I spent years in grad school developing specialized nanoparticles that could preferentially target lung cancer tumor tissues and release drugs only when there was an overexpression of cancerous enzymes—thus not affecting healthy cells and reducing the side effects of treatment. That work became the springboard for me to launch my own nanotech company.

Today, many educational programs are beginning to focus on the social impacts of STEM. For example, MIT offers D-Lab courses—the *D* stands for "development through discovery, design and dissemination"—that challenge students to tackle poverty issues around the globe. Participants apply their engineering and technology in impoverished areas in Latin America, South America, Africa, and Asia, doing fieldwork on projects to produce energy, process grain, diagnose illnesses, purify water, and tackle other urgent problems. Three-quarters of the two hundred–plus students enrolled are women, a rarity among engineering programs.

As the D-Lab projects illustrate, the impact of social entrepreneurship projects launched at colleges or universities extends far beyond the campuses themselves.

Dr. dt ogilvie is spreading the message that urban entrepreneurship can inject economic vitality into struggling neighborhoods. She started an urban entrepreneurship program at Rutgers University in New Jersey that attracts students not only from the university itself, but also from the surrounding community. Anyone in the neighborhood is welcome to attend Rutgers's entrepreneurial classes, kids included.

CONNECTING PEOPLE TO THEIR DREAMS

APPLYING ENTREPRENEURIAL TALENT AND STEM SKILLS TO TRANSFORMING the world doesn't necessarily have to focus on struggling inner-city neighborhoods, endangered species, or other social causes. Some idealistic entrepreneurial visions are simply about enabling people to fulfill their own dreams. It's not necessary for every project a girl launches to "make a difference in the world" (as some well-meaning school science fairs now suggest). All that's needed is for a project to have meaning that is *personal, intrinsic, and organic*. If it helps *one child* find her passions and discover the joy of scientific exploration and entrepreneurial creativity, that's good enough for me.

Randa Milliron is a rocket scientist and entrepreneur who has carved out a way to pursue her passion—making outer space accessible to more people. But back in middle school, a STEM career would have seemed the least likely option for her. She struggled with math and hated being forced to do problems on the blackboard in front of the class. "I had a sadistic math teacher who ridiculed and humiliated me," she now recalls. "Talk about being discouraged! It was mentally scarring." Despite her difficulties in math class, she graduated from college with a background in science, but those early classroom experiences caused her to focus mainly on languages and art.

After college, Milliron began a career in television and film. But then a visceral experience awakened her dormant interest in STEM:

I was in a video band that played industrial music, called H-Bomb/White Noise. A fan asked us, "Do you want to come to a rocket test?" Sure! So we drove to this godforsaken area hundreds of miles from anything, just a dry lake bed, scrub, and a desert outpost—a cool sci-fi setting. There was a rocket engine test pad, and five guys from the Pacific Rocket Society were going to be firing a rocket they had made.

Toward evening, we watched these guys—no women—setting up. They were not government, not military, just people you wouldn't think would have a rocket test area or the authority to do that sort of thing. They hooked up a two-thousand-pound-thrust rocket engine. Then we went into a blockhouse maybe two hundred feet away. When they hit the ignition, I fell to my knees. I thought the thing was exploding; the heat was passing over us. I rose along the cinder block wall up to the blockhouse window. Then I thought, No, it's not exploding—it's working! We watched a giant pillar of fire. That power! To harness it and get it working for you was beyond belief.

I respected those people so much. I wanted to do it, too . . . My husband, Roderick, was there, and we looked at each other and at that moment knew, we're doing nothing but this from now on![13]

In 1995, Milliron and her husband started Interorbital Systems, dedicated to the then-radical concept of making low-cost modular satellites. As CEO, she is involved in aerospace engineering assembly and design specializing in high-temperature composite materials. Today, for about eight thousand dollars, you can buy a personal satellite kit, assemble a small cube-shaped satellite, the size of a Kleenex box, and have it launched into space by Interorbital Systems. The least expensive comparable satellites cost a minimum of $250,000.

Originally, Milliron thought they would sell their kits primarily to graduate students. But almost overnight, space agencies, entrepreneurs, and schools were demanding them. Not only is Milliron an entrepreneur, her company *enables* entrepreneurs by making satellites more affordable than ever. The company also hosts interns from disadvantaged schools in nearby Los Angeles.

What I love about Milliron's story is her irrepressible spirit. She bounced back from the trauma of her discouraging math classes in middle school to discover that STEM can be an exciting, empowering field. As a result, many other young women and men are now able to spread their entrepreneurial wings via the space-orbiting ideas that Interorbital Systems makes possible.

TRY THIS AT HOME—AN ACTIVITY GIRLS WILL LOVE: WHAT IF I . . . ?

This activity gives you a chance to think about your wildest dreams and hopes—and to capture them in visual form.

TIME: 30—60 MINUTES

You Need

Something to write and draw with (pens, pencils, crayons, or markers)
Paper to write and sketch on

Directions

- Start by getting relaxed and thinking about your dreams. Ask yourself these questions:
    - What do I want to be?
    - What do I want to do?
    - What would I like to change to make the world better?
- As your dreams begin to emerge, start asking yourself "What if?" questions. Examples:
    - What if I started a ranch for homeless dogs?
    - What if I started a company and became a millionaire by the time I was in college?
    - What if I invented a way to travel the world instantaneously?
    - What if I could breathe underwater?
- Write down as many of your "What if?" dreams as possible. Remember not to limit yourself. Your dreams

can be anything. Some may seem impractical—but impractical doesn't mean impossible.

- Create a *mind map* of your dreams. A mind map is a visual way to represent ideas and concepts (see the sample below). Using colors and shapes, map out your dreams. Include words and phrases that suggest how you might be able to achieve them.

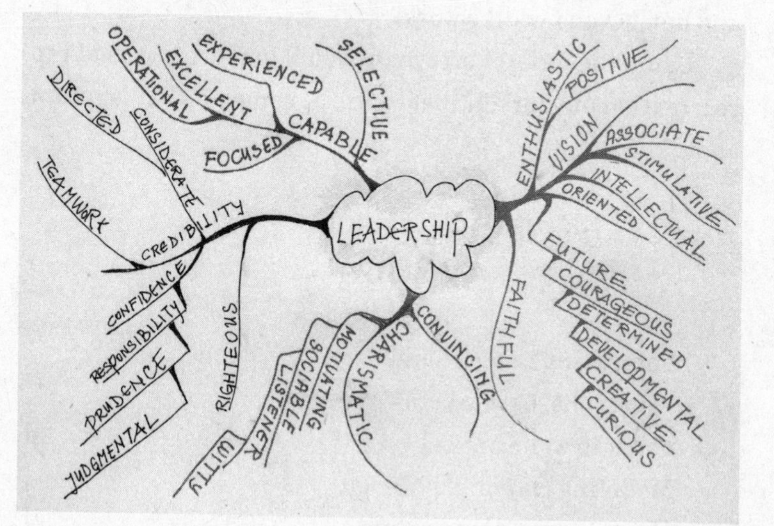

Image © leuviah

TRY THIS AT HOME—AN ACTIVITY GIRLS WILL LOVE: YOUR ENTREPRENEURIAL SELF

Wonder Woman and Superman have incredible strength. The Flash has super speed. Jean Grey and Professor X can control things with their minds. We are not all superheroes, but we all have unique strengths, talents, traits, and passions—things that make us uniquely us.

Maybe you have a special talent for singing, maybe you know everything about insects, maybe you have wilderness survival skills, and maybe you have a remarkable character trait like courage, kindness, or optimism. Maybe you are really good at knowing how to cheer people up. Maybe you are really good at convincing others to join your team. Many times, strengths are ways of acting that come naturally to us and don't even feel like work.

Using the tools of creativity, you'll create a physical representation of yourself that captures some of what is unique about you.

TIME: 30 MINUTES

You Need

Something to write and draw with (pens, pencils, crayons, or markers)
Paper to write on
Modeling clay or play dough
Magazines or newspapers
Scissors
Glue stick

Directions

- Put on some relaxing or fun music, and think about:
    - What you want to be
        - What you are passionate about
        - Your greatest strengths
        - Anything that captures your essence

- Come up with four words that represent you. Don't think too hard, just let the four words come to you.
- Spend 10 to 15 minutes using the clay or play dough to create a model, or the magazines or newspapers to make a collage representing you. Follow your gut instincts, and get creative! Suppose your four words are *adventurous, creative, helpful,* and *friendly.* Your collage might include pictures of people in outdoors activities, people smiling or helping others, people doing things that are adventurous or creative. Your play-dough model might be anything that represents those words to you.
- When you are finished, stand up and talk about your words and how the collage or model that you created represents you.

To discover the potentially wonderful future ahead of you, you need to start by understanding who you are today. This activity will help you do that in a fun and inspiring way.

10

Provide Role Models

On July 1, 2015, Colette Pierce Burnette became the first woman to serve as president of Huston-Tillotson University, the oldest historically black college west of the Mississippi River. Burnette is all the more remarkable because she is an engineer—an uncommon career choice for most women, and especially for women of color.[1]

In many ways, the young Colette was fortunate. In an era when many black girls were unable to experience higher education, going to college wasn't a choice for her. It was simply assumed that she and her sister would go to college—despite the fact that no one in their family ever had.

Burnette's father was born in Mississippi and moved to Cleveland, Ohio, in the 1950s, part of the Great Migration that brought millions of African Americans from the South to the North between 1910 and 1970. He had only a fifth-grade education, but he appreciated the value of education. "I remember sitting at the kitchen table with my father," Burnette recalls. "I was doing my homework as a seventh or eighth grader, while he was studying for his GED."

Actually, the entire family was engaged in the pursuit of learning. Burnette tears up when talking about her grandmother. "She would go to the butcher and ask for butcher block paper, and she wrote all of the times tables on it and posted them on the walls in the kitchen. During breakfast, my sister and I recited the times tables by rote until we got them right—five times five is twenty-five, five times six is thirty, and so on. As time passed, we couldn't eat breakfast without saying the times tables."

No opportunity to learn and practice was passed up. "Growing up, I could look in the grocery cart and add up every item in my head and tell you how much it was going to cost. My grandmother trained my mind to be a scientist."

Burnette was a terrific student in high school. She graduated in 1975, determined to become an engineer. But at Ohio State University, she discovered that the resources available at her high school had been far below standard, which left her at a disadvantage academically. The gleaming array of equipment in her first college chemistry classroom was unfamiliar to her; in fact, the only thing she recognized was the periodic table of elements hanging on the wall.

However, Burnette wasn't at a social disadvantage, because she believed in herself. Her parents had always told her and her sister, "You're smart, you're bright—apply yourself and you can do it." So she buckled down and worked hard.

In her first engineering summer job, she was working in

a power plant where she was the only woman. She spent long hours working in a basement that frequently flooded, with only a manometer (a gauge for measuring the pressure in a column of fluid) and a few mice for company.

Back at college, Burnette started dating an electrical engineering major. She did a homework assignment for both of them using a T-bar that she used to measure the drawings on the two worksheets to ensure they were exactly the same. Burnette's boyfriend earned an A on the assignment—while she got a C. She recalls:

> *I was crushed. I couldn't tell the professor that I'd done both assignments. I realized two things. One, that boy was going to have to do his own homework from then on! Two, because my name was on my paper, and I was a woman, the faculty member perceived my work differently. I realized that I would have to work extra hard because I was being measured using a different scale. It fired me up. I was going to go the extra mile to show that I was an A student. Grit gets you up off the ground and keeps you walking on the journey.*

As an upperclassman, Burnette got a summer job as a counselor to bridge students of color into the field of engineering. She found it fulfilling to check on students' progress and to guide them, and she decided to dedicate her life to mentoring others. But the tough times were far from over. Early in Burnette's marriage to a serviceman on active duty, she found herself working and pregnant:

> *When I was in my first trimester, I was so tired. My husband was stationed in Georgia, and I worked in the plant on the air force base, where we were building parts for planes. One day on a break, I put my head down on the table and the next thing I knew, the workday was over. When I realized I'd slept through the entire day, I thought I was going to be in big trouble. Instead, the men asked if I was all right. I realized they didn't really know how to treat me because I was a young, black, pregnant engineer. For the first time, it was a plus!*
>
> *Throughout my pregnancy, I was an anomaly to them. I think men don't realize that we're more alike than we are different.*

"You don't go through things, you *grow* through things," Burnette discovered. She kept growing. In time, she began taking business courses, then teaching them, beginning at the University of Colorado. She spent fifteen years in the corporate world, stretching herself as a leader with each workplace move—"constantly reinventing and rethinking myself so I could be marketable," as she now describes it. Then, in her fifties, she began work on a doctoral degree at the University of Pennsylvania. This was the final credential she needed to qualify for the job she'd decided she wanted more than any other in the world—president of a university.

To say that Burnette is now the first female president of Huston-Tillotson University is only partially correct. The university was formed in 1952 when Samuel Huston College and Tillotson College merged, and Tillotson had a woman president, Mary E. Branch, in the 1930s. Burnette keeps a portrait of Branch hanging on the wall of her office:

> *I often think about what made her tick. That type of perseverance and grit. It was a time when she couldn't get on a train and ride in front. She was up against tremendous odds yet maintained the school so that it could become a well-known institution. When I get discouraged, I look up there and think, if Mary Branch can do this, then I can do this.*
>
> *Even university presidents need role models!*

As president of Huston-Tillotson, Burnette is especially dedicated to encouraging minority women and men to pursue STEM careers—a natural focus for this engineer and self-described techie. "We need to instill in all of our students the message, 'You are good in math, you are good in science. You can go out and become an engineer or mathematician. And we expect you to succeed.' "

Colette Pierce Burnette is making a big difference every day in the lives of students whose futures she is helping to shape. But her influence extends even beyond the campus of Huston-Tillotson University. She serves as a role model for girls who aspire to succeed in science, technology, and leadership—which means that she instills a measure of her dauntless spirit into many young women who will carry forward her work in generations to come.

THE ROLE OF THE ROLE MODEL

WHO ARE THE ROLE MODELS THAT YOUNG GIRLS IN AMERICA LOOK UP TO? Are they beautiful Disney princesses like Cinderella, Belle, Ariel, and Elsa? Are they glamorous pop stars like Beyoncé, Katy Perry, and Taylor Swift? Or tough-minded heroines from young adult fiction like Katniss from *The Hunger Games,* Tris from *Divergent,* or Lyra from *The Golden Compass*?

There's nothing wrong with any of these kinds of role models. But they need to be supplemented with others whose lives represent what young women can really aspire to in today's world—women scientists, engineers, mathematicians, computer programmers, inventors, entrepreneurs, and business founders.

Where are these female role models? There are plenty of them, and at VentureLab, we make a point of seeking them out and integrating them into our camps and classes. They visit with us, talk about their lives and their work, and display some of their accomplishments. For many girls, it is the first time they have ever met a woman scientist . . . a woman company president . . . a woman entrepreneur. And honestly it is as thrilling for me as it is for them. It's magical to see their eyes widen and their mouths open as a woman describes how she got into engineering, the teams she leads, the mistakes she's recovered from, the failures she learned from, the successes she has achieved, and the cool projects she gets to work on every day.

Later in the program, when our female students are ready to present the products they've developed as part of the entrepreneurial process we teach, they are focused and excited partly because the audiences include not just friends and parents but often actual entrepreneurs and STEM professionals, many of them women.

We all need role models we can identify with and aspire to emulate, and female role models are all around us if only we make the effort to find them. That's why, with both girls and boys, I do my best to balance the well-known faces of successful male entrepreneurs and innovators—Steve Jobs, Elon Musk, Bill Gates—with those of equally accomplished women whose stories are often less well-known. Some women whose stories I love to share with my children include:

- Mae Jemison, an engineer and physician who became the first African American female astronaut when she flew on the Space Shuttle *Endeavour* in 1992
- Megan J. Smith, an MIT-trained engineer who participated in the world's first cross-continental solar car race across two thousand miles of the Australian outback, then served as the nation's third chief technology officer under President Barack Obama
- Wanda Austin, a PhD in systems engineering who served as CEO of the Aerospace Corporation, the leading architect of America's space security programs
- Meg Whitman, the business executive who as CEO of eBay led that company's phenomenal growth over the course of a decade and today serves as chairman and CEO of Hewlett Packard Enterprise
- Cornelia "Cori" Bargmann, a biochemist who founded

and leads the Brain Research through Advancing Innovative Neurotechnologies (BRAIN) Initiative, which researches the root causes of conditions such as Alzheimer's and autism by studying connections between brain function and behavior

- Emily Levesque, a Hubble Fellow at the University of Colorado at Boulder, who is discovering the hidden mechanisms driving the formation and collapse of massive stars and galaxies

Sometimes the stories of the most remarkable role models remain obscured during their lifetimes, like those of the brilliant African American mathematicians at NASA—Katherine Johnson, Dorothy Vaughan, and Mary Jackson—whose work made possible the first orbital flight of astronaut John Glenn. They only became famous thanks to the acclaimed 2016 book *Hidden Figures* by Margot Lee Shetterly, which became the basis of an Oscar-nominated movie.

Another often-overlooked example: Hedy Lamarr, the famous Hollywood actress who—in her spare time—used her interest in science and math to work on a string of inventions. During World War Two, she codeveloped a "frequency-hopping" signal system to enable torpedoes to reach their targets without being tracked or jammed. "Improving things comes naturally to me," she once remarked.[2] As for the acting career that earned her fame and fortune, she was much more dismissive. "Any girl can be glamorous," Lamarr said. "All you have to do is stand still and look stupid."

Role models needn't be famous or wealthy—just willing to share their stories with the girls who look up to them. An entrepreneur who speaks to a fourth-grade class may learn much later that one student treasured her business card for years as a talisman reflecting what she, too, could achieve.

FINDING ROLE MODELS

It is up to grown-ups to help the girls in their lives to find role models who can inspire them—and, if they are especially lucky, who may help to teach or guide them.

Throughout my life, I have had role models who have allowed me to see myself following my passion. When I was thinking about starting a nanotech company, it was Becky Taylor, an accomplished female mentor, who encouraged me to leave my comfort zone. She introduced me to Springboard, a program that supports female CEOs in building high-growth tech companies. Meeting extremely successful women in tech gave me the confidence to believe that I could do the same things.

The life stories of many successful leaders in STEM or entrepreneurship include tales of encounters with inspiring or helpful role models. Steve Jobs was in the eighth grade when he was bitten by the computer bug. Uncertain where to turn for help, he looked up the home phone number of Bill Hewlett, CEO of Hewlett Packard, who lived not far from the Jobs family. Young Steve asked Hewlett to donate parts so that he could build a frequency counter for a school project. Jobs got the parts—and a summer job at HP. His historic career as the founder of Apple was the ultimate result.

How perfect it would be if female CEO technology entrepreneurs lived next door to each of us! Since most of us aren't so lucky, I encourage girls and their parents to seek out role models rather than waiting for them to appear.

Sometimes a role model can be found right across the dining room table. Kennon Lydick, a high school junior, is interested in engineering. Her role model is her older brother Hayden, a college student majoring in biomedical engineering, who encourages her interest in engineering. As far back as elementary school, Hayden worked with his sister on projects, like an elaborate tree house that called for pylons and concrete. Now he encourages her not to let a poor grade set her back:

> *Engineering is perceived as a very difficult major, so the fact that you don't succeed is expected. I think Kennon would be a good engineer, I truly do. But she has it in her head that she wouldn't be good in engineering. I lean more toward math and science when it comes to my intelligence, and she feels that's the type of person she has to be to achieve at engineering. But she's a very well-rounded person who will beat her head against the problem until she solves it. That's all it takes.*[3]

That kind of encouragement can make all the difference in the life of a young woman who is wondering whether she's really cut out for a future in STEM.

It doesn't take a STEM superstar to be an aspiring girl's role model. Parents, relatives, friends, neighbors, teachers, tutors, and community members—such as the local leader of the YMCA, 4-H club, or scout troop—can help simply by taking an interest in the dreams of the girls they know. They can ask questions, offer encouragement, and sincerely seek to understand a girl's fascination with science, math, technology, or business. They can cultivate the curiosity, creativity, and willingness to experiment that open doors to achievement. By their words and actions, they can demonstrate a growth mind-set—illustrating by example the fact that practice and diligence can help anyone develop new capabilities and accomplish things that might seem impossible.

Of course, it's also worthwhile to seek out role models who can talk about STEM and entrepreneurship from personal experience. Think about friends of friends who have pursued careers in science or technology, or who have launched businesses. If you call and say you have a daughter or a young friend who wants to learn more about the world of STEM, they are likely to be flattered and pleased to help. An invitation to visit an office, lab, or workshop may result.

Another option is to look for opportunities to encounter role models at community events—a presentation at the local science museum, an author appearance at a neighborhood bookstore, a space show at the planetarium, or a talk about animal behavior at the zoo.

Role models are all around—you just need to find them!

FROM RANCHER TO ENGINEER—ROLE MODELS IN UNLIKELY PLACES

For almost nine hundred miles, the Rio Grande flows as a natural border between Texas and Mexico. Spanish conquistadors began to settle the region centuries ago, long before Texas came into existence. Among the first waves of settlers in the 1700s were the ancestors of Kathy Garza Smith. When Smith talks about "the Valley" with her fellow engineers, she's not referring to Silicon Valley—she means the Rio Grande Valley.

Smith grew up as the oldest of six kids, in a small community, spending weekends and holidays on her family's thousand-acre ranch, where she was free to roam—perhaps a little too free. Smith first got behind the wheel of her family's ranch equipment at age nine:

> *I would drive on the dirt roads to get the mail, and sometimes I would drive to see our relatives on the family ranch. My dad's siblings had houses on the ranch. Sometimes I would venture farther, without asking my dad's permission. He would ask me, "Why did you go to Tio Lupe's house?" I would ask him, "How did you know I went there?" It was the tire tracks that gave me away.*[4]

Those early lessons in self-reliance and managing technology served Smith well. Today, she is a traffic engineer with

HDR, one of the largest engineering, environmental, architectural, and construction firms in the world, with more than eight thousand employees on five continents.

Smith recalls the spark that set her career in motion when she was still in eighth grade. By then, of course, she'd been driving pickup trucks for years:

> *I was in an occupation orientation class, where they show you pictures of people in different professions that you can strive for. I saw the one with a guy wearing a hard hat and a vest on a construction site, and I thought, "That's what I'm going to do." It was considered the craziest thing. Everybody said, "What are you talking about?" But I thought it was so cool. To me, it was a creative job that used math in a creative way—math and a hard hat. It clicked with me, being able to see something built from the ground up, to be a part of it.*

Starting at age fourteen, Smith was thoroughly immersed in entrepreneurship through 4-H Club, a nationwide youth organization administered by the Department of Agriculture. Smith raised and sold lambs as a young entrepreneur, earning money that was hers to keep:

> *The leaders in 4-H didn't just focus on animals. They took us to competitions all over the country. When other teams would come to the Valley, we'd take them over the border and show them Mexico. We did a lot of public speaking, which was amazing. The leader of our*

club was one of the most influential people in my life. We were just these little Hispanic kids, but we became junior leaders and got to run a camp. We decided what activities to have, what the daily program was. I organized arts and crafts. I don't even really know where the adults were, honestly.

As with so many girls destined for careers in STEM, Smith's father treated her as if she could do anything that a boy could do—including fixing things and getting dirty. She got her hands on a lot of ranch equipment, including combines and tractors. "My dad was constantly working on some hands-on projects, so I was exposed to a lot." Her entire extended family also prioritized education. "My dad started his career driving the school bus in the mornings. He became a counselor, teacher, and principal. He taught adult education in the evenings." She and her siblings were all expected to go to college—and they all did.

At the University of Texas, Smith began in electrical engineering. Other students helped one another, but as the only woman in class and sometimes the only American-born student, she often felt alone and isolated. "I was completely lost and out of my element for three years" until she changed her major to civil engineering, which had always been her first love because of the "guy in the hard hat." Soon she was president of the student chapter of the American Society of Civil Engineers.

And then came the role model in the form of a guardian angel. "I had a probability and statistics professor who was trying to get women to get a master's degree in transportation," Smith said. "He told me to take the GRE, and if I did well he would essentially give me a scholarship and pay for my tuition, my books, and give me a salary, and then I could get a master's in transportation." And she did.

Kathy Smith's story resonates with Robert Scherrer, chairman of the Department of Physics and Astronomy at Vanderbilt University. "It's no accident that an unusually large number of twentieth-century scientists grew up on farms or ranches, where they had to learn to fix the tractors and planters without outside help," Scherrer says. "Now most of us don't even change our own oil."[5]

There's something about living outdoors, among machines in need of maintenance, that inspires self-confidence and risk-taking. One of my favorite photos is of an outdoorsy girl, Joely, age eleven, with bicycle grease smeared on her face, beaming because she fixed the gears by herself. She'd gotten down on the sidewalk to learn what did and didn't work. It took her an hour. She tried to fix the brakes, too, but she hadn't—yet.

Joely's mother, Susan Engelking, took that photo. She encourages her daughter's experiments, which always begin with the sentence "I think I can fix it." Recently the two of them learned how to change their car's windshield wipers and fluid, which required them to go to an auto parts store and open the car hood, something they'd never done before. Hand in hand, they tried to figure out what all of the engine parts were.

Says Engelking, "I'm not comfortable under the hood of

a car, but I got over it by reminding myself, I need to be her role model." The experience saved them twelve dollars and sparked her daughter's interest in engines.[6]

Next, they plan to try plumbing.

SELF-CASTING: IMAGINING AN AMAZING FUTURE

IMAGINING YOURSELF IN THE FUTURE CAN BE A POWERFUL STEP TOWARD making your dreams come true. I call this process *self-casting*. It's a long-term form of "visualization," which experts on human behavior have long identified as one of the keys to improving personal performance in any field. Just as a pro golfer can improve her swing by visualizing herself hitting a perfect drive, or a public speaker can boost her self-confidence by visualizing the smiles on the faces of the audience after she delivers an inspiring speech, so an elementary school girl can charge herself up for future STEM success by visualizing herself carrying out brilliant experiments in a physics lab or designing an electronic device that will make life better for millions of people.

That's what self-casting is all about—it's about seeing yourself in a role that you hope to fill in real life someday. More than just having a career goal, it's about a girl vividly imagining herself actually playing the part of a college engineering student, a computer scientist, a cancer researcher, a civil engineer, a genetic scientist, a computer game designer, a technology inventor, or any other occupation that fascinates and excites her.

Role models play a huge part in our ability to self-cast. If a girl sees a woman engineer or a woman CEO, she can see herself in that role. She can cast herself in that role. It's the old mentality of "If she can do it, I can do it!"

After I started VentureLab, people began asking me whether I'd had an entrepreneur in my family. I used to say no—but then I remembered that my dad had started and run the Amigos Soccer Camp. My sisters and I watched what he did and learned from it, an experience that made it easier for me to see myself doing something similar years later. That's exactly how self-casting works.

Self-casting helps turn dreams into realities in a number of ways. One way it helps is by encouraging a girl to think through the various steps in the process of getting from here to there, including education, first jobs, experimentation, risk-taking, failures, and ultimate success. Visualizing a career with all its ups and downs makes the hard work ahead simply part of the process, including the rough patches one should expect along the way. A student who has practiced self-casting finds it easier to keep her eyes on the prize; she is less likely to be derailed by a poor grade or discouraging feedback from "negatrons"—the inevitable skeptics whose feedback will always be a downer. Self-casting lets girls imagine their futures as accomplished, successful women doing what they love—a powerful stimulant for signing up for tough classes and sticking with them because the rewards are worth it.

Part of positive self-casting is overcoming negative stereotypes that can create barriers to girls' visions of themselves in STEM or entrepreneurial careers. Rachel Kast is an accomplished female engineer, but she nearly missed out on that achievement because of the negative stereotypes surrounding the field:

> *Growing up in Detroit, you have a vision in your head of what an engineer is. The ones that you think of, they all work on cars—or you think of the traditional scientist, usually a crazy old man in a laboratory. And neither one was something I was interested in. It really took going to college and meeting people who aren't in those stereotypes to make me see that engineering was something that I could do, even though I didn't fit the stereotype in my head.*[7]

Notice what happened to Kast: Encountering positive role models in college helped her escape the negative stereotypes surrounding science and engineering, and made it possible for her to finally self-cast in the role she was always meant to play.

As a society, we've got to pay more attention to the counterproductive casting signals that girls like Rachel Kast receive. In the meantime, all of us as parents and friends of young girls can help them self-cast in the shape of their dreams by exposing them to role models who show the way.

CREATING AN ECOSYSTEM THAT ENCOURAGES GIRLS TO EXCEL

Based in Atlanta, Georgia, Techbridge is an award-winning national nonprofit dedicated to inspiring girls to pursue careers in STEM. In 2016, Techbridge published a white paper that described ways to encourage girls by designing and developing girl-centric communities—what the experts call "learning ecosystems"—that provide environments in which it's easy for girls to achieve and thrive.[8]

The ecosystem model emphasizes the fact that positive role models can and should be found everywhere in the life of a girl—at home, at school, in the media, and throughout the community. At the same time, negative experiences that overtly or subtly discourage her from pursuing her interest in STEM or entrepreneurship can also crop up almost everywhere. Parents and others who want to encourage girls to follow their dreams with confidence should pay attention to the signals emanating from every corner of the ecosystem, and try to counteract the negative signals with positive ones.

College student Grace Frye, who interned at VentureLab, says, "Something that has always defined me is how much I love school and how much I love learning." But when she enrolled in computer science at Trinity University in San Antonio, Texas, she had the discouraging experience of finding herself as one of only a few female students in a computer science department that intimidated her. In other classes, she'd experienced the fun of students building relationships and camaraderie around achievement and helping one another. That sense of mutual support was missing in her computer science classes, replaced by an intense feeling of cutthroat competition, "where you feel like you're immediately wrong because you don't know [the answer]. I consistently felt like the only one who had questions, and therefore I didn't ask a lot of them. It was very discouraging, especially in such an important field, where I really wanted to succeed."[9]

Fortunately, the leaders of the university's computer science department recognized the problem and made an effort to transform the ecosystem around Grace. One piece of this effort was sponsoring her to attend the Grace Hopper Celebration of Women in Computing. At the celebration, Grace was surrounded by role models. Seeing herself as a part of a global community of computing women lifted her spirit. It's an event that leaves no question that computer science is as much for women as for men.

The Anita Borg Institute, which sponsors the celebration, encourages women to set stretch goals and to support one another through the travails of their tech callings. It was founded by the late Anita Borg, an entrepreneur and one of the first women to earn a PhD in computer science. The celebration itself is named after Navy Rear Admiral Grace Hopper, who once said, "Big rewards go to the people who take the big risks." Grace Hopper would know. She invented the first compiler for a computer programming language, and her work led to the development of COBOL, one of the most widely used computer languages in business and defense. Hopper was buried at Arlington National Cemetery in the 1990s, yet she lives on, with a guided missile destroyer named for her—as well as the largest event for women in computing in the world.

Events like the Grace Hopper Celebration illustrate the kinds of activity we need to create for girls and women of all ages. Once every female is part of an ecosystem that makes role models available, encourages self-casting for success, and demonstrates the potential for achievement in STEM and entrepreneurship, our society will have opened the doors for millions of girls and women to play their destined parts as leaders of tomorrow.

TRY THIS AT HOME—AN ACTIVITY GIRLS WILL LOVE: MY DREAM/IDEA/GOAL JOURNAL

One of the best ways to keep track of dreams, ideas, and goals is to have a journal that you can look back on, whether it is written or drawn with pictures. A VentureGirl can buy a journal at a store or make her own journal out of paper and cardboard, and then decorate it.

TIME: 30—60 MINUTES

You Need

8½ × 11-inch heavy stock paper, construction paper, or thin cardboard
10 pieces of 8½ × 11-inch printer paper or notebook paper

Duct tape
Scissors
Ribbon, yarn, or thread
Large needle
Hole punch or utility knife
Optional: Fabric for cover; markers, glue stick, and stickers for decoration

Directions

- Cut the stock paper/construction paper/cardboard in half. These two pieces are your journal covers. If you like, you can glue some fabric or decorative paper on the inside and outside of your covers. You can also decorate the covers however you like.
- To create the journal binding, place the covers about a half inch apart (along the longest side) and wrap with duct tape to join the two pieces. Make sure to wrap the duct tape all the way around so there are no sticky sections exposed.
- Take 10 pieces of paper and fold them in half horizontally. Then unfold them and line up the crease of the paper with the middle of the duct-taped covers.
- Use a hole punch or a utility knife to create two, three, or four holes through the paper and the duct tape. If your paper is moving around a lot, you can use a paper clip to hold it in place on the journal covers.
- Cut an 18-inch length of ribbon, yarn, or thread, and use a large needle to thread it through the holes that you created.

- Tie the ribbon, yarn, or thread in a knot or bow on the outside portion of the journal and trim any excess.
- Now you have a 20-page journal in which to record your dreams, ideas, and goals—as well as the actions you take to make them come true.

TRY THIS AT HOME—AN ACTIVITY GIRLS WILL LOVE: BRAG ABOUT YOURSELF

It's time to toot your own horn! No time for modesty. You are a rock star, and people need to hear what you have done.

Many times it can be hard for us to talk about ourselves and our accomplishments, and this is true in particular for girls. But it is really empowering to be able to tell others what you have done and hear yourself speaking about your accomplishments out loud. It's also necessary as a step toward many important accomplishments, whether it's getting a position in a student club, being elected to a role in student government, or being offered an internship.

TIME: 15—30 MINUTES

You Need

Something to write with (pens, pencils, crayons, or markers)

Paper to write on

Directions

- List your proudest accomplishments. Think of as many as possible. Some may seem small, like remembering to feed the dog before you leave for school or having a supporting role in a school play. Others may be more impressive, like earning an A grade in the toughest science class you took or being named "Employee of the Month" in a part-time job after school. Big or small, list them all.
- Pick out your favorite accomplishments from the list. Then stand up in front of your parents, family members, or a small group of friends, and take two minutes to brag about yourself.
- You'll find that it is uncomfortable at first, but you'll gain confidence the more you practice. And many times, people in your audience will remind you of accomplishments that you didn't even think about!
- Afterward, take the time to experience the positive emotions and appreciate yourself for all of the hard work you did to achieve what you have done.

This activity is great practice for some of the most challenging and important things you may do in the future, such as college interviews, job interviews, and pitches to investors considering your startup company.

11

Get the Whole Family Involved

The year I was born, a Latina girl in Texas had less than a 2 percent chance of graduating from college. The obstacles were formidable. There was no support system, no role models, no positive societal expectations. Unless a family believed that their daughters would go to college and constantly reinforced that belief—as my family did—it was not likely to happen.

One early challenge, and my family's response, was especially crucial. There were no bilingual programs in public schools at that time—so when the school administrators discovered I spoke Spanish, they tried to put me in remedial classes. Thankfully, my parents protested and insisted I be given a seat in a regular classroom. Looking back, I can see how their support completely changed my life trajectory.

Because I was raised in such a special family, I didn't even fully realize how lucky I was. Not until I completed my doctorate did I grasp how unusual it was—and is—for a Latina to earn a PhD in a STEM field. In 2015, just 2 percent of all PhDs in science and engineering went to Latinas.[1]

Yet the Hispanic population is growing rapidly, now numbering more than 17 percent of the US population. In San Antonio and Austin, Texas, the two cities where I live and work, more than half of the public school population from kindergarten through high school is Hispanic. It is crucial to our future that every student has dreams and aspirations that include proficiency with STEM—and Latinas must be part of that equation.

This is where family support is crucially important. Unfortunately, making sure that support is available to every child isn't simple.

For decades, Hispanic adolescent girls have had an unusually high rate of suicide attempts. Undoubtedly a number of factors are involved. But research suggests that many Hispanic girls experience an emotional struggle as they try to manage growing up in two different cultures.

This culture clash can impact the way Latina girls feel about education, college, and subjects like STEM and entrepreneurship. Torn between their desire for a "modern," "American" lifestyle and the more traditional values of an older Hispanic generation, some Latinas avoid thinking about attending university and studying fields like engineering as a way of remaining close to their conservative parents. In the process, however, they shortchange their own potential.

THE POWER OF MOM

The Junior League of Austin has always been activist- and entrepreneurial-minded. It is also a strong advocate of female empowerment, as you might expect of an organization whose motto is "The Strength of Women—The Power of Community." In 2008, women of the Junior League concerned about the future of young Latinas started a Hispanic mother-daughter program designed to tap the cultural strength of Latino families. The goal: to provide Latinas pursuing higher educations with strong family ecosystems to support them.

The program worked so well that it evolved and spun out to become a nonprofit organization called Con Mi MADRE, in which MADRE stands for Mothers And Daughters Raising Expectations. Of course, the name also means, in Spanish, "With My Mother." Con Mi MADRE invites Latinas and their mothers to join in the spring of fifth grade and continues working with them through college graduation. This longitudinal commitment among organizations working to support students and families is uncommon. It's also very effective. So far, Con Mi MADRE has worked with thirty-five hundred Latina girls and their mothers (six to seven hundred girls per year), virtually all of whom have graduated from high school. Only about 1 percent of Con Mi MADRE teens experience pregnancy, just one-tenth of the rate for Texas Latinas. Three-quarters enroll in college, as compared with the average of about half of Latinas in Austin. Most are the first in their families to go to college, and about one-third are pursuing STEM degrees.

The organization's executive director, Teresa Granillo, used to be a professor of social work at the University of Texas at Austin. Her research examined the connections between mental health and academic success in Latinas, with an eye toward understanding how to help these young women survive and thrive during adolescence. She was hoping to build a program that would keep Latina girls in school and set their sights on higher aspirations when, one day, she noticed a door on campus with the nameplate "Con mi MADRE."

When she learned about the organization, she recognized that it had created exactly what she had imagined—a program for the whole girl, supporting her academically, socially, and emotionally, and deepening her ties to her family. It was the perfect program to help young Latina women manage stress, do better in school, and stay on course to realize their dreams. "It was doing everything I wanted to do," Granillo says. She left academia to take the helm.[2]

One key to the success of Con Mi MADRE is in the name: the influence of mothers. Many of the mothers involved in the program are immigrants or the children of immigrants, people who came to the United States so that their children would have a chance at an education and a better life. Con Mi MADRE helps make these dreams into concrete realities.

The essence of Con Mi MADRE is self-casting—mothers and daughters together envisioning what they can become with determination, knowledge, mentoring, financial assistance, and a support system. All programs are bilingual and culturally sensitive so mothers can fully participate. Mothers are involved at every step. Young Latinas meet successful role models who graduated from college and now earn good incomes as professionals, many in STEM fields. A student gets to make informed decisions about her future while holding hands with "the president of her fan club"—her mother. Meanwhile, mothers bond among themselves to support their daughters' educational ambitions.

"My mother didn't even know it was a possibility for me to go to college until we joined the program," says Karen Gonzalez, who signed up for Con Mi MADRE when she was in the sixth grade. "We're immigrants. My mom didn't know how to help me or where to start. It was really important for her, because I was the number one reason she and my father came to this country. Once I entered the program, and she saw all of the resources and opportunities that it was giving us, my sister joined, too. She's graduating from high school this year."[3] Gonzalez is now a program director for Con Mi MADRE and a role model for Latinas in her own right.

A Latina mother's example can have tremendous influence. Ask Desiree Prieto Groft, whose mom has been in college since Desiree was in kindergarten:

> *A traditional, hard-working Hispanic woman, my mother didn't finish college until after she'd had all four of her demanding children. Since I was the youngest, I went to college with her. She'd pick me up at noon from kindergarten in our old red Chevelle, and we'd*

park at the base of a pebbled promenade and hustle up to the campus. My mother and I would sit at the top of a large, windowless lecture hall, where I smelled library for the first time. I watched her open her notes, pull a pen from her purse, and press play on her tape recorder. I'd pull out my colors and my Snorkels coloring book, while an itty-bitty male professor spoke on a stage below us. Perhaps I'm so smart because I've been going to college since I was five.[4]

Now in her thirties, Prieto Groft has earned two master's degrees, and imagines a PhD in her future. "I might wait until I have my own daughter and can bring her to large lecture halls, so she can smell her own version of education for the first time."

The success of Con Mi MADRE demonstrates that when it comes to raising girls with the curiosity, courage, and gumption to embrace their inner entrepreneurs, moms can play a crucial part as role models, facilitators, and cheerleaders.

There's ample evidence that this truth applies not only in Latina families but among people of every ethnic, national, and religious background. For example, psychologist Margaretha Lucas of the University of Maryland found in her work that teenage girls who trust and confide in their mothers are able to make better career choices. Thus, emotional relatedness between mothers and daughters is key when constructing a young woman's career path.[5]

The Moms as Mentors Project, based in Boston, was founded upon the concept that moms can make a true impact on their daughters simply by being cognizant of what they say and how they act around their daughters. Small daily adjustments to a mom's words and actions can make a big difference in her daughter's life and career outcomes. Leslie Coles, executive director of Moms as Mentors, explains some of the insights they share with parents:

> *Mothers' attitudes can get passed down to their daughters unintentionally. Let's say a girl comes home very upset because she didn't do well on a math test. In an attempt to comfort her daughter, a mom who has her own math anxieties might say, "Oh, honey, don't worry. You are just like me. We aren't math people. But you are so good at art and languages!" Without realizing it, this mom can narrow how the girl views herself—when, in reality, we know that with the right support, this girl could improve her math skills and go on to become successful in any one of the STEM fields.*[6]

Moms truly are an important factor in mentoring and fostering confidence in their daughters. Luckily, my mother has always served as a strong role model for me. She raised three girls while working full-time and achieving success in her career. She headed the cataloging department at the Texas State University library and would take us to work with her on many occasions (something I now do with my own kids). I still remember building a fort under her office desk, and Mom bringing all genres of books for us to read. If we were ever curious about something or struggling with a problem, she was there to encourage us and tell us that we could learn anything. She modeled the growth mind-set and taught me that I could be a strong, successful woman and raise a family. And I hope to pass this attitude on to my own daughters and to the girls across the world whom I am fortunate enough to mentor.

DADS MATTER, TOO

MOMS AND OTHER FEMALE RELATIVES—OLDER SISTERS, AUNTS, GRANDmothers, cousins—can all serve as powerful role models and guides for girls who are seeking pathways to success. But dads, uncles, grandfathers, and other males in the family also matter—especially in today's world, where most of the people who are deeply engaged in business leadership and technology creation are male.

Research shows that girls with fathers who are actively engaged in their lives and who encourage their accomplishments achieve more in school and in their careers. According to one expert, "This helps explain why girls who have no brothers are overly represented among the world's political leaders: they tend to receive more encouragement from their fathers to be high achievers. Even college and professional female athletes often credit their fathers for helping them to become tenacious, self-disciplined, ambitious, and successful."[7]

Many successful women in science and technology, like me, have had dads who encouraged their achievements and dreams. Growing up in a household with no brothers, I was taught by my father to be assertive and ask for what I need—a skill that can be particularly unfamiliar to girls, as Nick Hahn and Graham Weston discussed in Chapter One. Nick Longo, cofounder of Geekdom and founder of CoffeeCup Software, teaches his daughters how to present themselves confidently. He expects them to have a firm handshake and to look people in the eyes.[8] It is part of the entrepreneurial learning experience for girls to imagine, ask for, and compete for what they need—whether it's funding for a startup business, advice that can help them solve a thorny problem, or the recommendation that can open doors to an internship or a school scholarship.

When Mary Barra was named CEO of General Motors in 2014, it made history. She's not simply a woman at the helm of a $150 billion company, nor simply the first woman to lead a major automaker. As an electrical engineer, she is one of today's relatively few CEOs who come not from finance but from product design and manufacturing. Barra seems most comfortable on the shop floor. She *makes* things.

Barra's father was one of the crucial forces that helped fuel her ascent. He worked as a journeyman die maker for GM's Pontiac division for thirty-nine years. When Mary was growing up, he helped his daughter explore her interests. When her curling iron broke, she and her father took it apart in their basement workshop and tried to put it back together—which didn't always work out. But no matter—those early experiments sparked Mary's interest in engineering.

Of course, Barra has faced all the cultural and social barriers that women leaders commonly confront. Former GM vice chairman Bob Lutz expressed doubts as to whether she was tough enough to implement the changes needed to position the company for the coming decades, saying, "I didn't see her as one of the disruptive people in a meeting who would raise their hands and say, 'Excuse me, Bob, but I don't think, with all due respect, that's going to work. She always came across to me as being nonconfrontational."[9] But Barra is just one of countless female executives who have adopted a nonconfrontational style as a way of winning acceptance from her male colleagues. Could Barra have risen within GM's ranks had she been seen as aggressive and confrontational? The answer is obvious. Women have to walk a fine line when it comes to assertiveness.

And then there is the media treatment that female executives typically receive. In its cover story on Barra, *Time* magazine reported that Barra wore "killer black suede heels" to an interview, and even named the brand, despite Barra's request that they not do so.[10] I like fashion myself, but just once, for balance, I'd like to read a story about a male CEO in which he is pressed to comment on his shoes!

Mary Barra's story illustrates how fathers can make the difference in whether their children dare to tackle complex, challenging problems and subjects that they're drawn to.

Would Google exist without the positive influence of Carl V. Page on his son Larry? Carl Page was a professor of computer science at Michigan State University. Years after becoming the cofounder of the Internet giant, Larry recalled, "My dad was really interested in technology. He actually drove me and my family all the way across the country to go to a robotics conference. And then we got there, and he thought it was so important that his young son go to the conference, one of the few times I've seen him really argue with someone to get in someone underage successfully into the conference, and that was me."[11]

Fathers can help set the trajectory for their daughters' lives in much the same way. When they believe in their daughters and encourage them, those girls learn that they can do anything a boy can do—maybe better. Girls need their fathers to share what they know. "I'm interested in technology and entrepreneurship. So I don't hide it from my daughter. I share it with her," says Frederick "Suizo" Mendler, cofounder and chief executive officer of TrueAbility:

> *I tell her what I am doing, how I am doing it, and what is going on. She came with me to pick up an investor check once, and I handed it to her. It was a relatively large sum of money, more than she has ever seen. She asked what we would do with the money, and the subsequent conversation was a good one about staffing, marketing, and product development. I talk to her about wins, and about struggles as a business. I love getting an eight-year-old's perspective on how to solve my business problems. Her ideas may not be one hundred percent on point, but I encourage her to think through them.*[12]

BE AN ADVOCATE FOR YOUR DAUGHTER—AND FOR EVERYBODY'S DAUGHTER

ENTREPRENEUR JOHN WOOLEY WORKS WITH HIS ELEMENTARY SCHOOL–age daughter CaryBeth on her school science fair project every year. It's a bonding experience that extends over the course of several weeks, allowing her hands-on experience with science as well as a glimpse into the entrepreneurial process that is her father's world. She knows that when science fair day arrives, she will have to present her project to the judges much the way an entrepreneur might demonstrate a product prototype to investors. So she works with her dad in advance to practice speaking clearly and persuasively about her work.

CaryBeth struggles with dyslexia, and John sees the science fair project as an opportunity to show his daughter that she can still do anything she sets her mind to. She is learning that just as dyslexia doesn't hold her back as she works hard on her science fair projects, it won't hold her back in life—because she won't let it.

For the past few years, CaryBeth has won or placed in the science fair for her grade at school, recently winning first place in fifth grade and proceeding to the citywide science fair. But her father sees a disturbing trend. Each year as CaryBeth's cohort advances to the next grade, fewer students compete. Worse, even fewer girls compete. Before they've left elementary school, most girls have begun to shift gradually away from science.[13]

One of the most important things that families who

hope to raise VentureGirls can do is to support greater equity for kids of both genders and from every background when it comes to STEM and entrepreneurial studies. We all need to set an example of fairness and non-bias in the way we treat the girls and boys around us. And as citizens, we need to advocate for having greater resources dedicated to the teaching of science, technology, engineering, math, and entrepreneurship in our public schools. This is a cause you can support in many ways: through the vote you cast every year when the local school budget comes up for approval; through the comments you make at school board meetings, town hall gatherings, PTA events, or just among your circle of friends; through letters to the editor and Internet comments you write; and through the encouragement you offer to local political leaders about devoting the money needed to make sure our schools are well equipped to produce the STEM- and entrepreneurship-savvy young people we'll need in the future.

And being an advocate for kids—especially girls—can also be expressed in small, simple, yet important ways in your daily life.

Sue Kolbly once attended a middle school robotics exhibition where her son had a project on display. She couldn't help noticing the only girl in the exhibition. Her name was Gabrielle, and her father was there with her. Gabrielle's team demonstrated their robot for the gathered parents, and Gabrielle went to join her father on the sidelines.

Kolbly was taken aback to overhear Gabrielle's father say

to his daughter in a snarky tone, "*That*'ll get you invited to the prom." Gabrielle's expression fell.

Kolbly said nothing, and later she regretted it. "Here is his daughter, taking a course that requires courage and hard work," she told me later. "And instead of expressing admiration or support, he jabs her with a sexist, juvenile, sarcastic remark. It wasn't humor. It was just mean. As if her worth is determined by whether or not she gets invited to the prom. As if being smart would hurt her chances with boys."[14]

I wonder whether Gabrielle's father would have made that remark to his son. I strongly doubt it.

But there's a happy twist to the story. Kolbly's older son, Lane, had aced his high school robotics class years earlier. When he learned what that father had said, he laughed and told his mom that, while there weren't many girls in his class, "*Every* girl in my robotics program got invited to the prom."

The story illustrates the truth that we all have a role to play in helping to overcome bias, prejudice, and needless limitations.

Here's what one nineteen-year-old male computer science major at the University of Texas wrote in response to an assigned reading about women in computer science—the assignment itself a sign of progress:

> *There's a large movement to get more women into the tech field. You hear this in the government, the private sector, and education—so why isn't it happening? The general consensus seems to be that a lot of the "sexism*

in the workplace" is due at least partially to women being timid. As Sheryl Sandberg describes her experience at Google, "The men were getting ahead, banging down the door for new assignments, promotions."

Before I get assassinated by any one of my female friends (all of whom are strong, smart, self-empowered women who are totally capable of killing me and getting away with it), I realize that it would be naive to say "the issue is that women aren't pushy enough" and stop. It's deeper than that. The issue is how we raise our daughters and sons.

Read this, from an online store: "The Boys' Store showcases all the best in action figures, hobbies, construction, blasters, and outdoor play. The Girls' Store is perfect if you're looking for dolls, plush, dollhouses, and pretend play."

Is it just me, or is there a slight gender bias there?

So you argue, hey, that's just one company, it's not like they're the largest Internet-based retailer in the United States or anything.

Oh, wait, they are. Never mind.

Gender equality will not be solved by telling programmers to put women on equal footing with men. I've met lots of programmers and found in general that they put women on an equal footing.

The issue is with society.

The author of the paper? Lane Kolbly, the onetime middle school student who'd already learned that all the girls in his robotics class were eminently prom-worthy. He's now a computer science major and steadfast advocate for women in the program.[15]

Kolbly titled his paper "Male Seeks Terrible Female Engineer." *Terrible,* he explains, because women don't need any more pressure to be perfect. I have a feeling he will find a terribly wonderful engineer.

Lane Kolbly is on track to be a tech leader who respects and appreciates the talents and insights of everyone he works with, no matter their gender or background—the kind of advocate for fairness and equality we need by the millions, in every walk of life.

Men can also serve as advocates for women's wage equity and fair treatment in the workplace. An interesting study demonstrated a phenomenon called the "daughter effect" in which women's wages in a company rose relative to men's after the male CEO had a daughter. There was no effect if the CEO had a son. The researchers concluded that once men had daughters they were able to envision a female employee as if she were their daughter.[16] Let's all make sure that we are raising awareness of unconscious bias and creating a safe and friendly environment for our girls to enter into successful careers.

TRY THIS AT HOME—AN ACTIVITY GIRLS WILL LOVE: LET'S GET TO KNOW EACH OTHER

If you are serving as a mentor to an ambitious young woman, here's an activity that will help you think about how to build rapport and a relationship with your VentureGirl.

TIME: 45–60 MINUTES

You Need

Time and space to meet comfortably with the young woman who is your mentee

Directions

- Start by asking yourself and your mentee what your expectations are and what you want to accomplish together. What are some of the goals of your mentoring experience—for each of you?
- Continue the dialogue by mutually exploring your personalities, interests, values, experiences, and dreams. Here are some questions you may want to ask each other:
  - What achievement in life are you most proud of?
  - What do you like doing? What are you really good at? What would you like to do more of?
  - What don't you like doing, and why?
  - Tell me about a time you failed. What is something you've learned from failure?
  - What is something you did that helped someone?

    - Tell me about a time you were courageous. What is something that you are afraid of?
    - What would you like to learn? What would you like to improve at?
    - What are your favorite things? Think about books, movies, places, games, pastimes, hobbies, and so on.
    - How would someone who had just met you describe you? How would your closest friends describe you?
    - Who is your favorite person in the world, and what do you like about them?
    - If you could change anything in the world, what would it be?
    - If you could do anything, what would it be?
- As you continue your mentoring relationship, try using the following questions when you meet each week:
    - What was the best part of your week? What was a success for the week?
    - What was the hardest part of your week? What did you fail at? What did you learn from your failure?
    - What are two or three choices you made this week, and what happened because of your choices?
    - What goals did you achieve this week?
    - What do you have planned for next week?
    - What do you need to work on?

TRY THIS AT HOME—AN ACTIVITY GIRLS WILL LOVE: FLY YOUR BRAND

In this activity, parent(s) and kid(s) create their own family or personal flag, representing their personal brand, using colors and pictures that convey their unique strengths and traits.

TIME: 15—30 MINUTES

You Need

Something to write and draw with (pens, pencils, crayons, or markers)

Something to draw on: 8½ × 11-inch paper, a large piece of butcher paper, poster board, or cardboard

Optional: Magazines to clip out images, scissors, glue or tape

Directions

- Plan your flag. Think about what you'd want others to know about you. Consider your interests and personal qualities. Think about things you do with your family or things that are important to you.
- If someone were to use three or four words to describe your personal traits, what might those words be? What symbols, pictures, or colors could you use to represent these traits?
- How might you describe the things that are most important to you? What symbols, pictures, or colors could you use to represent these things?

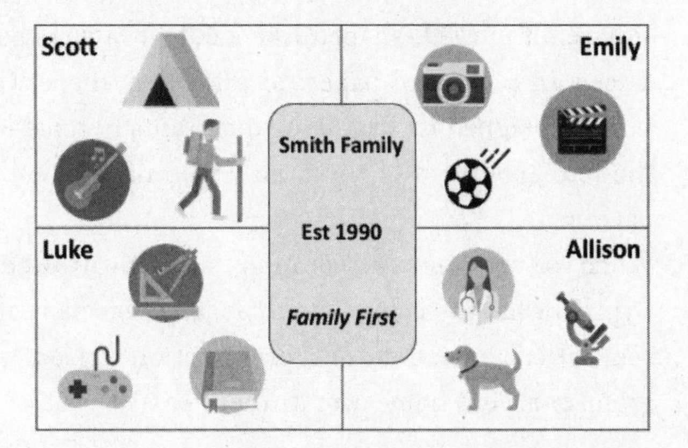

The flag created by a family with four members,
each with his or her unique interests and qualities.
Image © Luz Cristal Glangchai

- Think about some of your favorite things to do—activities, hobbies, or pastimes. What symbols, pictures, or colors could you use to represent these things?
- When thinking about your future, what are some of the goals that you would like to accomplish? What symbols, pictures, or colors could you use to represent your interests for the future?
- What are some careers that you might want to pursue to make positive changes in our world? What symbols, pictures, or colors could you use to represent those future careers?
- Now design your flag. Include symbols, objects, and colors that symbolize who you are or what you find enjoyable or important.
- The flag can be any shape you like: rectangular, like most flags used by nations or states; triangular,

square, or curved; shaped like a cutout of your body traced on a piece of paper; or any other shape. One family designed its flag using quadrants to represent the four members of the family (see illustration on page 277).

- When you are done with your flag, share it with others! Explain what the colors, symbols, and objects represent. This can be done as a presentation in front of a group or at your home over dinner.

Creating a family or personal flag is a great way for a kid or a family to think about what they stand for, the things that are important to them, and the best ways to communicate those values through symbols. These are all activities that entrepreneurs must do as well.

12

High School and Beyond

No girl is too young to begin enjoying the fun of math, science, and entrepreneurship. But no girl is too old, either. Even teenagers who may have struggled throughout elementary and middle school can catch the spark of entrepreneurial creativity and use it to ignite a flame of lifelong excitement. At VentureLab, we've seen it happen countless times.

One summer, we held our High School Startup camp in downtown Austin, Texas, at the Capital Factory, a hub for ambitious startups from around the nation and the world, whose inhabitants include migrants from the overcrowded tech community of Silicon Valley. Upon arrival, the high school students were thrilled to learn that they would finish their two-week program by pitching their products and companies to real-life angel investors, venture capitalists, and high-tech business experts.

Some of the projects the high school teams created in response to this challenge were simply amazing. One all-girl group of teenagers decided that geography lessons in school weren't really teaching significant cultural aspects about cities, states, and countries, which the girls had learned while on their own travels. The girls decided to create a subscription service that would send kids a box of educational cultural artifacts from a new destination every month. The girls visited the gift shop at the nearby state capitol and bought items to fill the first monthly gift box. They loved exploring and sharing history through artifacts like a replica Texas dollar, dating from the time when the Republic of Texas had been an independent nation with its own currency.

Another team was made up of a group of diverse students from the Austin, Boerne, and San Antonio areas who decided they wanted to build a product that would help parents and children get along better. They came up with the idea of an app that allows kids to earn points and win prizes by doing chores—a way of teaching household responsibility while helping families run more efficiently and cooperatively.

Ironically, the team itself had problems at first operating in an efficient and cooperative fashion. One of the students in the group was disruptive, insisting on his own ideas about prototype function and product design, and working on his own to assemble batteries and wires while the other members of the group thought the product could be improved through digitalization. The VentureLab teachers began to intervene, but then decided to stand back and let the team members discover on their own how business founders must navigate the tricky waters of partnership.

Eventually the group turned into a cooperative team. They called themselves Toucan Technologies and named their app ChoreBound. On pitch day, they presented their product prototype, website design, and social media marketing kit before a group of judges that included a real-life entrepreneur who'd produced a similar product—an app called ChoreMonster. In effect, the team had to convince a competitor that their product was better!

Our experience with the High School Startup camp convinced us that girls well beyond elementary school are still capable of "unlearning" the negative messages about science, math, technology, and entrepreneurship that they've absorbed from the media or their educational environments—and of unleashing the potential for leadership and creativity that exists in all of us.

WAYS TO ENGAGE YOUR TEENAGE DAUGHTER

MANY OF THE RECOMMENDATIONS I'VE ALREADY PROVIDED IN THIS BOOK for helping girls become excited about STEM and entrepreneurship apply equally well to teenagers of high school age and beyond. Encouraging curiosity, modeling a positive attitude toward failure, showing teens the idealistic and socially beneficial uses of science and technology, and helping them find role models who will inspire them—all of these approaches are just as important with kids as they get older and begin to explore their options for college and careers.

Engage your teenage daughter in a conversation about

her values and the things that are important to her. Actively listen to her dreams, and help her set goals to achieve them. Maybe your daughter has a talent for art, is really good at convincing others to join her team, or has the organizational skill to plan and execute complex projects. When a girl works in her areas of strength, success comes naturally and helps builds confidence. Help your teenage daughter identify her strengths and find opportunities to employ them.

I always had a talent for building things, and my parents encouraged this. When I was in the engineering and robotics clubs in middle school and high school, it was definitely not the cool thing for a girl to be doing, but I loved it and didn't care what others thought. Help your daughter stay true to her interests despite social pressures to conform.

Shari Ballard, senior executive vice president of Best Buy, says it this way: "Be clear on who you are and what you're serving with your life. Then, get ready for the world to relentlessly test you on how much you really mean it."[1]

I've discussed the relative paucity of scientist, technologist, and entrepreneur role models who are women, people of color, and others from the majority of Americans who are not white males. It may be that your daughter feels alienated from science and tech, in part because she just can't see herself in an array of media images that is dominated by people like Steve Jobs, Elon Musk, and Stephen Hawking.

The good news is that high school is not too late to take steps to remedy the problem. Most teenagers approaching their college years begin thinking for the first time about the career options they'll face. Many are very receptive to sources of information that may broaden, and brighten, their idea about the future.

Fortunately, there are a number of such sources specifically designed to captivate the interest of high school–age students. Show her geeky women role models with similar passions and interests who are doing impactful things in the world, whether in tech, or art, or music.

For example, *The Secret Life of Scientists and Engineers* is a highly engaging, Emmy-nominated video series by the makers of the famous public television series *NOVA*. *Secret Life* provides behind-the-scenes profiles of real-life science and tech masters, including many from diverse backgrounds—people like African American neurobiologist André Fenton, Hispanic experimental psychologist Laurie Santos, Asian American physicist Michio Kaku, and a long list of inspiring female scientists and engineers from many different fields.

Sada Ganske, a middle school science teacher in a Minnesota community where 37 percent of adults don't even have a high school diploma, struggled to find role models her students could identify with. The *Secret Life* videos have made a huge difference in her classroom:

> *Students can now see the connection between their interests (e.g., sports, music, art) and STEM subjects. They have adult role models that they can reference who didn't have to choose between their passion or "doing science," but rather were able to embrace both. Watching students connect with the videos and stories and develop a sense of hope about their future choices or*

> *paths is empowering. They're saying that they can now picture themselves as scientists or engineers.*[2]

The *Secret Life* series is available to teachers for use in middle schools and high schools. If the videos are not being used at your kids' school, try recommending them.

It's also important to help teenage girls to see the relevance of their math and science classes to their long-term educational and career plans. Too many girls excel in STEM classes during their elementary school years, then drift away as they get older, gradually becoming convinced that their futures lie in "soft" subjects like English, foreign languages, history, and the arts. Those non-STEM subjects are important and useful, of course. But as I've pointed out throughout this book, in the world of the twenty-first century, even professionals in fields like media, law, counseling, teaching, and the arts need to know how to use scientific and technical knowledge, as well as entrepreneurial skills, in order to be successful.

Encourage the girl in your life to keep pursuing the math and science classes she may have enjoyed in her earlier grades. Rather than stopping short at algebra and earth science, urge her to move on to calculus and physics, including classes at the Advanced Placement (AP) level that may be available at her high school. And introduce her to friends and acquaintances with careers in many arenas who can show her exactly how skills from STEM and entrepreneurship are vital to their everyday work—as well as how fun they can be to learn about and to apply.

BARRIERS TO GROWTH: GATEWAY COURSES

As a parent, friend, or supporter of a teenage girl, you also have to help her overcome the barriers that continue to discourage females from pursuing their STEM and entrepreneurship dreams. One of these barriers is the unfortunate tradition of gateway courses, which I discussed in Chapter One.

Parents, relatives, and friends can help teenage girls deal with the scourge of gateway courses. When your daughter or a girl you support is applying to colleges, encourage her to ask about gateway courses and seek out schools where such courses are being discouraged or eliminated. If she finds herself in a gateway course, help her to recognize the fact and to understand what her experience is telling her—the problem is not her lack of ability but rather the course design, which has been deliberately skewed to make learning all but impossible for a subset of students.

Then, rather than becoming disheartened and dropping out, help her to push back against the system. Support her in finding tutoring help or creating a study team made up of other students determined to beat the odds. In many gateway courses, if a student who feels challenged is able to survive the first couple of exams, the rest of the semester is more manageable. The key is to resist the temptation to give up during the first month or two.

BARRIERS TO GROWTH: HURDLES SET TOO HIGH

Another way teenage girls get discouraged from continuing to pursue STEM and entrepreneurship studies is through the emergence of a "culture of hyperachievement" in certain high schools and colleges. Aspiring to high achievement, of course, is a great thing—but not when it involves setting hurdles that are absurdly, arbitrarily, and pointlessly high. When that happens, it leads to serious drawbacks, including high rates of depression and suicide. It also causes thousands of talented girls to simply stop trying to pursue dreams that might force them into competition with their "hyperachieving" peers.

An example of this destructive syndrome can be seen in the city of Palo Alto in the heart of Silicon Valley, where Facebook, Google, Pinterest, Hewlett Packard, Tesla, and Skype either began or relocated early on. It's ten miles from the garage where Apple started, and it's where Steve Jobs chose to live. The average home there is worth millions of dollars.

Palo Alto High School is centered in this technology haven. Roughly one-quarter of the students score in the 99th percentile on the SAT college entrance exam. In other words, about 25 percent of the students at Palo Alto High would rank in the top 1 percent of students in the rest of the United States.

At first glance, you might assume that a school like this might be an ideal place in which to study challenging courses. But hyperachieving schools pose serious problems for the majority of their students. Are the students in such a school district encouraged to try studies in which they might fail at first? With the pressure on to compete against a classroom full of apparent "geniuses," will they readily risk a course where they might get a poor grade? Will they dare to turn in a project that is so offbeat and creative in its thinking that the grade it will earn is completely unpredictable?

Palo Alto High School is a place where a few students can flourish brilliantly . . . but where many others are apt to be paralyzed by the fear of failure, which society has already given too much power over our lives.

In Malcolm Gladwell's 2013 book *David and Goliath,* the author identifies a "phenomenon of relative deprivation" that he calls "the Big Fish–Little Pond Effect":

> *The more elite an educational institute is, the worse students feel about their own academic abilities . . . Students who would be at the top of their class in a good school can easily fall to the bottom of a really good school [like Harvard] . . . [T]hey can have the feeling that they are falling farther and farther behind in a* really *good school. And that feeling—as subjective and ridiculous and irrational as it may be—*matters. *How you feel about your abilities—your academic "self-concept"—in the context of your classroom shapes your willingness to tackle challenges and finish difficult tasks. It's a crucial element in your motivation and confidence.*[3]

Gladwell believes that the Big Fish–Little Pond Effect is one of the driving forces behind the shortage of qualified scientists and engineers in the United States. Discouraged by the prospect of competing against the hyperachieving students found at elite schools like Palo Alto High—and even more at elite universities like Harvard and MIT, Stanford and Chicago—too many talented young people simply give up. As a result, Gladwell says, "large numbers of would-be STEM majors end up switching into the arts, where academic standards are less demanding and the coursework less competitive."

Gladwell illuminates the impact of this destruction of confidence at our top universities, where many members of the bottom third—all of them really smart students—decide that they don't have what it takes to succeed in STEM. Thus, *where* a girl goes to college, and the effect on her confidence—whether it is reinforced or crushed—is a huge determinant of whether she is likely to continue in science, engineering, math, and entrepreneurship. Of one student who changed career directions after getting a B-minus in quantum mechanics, Gladwell writes, "Harvard cost the world a physicist and gave the world another lawyer."

You can help the girls you care about avoid the destructive impact of the Big Fish–Little Pond Effect by helping them recognize and avoid its worst effects. Learn to recognize the symptoms of a culture of hyperachievement, such as a drastically skewed bell curve of academic results. (For example, it's a bad sign, not a good one, when a large fraction of a high school's graduating class boast grade point averages of 4.0—the equivalent of a perfect A—or even better.) Unless a girl has a very strong sense of self-awareness and self-confidence, such an environment may be counterproductive for her rather than encouraging.

Similarly, discourage a girl from assuming that she should automatically accept admission to the "best" or most competitive college that will accept her. Many factors should be considered, including the size of the school, its location, the campus culture, the teaching styles of various departments, the access of students at all levels to the leading instructors, and so on. For some students, the most competitive college ends up being a place where their self-confidence gets broken and their dreams collapse. By contrast, a college with a slightly less exalted reputation might have provided a more supportive atmosphere that would have led to a very successful educational experience and, ultimately, a rewarding life and career.

LET'S GET BACK TO BUILDING THINGS

MALCOLM GLADWELL'S SARDONIC QUIP ABOUT HARVARD'S HYPER-achievement ethos turning physicists into lawyers has more than a grain of truth. Women are now well represented in law, some say partly as a product of the many women playing lawyers on television shows for the last two decades—another reminder of the shaping influence of media images. Some smart women drift into law having left high school ungrounded in science and computing. But as a society, we don't need more lawyers. We need more innovators, engineers, creators, computer scientists, and entrepreneurs.

Andrew Yang, founder of Venture for America, puts it bluntly. "We've got a problem: *our smart people are doing the wrong things*. We need to get our smart people building things again. If we can accomplish that, it will transform the country."[4]

Yang's personal story is one he shares with thousands of others. He is a supersmart guy who went to law school and became a corporate attorney because of some vague notion of prestige, success, and money. But soon after he joined a New York law firm, he noticed "the people around me seemed pretty unhappy. The work was entirely uninspiring, detail-intensive, and dull. I pretended my work had meaning; it didn't. Then I pretended meaning didn't matter; it did . . . Most worrisome of all, my brain started to rewire itself after only the first few months. Holy cow, I thought, if I don't leave soon, I'll be doing this for life."

Notice his growth mind-set? He felt his brain was growing, but not in a good way.

Companies engaged in providing "prestige services" like law, finance, and consulting send legions of suit-wearing recruiters and spend millions on internships to recruit the best and brightest Ivy League students to their luxurious lairs. As a result, roughly 40 percent of Harvard graduates in recent years have gone on to careers in law, finance, or consulting. These are academically gifted graduates who *don't* go into engineering, computer science, math, sciences, or technology innovation. They *don't* start companies, they *don't* innovate or design, they *don't* create jobs, and they *don't build things*.

Frustrated and unfulfilled by his work as a lawyer, Yang

made the decision to quit the firm and set about building a different kind of company, one that contributes to the world by channeling talented young people to early-stage companies where they acquire skills necessary to start companies and create jobs. This is his second entrepreneurial venture; his first one failed. As for the title of his book, *Smart People Should Build Things*—I couldn't agree more.

As it turns out, acclimatizing girls to failure, letting them experience the accomplishment of overcoming failures, concentrating on *learning,* and cultivating a growth mind-set are important not only to girls' future, but to our collective future as a country.

It's a loss any time young women take "easy" courses to keep their grade point averages high and avoid challenges that could knock their grades down a notch. Why not help girls set sights differently? Instead of focusing on perfect grades, let's encourage them to cast themselves in a future that takes hard work, resilience, and creativity to achieve. And that's a future in which STEM and entrepreneurship will play major roles.

BEYOND HYPERACHIEVEMENT: GIVE TEENAGERS PERMISSION TO PLAY

One of the themes of this book has been the importance of play. Unstructured, open-ended, freewheeling play is crucial to growing hearts and minds. And the need for play doesn't end when kids enter high school. In fact, people of all ages need play as a way of unleashing their creativity. This is why Tim Brown, president and CEO of the famous "design thinking" company IDEO, gave a TED Talk in which he said that we all need to learn to "think with our hands," whether that means playing with Legos or clay or tinkering with prototypes while imagining fresh solutions to thorny problems.[5]

The biggest obstacle to teenagers' taking advantage of the power of play to stimulate their creativity muscles is the rigidity of our social expectations. As writer Lisa Rivero puts it,

> *This kind of hands-on play, however, often requires that we give ourselves and our children permission to engage in activities that can look like a waste of time. For a sixteen year old who has a full schedule of AP classes, sports practice, and orchestra rehearsal, half an hour spent building a snowman in the backyard with young siblings can seem a luxury, but parents can help to shape good life-time habits by encouraging their children and teenagers to build in time for just such free play, and by setting a good example by turning off their cell phones and joining in.*[6]

Who knows? If you're the parent of an overscheduled, overstressed teenager, you may find that sharing the gift of freewheeling play turns out to be a liberating experience for *both* of you!

TRY THIS AT HOME—AN ACTIVITY GIRLS WILL LOVE: THE PITCH CARD CHALLENGE

In this activity, parent(s) and kid(s) will create a new product, company, and logo using three randomly chosen words: one noun, one verb, and one adjective, and pitch it to an audience. The product ideas that come out of this activity are usually truly creative and imaginative!

TIME: 15–45 MINUTES

You Need

Something to write and draw with (pens, pencils, crayons, or markers)

Something to draw on: 8½ × 11-inch paper, a large piece of butcher paper, poster board, or cardboard

Slips of paper or index cards with random words written on them, in three categories: nouns (such as *bicycle, shoe, headphones, desk, pancake*), verbs (*mix, eat, wear, listen, repair*), and adjectives (*green, tiny, sturdy, delicious, lightweight*).

Directions

- Each participant should select a random noun, verb, and adjective. Based on those three words, each participant will brainstorm a product and company name, create a poster with a company logo and information about the product, and develop a brief sales pitch for the product.

- Start by brainstorming a product that uses the three words you picked. For example, if your three words were *bicycle, green,* and *mix,* you might come up with a bicycle that mixes a salad as you pedal, a service that delivers mixed salads to your home on a bicycle (it's "green" because it doesn't use a car or gasoline), or a spin class that powers a blender to mix green smoothies. Get creative!
- Now brainstorm a company name and logo. Both should capture what makes your product idea unique, useful, and special.
- Now think about who your customers are and how much they might pay for your product. You may want to do some research on the Internet to see if there are other companies doing something similar. Who are they selling to and how much are they charging? How are you different or unique? Based on this information, decide on your product's price.
- Now write a script for a sales pitch that will last between ninety seconds and two minutes.
- Start your sales pitch with a hook. What is the problem you are solving? You might choose to dramatize the problem by having people act it out, like a scene in a play.
- What is your solution, and why is it unique? Describe your company and product, and show your product picture and logo.

- Who is your customer, how much are you selling your product for, and why should your customer buy it?
- Once you've scripted your pitch, practice it until you can deliver it smoothly and persuasively. Time yourself to make sure the pitch fits the allotted period.
- Now it's time to pitch! Have your poster with the relevant information and company logo and product drawing displayed. Deliver your pitch, and see whether you can convince your audience to buy your product—in two minutes or less!

This activity helps kids learn and practice how to brainstorm a solution to a problem, perform market research, and present their ideas to others. Later, they will feel more confident when they use the same techniques at school, in the community, or on the job.

TRY THIS AT HOME—AN ACTIVITY GIRLS WILL LOVE: ENTREPRENEURIAL GOAL SETTING

Creating goals and planning to achieve them is how we bring our dreams to life. This activity will help you get started on a lifelong habit of setting goals and turning them into realities.

TIME: 30—60 MINUTES

You Need

Something to write and draw with (pens, pencils, crayons, or markers)

Paper to write on

Directions

- List the values and priorities that you care about and that are important to you. For example, is it important for you to spend time with your family? Is it important to have a lot of friends or a few close friends? Is it important for you to help others? Do you want to take care of animals or the environment? How high on your priority list is making a lot of money? Do you care about being famous and widely admired? Would you like to have the power to influence the world?
- With your values and priorities in mind, think about your dreams and hopes. What do you want to do in life? What do you want to be? What do you wake up wishing you could do each day? Write out what your most important dreams and hopes are.
- Think about where you want to be and what you want to be doing one year, five years, and ten years from now.
- Write down your goals for the years to come, and choose one to focus on.
- Write down why you are passionate about that goal. How does it make you feel to think about achieving that goal?

- Brainstorm some practical ways that you can try to achieve the goal. Write down all the ideas you can think of.
- Write down some possible obstacles to reaching your goal.
- Write out some actionable ways that you could overcome the obstacles you've listed.
- Envision yourself having accomplished your goal. Pretend you are a journalist writing a front-page story for a newspaper that features your achievement. Write out a headline and a few sentences that describe how you achieved your goal. Having done this, notice how you feel and your confidence level.

CONCLUSION: WHAT WE CAN DO

I WROTE THIS BOOK BECAUSE I BELIEVE THAT THE ENTREPRENEURIAL mind-sets and skill sets are critical to raising our next generation of leaders and innovators, and are paramount to decreasing the gender gap. Many people are working to solve the problem of the gender gap in leadership and STEM at many different levels of the pipeline. I believe that if we really want to create a culture change, and to create a world where both women and men create the future, it has to start by giving our girls confidence at a young age and by teaching boys that girls are equally as capable. The girls and young women in your life *need you*.

Our crazy world is their context—think about that. If alien sociologists landed in the United States and spent one week on our planet, they would likely conclude that the Kardashians are the most prominent people on the planet, girls are weaker and less accomplished than boys, difficult subjects are for men, a person's value is measured in "hits," politics is a spectator sport, and women must wear fragrance.

We can instill *entrepreneurial life skills* in girls so that they are curious, creative, resilient, collaborative, inventive, optimistic, persevering, technologically savvy, critically thinking problem-solvers, and leaders in whatever direction they choose to go in life.

Our schools are neither equipped nor organized to ensure that girls acquire these crucial lessons. Many talented teachers and educators who care mightily about girls work in our schools—but it is not always enough. The task is ours—yours and mine.

As a mom of two boys and two girls, I don't just talk about this; I practice it religiously at home. Here is my top ten playlist to encourage the entrepreneurial mind-set and a curiosity for STEM in my kids. You can use these ideas and tips with your girls at school and at home.

1. ENCOURAGE CURIOSITY, EXPERIMENTATION, AND PROBLEM-SOLVING

Think like a scientist. Encourage curiosity. Encourage your kids to ask Why? How? What if? When something mechanical breaks, consider its teaching value. Look for older or broken appliances to take apart and discover what made them work. When my kids ask me questions, like why is the sky blue, or what makes thunder, we go and look the answer up online and talk about the science behind it. Also, when they ask those questions you sometimes dread, like how are babies made or what is sex, I handle them with the same approach: I go online and talk honestly about the science behind them.

Encourage at-home science projects. I had a blast with my chemistry set as a kid, but times have changed. The chemistry sets of our current time can be found in your household. Check out YouTube videos for home science projects using materials and liquids you already have at home. Spend some time over the weekend and clear your kitchen table or go outside and get ready for a mess. My kids love the milk, food coloring, and dish soap experiment. It's a fun way to create art using science. You can also go outside and make a volcano using baking soda, vinegar, and a two-liter bottle. It's fun to change the amount of baking soda, vinegar, and water and measure how high you can get liquid to go up in the air. You can even put masking tape on the side of your garage every one to two feet to get a better idea of how high it's going.

Help your kids become makers. Outfit a "maker space" with books, arts/crafts supplies, and tools for girls and their siblings to construct and deconstruct whatever they can imagine and to learn new skills and hobbies—drawing, sewing, measuring, cooking, stargazing, writing, crafting, crystal making, rock polishing, etcetera . . . It needn't cost a lot of money. A lot of these items are lying around your house or offered at garage sales for pennies on the dollar. And the size of the space doesn't matter; it can be large or small, but should be a place for creativity and messiness. We have a large table, a cabinet with a variety of arts/crafts supplies and gadgets, and a little sink for cleaning up in our garage. It's hidden away so the kids can keep their works in progress without making a mess in the house, and it gives girls a sense of autonomy. Sometimes my kids will build cities or structures out of leftover cardboard or Styrofoam for their play figures and stuffed animals. We also painted a wall green so that the kids can use it as a green-screen for any sort of movies they want to create.

Go to a museum. At many of the country's more than 250 children's museums, you will see marvelous hands-on exhibits where children can experiment. When my kids were younger we spent a lot of time at our local children's science museums learning about magnetism and making larger-than-life bubbles. We've also taken vacations specifically to take the kids to some amazing museums. My kids enjoyed the life-size Lego structures at Legoland in Carlsbad, California, and loved going to the National Museums in Washington, DC, like the National Air and Space Museum and the Museum of National History. Chicago's Field Museum of Natural History, the Art Institute of Chicago, the Museum of Science and Industry, and the Adler Planetarium were also hits. Many of these are free, but if you cannot afford admission, ask for a scholarship, or go during free admission times.

Enroll kids in a program or class. Find a STEM, creativity, or entrepreneurship program like VentureLab in your area, or look into camps, classes, or clubs at your local library, their school, or even a nearby community college or university. These can give your children an opportunity to meet other like-minded individuals, as well as inspire their inner creativity and drive.

Encourage kids to embrace math and science. Many times we may unconsciously put a negative spin on math or science, especially if it is not something we ourselves are comfortable with. Girls pick up on that and start to internalize it. So make math and science fun and understandable. Encourage girls not to drop AP calculus; change the problems in their textbooks so they don't presume an interest in football or war; allow them to appreciate the joys of designing a computer game that doesn't involve blowing up people's heads.

My kids and I will sit around the dinner table and practice multiplication or division. I will turn it into a game or I will turn their math problems into real-world problems that they understand. For instance, they want to start a dog-walking company. So I will say, okay, if you charge five dollars a dog and you walk fifteen dogs, how much money will you have made? Augment their math with online programs like Khan Academy, Prodigy Math, or XtraMath.

Teach kids to code. All right, most of us can't do that. But we can jump in and help by encouraging them to sign up for classes and try their hand at KidsRuby, Codecademy, Code.org, or Scratch. There are a multitude of sites and programs with free learn-to-code exercises that are fun even for parents. At my VentureLab camps my kids learned to create their own games and become more comfortable with the concept.

Experts now speak of coding as essential, the technical world equivalent of reading, writing, and math. Understanding the basic problem-solving skills and logic of coding will be important in our future because everything will be technologically enabled. Kids will need an understanding of this to understand how the world works.

Help girls develop spatial relations skills. Engineer Sheryl Sorby's years of research funded by the National Science Foundation proves that girls' relatively poor spatial relations skills can be greatly improved with roughly sixteen hours of specifically designed coursework. Go to your local library, museum, or maker space, or buy or make your own 3-D printer, and suddenly spatial relations is fun, relevant, and playful. My kids have enjoyed printing out their own iPhone cases or Minecraft figures. They can design whatever they want or find things to print on Thingiverse.com.

Embrace the outdoors. The outdoors offers many openings for the Medici effect—breakthrough thoughts that come from mixing disciplines. A sense of the outdoors, a sense of wonder, and keen observation equip children with ideas and analogies that they could never acquire if stuck indoors. My kids and I will take walks or bike rides along a creek by our house and will just observe nature, or during the fall, we will collect leaves and categorize them. Sometimes, like my mom did with me, we will lie down and look at the stars. The act of actively observing brings up so many questions for kids, which then allows for a discussion of science and developing of new ideas.

2. FIND VALUE IN FAILURE

Celebrate failures. Don't we all love the triumph of a comeback? In films like *Rocky* or *Erin Brockovich,* and in lives like Nelson Mandela's, seeing someone persist after repeated failures and setbacks makes the ultimate accomplishment all the more meaningful. We *know* this.

Celebrate achievements that required perseverance and learning from failures—not just talent or luck. Celebrate exhibits of emotional maturity in the face of a loss. Celebrate the events that mark the development of resilient, gritty character traits. Say "I am proud of you" when a child makes a mistake and accepts it in the right spirit. Home should be a safe place for children to tell you the truth about the parts of their lives that aren't going so well.

Make it clear that your love and admiration do not depend on grades and test scores, as long as your kids are trying their best.

"What have you failed at today?" Turn your dinner table conversations into a time for learning from your failures. Talk about what was hard for you today and times that you failed. Instead of asking "How did you do on that test?" try asking "What's the most difficult problem you had today?" Or, like Sara Blakely's father, "What have you failed at today?" If your kids aren't failing or struggling at something, then they aren't being challenged enough. By your questions and conversation, you can build a true rapport with your kids, and they absorb the message that learning isn't something that's jammed into their minds, but a process of trials, errors, and creative problem-solving.

Let kids cook. Let them get messy and see what they can create while feeling free to make mistakes. My daughters and I love to experiment with food and even create our own recipes. The girls especially love making different kinds of drink concoctions or frozen popsicles using whatever fruit we have on the table or whatever drinks we may have in the refrigerator. It's not unusual for my husband and me to find an array of glasses with beverages of varying colors and textures waiting on the kitchen counter for us to taste test. The kids get sheer joy out of their creations (and our reactions) and are learning valuable lessons in creativity and experimentation.

3. PLAY TO LEARN

Adopt the spirit of improv. Improv performers have to think on their feet. Improv language encourages brainstorming without judgment. Sometimes their skits work and sometimes they don't. They have fun with the unknown and with failure. My kids and I love to play charades. And usually around the dinner table we will each take turns building a story, with each person coming up with a new twist or turn. Sometimes we will have an impromptu play and the kids will record themselves and turn it into a movie using iMovie.

Play with techie toys. Girls need to have a level of comfort with technology, so it's good to expose them to techie toys that teach concepts of coding and logic. Some libraries have even started lending these types of toys. My kids enjoy playing with little toy robots like Dash and Dot who you can control with your iPad, or building circuits with Snap Circuits or littleBits that can enable all sorts of inventions.

Just play games. We don't have many opportunities in life where there are no grades, no penalties for "coloring outside the lines," no possibility of a humiliating failure—but this is exactly the environment needed for creativity to flourish. With play there is no judgment or failure; yes, some games have winners and losers, but that is part of a game and has its own way of teaching strategy and how to follow rules. My kids love playing two truths and a lie at dinnertime. They also enjoy playing Werewolf, a mystery game where you have to guess who the murderer is. And we have made Sundays our family game day when we will play Monopoly, Life, dominoes, or card games like gin rummy. Sometimes we just stand the dominoes up in a line and create cool designs, and then just watch the dominoes fall.

4. BUILD CONFIDENCE

Teach girls to be assertive and ask for what they want. The ability to ask for what you need seems so basic, doesn't it? Yet many girls and women are hesitant to do so. Many times women are afraid that if they are too assertive they will be seen as aggressive, and sometimes the impostor syndrome kicks in and women think they may not be deserving.

I believe the whole notion of asking for what you want can be practiced and taught. It begins with you as a parent and teacher modeling it for your children. I always tell my kids, "It doesn't hurt to ask because if you don't ask you will never know. And what's the worst that will happen? Someone may say no. But if they say yes, it may lead to a great opportunity." Help your children verbalize what they want and practice asking for it. And if your kids are young, sometimes they can demand things, so teach them to ask in a courteous way.

Focus on strengths. Schools are not always equipped to teach kids who learn in different ways, and kids are always comparing themselves with each other. Many times kids will lose confidence if they are not keeping up with their peers. What I tell all of my kids is that they each have their own strengths and learn in different ways.

I try to push them to do more in their areas of strength and let them know that it's okay not to be as good as others in different areas. I encourage them to be great at what comes naturally to them, because I know that is where they excel, and little wins build their confidence, and build a potential career opportunity in the future.

Stick kids in front of people. It is important that girls learn how to present themselves confidently. An ongoing lesson at my household is that we expect our kids to introduce themselves to guests. We teach them how to shake hands with a firm grip, look people in the eyes and say nice to meet you, or carry on a brief conversation. We also have our kids order their own food at restaurants. My kids have been doing this since about five, and sometimes they may be shy or talk quietly, but it is good practice, and now they are much more confident.

Help girls develop a more powerful presence. It is hard to lead from a posture of powerlessness. Teach girls to adopt more powerful physical postures that use more space and express their personal power. Together, watch Amy Cuddy's remarkable TED Talk and practice her lesson on how to pose for presence. A positive response from others can build girls' confidence and optimism.

Prompt girls to notice what is happening in the moments when they begin to contract, collapse, and disappear. Ask, "What are the situations and stimuli that cause you to shrink and fold in?" This awareness alone will help girls avoid "falling into the powerless poses we often mindlessly inhabit."[1]

Encourage kids' ideas and passions. A few encouraging words can change a kid's life. No matter how crazy your kids' ideas are, encourage them. Whatever it is, get actively involved, and help guide their way through the process. Even if the idea doesn't pan out, your encouragement and support will help give them the confidence they need to continue creating and innovating later on down the line. Encourage them to try new things that might be out of their comfort zone. And if your children show an affinity for science or math, encourage them to take more challenging classes.

Encourage girls to be themselves. With puberty and transitions of schools and peer groups, junior high and high school can be difficult times for girls. Girls begin to lose confidence and trend toward following the "herd" mentality. That is why it is so important that we encourage girls to be themselves during this time, and even more so while they are younger so that they have a confidence buffer prior to entering junior high.

I grew up as a nerd in the robotics and engineering club in junior high and high school. It definitely was not the "cool" thing for girls to be doing, but I knew who I was despite the social tests that were thrown at me. With geeks designing a better world—Elon Musk, Steve Jobs, Marissa Mayer, Meg Whitman, and change agents like Bill and Melinda Gates—people should want to be geeky.

Show girls that people like them, with similar passions and skill sets, are doing impactful things in the world.

5. BE OR FIND MENTORS AND ROLE MODELS

Help girls find role models. Many girls—and boys, for that matter—have never met a female computer scientist, engineer, or CEO. They don't know what the work requires or how to get from where they are to where they want to be. Reach out to a local woman entrepreneur, engineer, or computer scientist. They are usually excited to give back and visit with a girl or a classroom and talk about their career and experiences.

Likewise, distant role models can be just as inspiring—Mae Jemison, the first African American woman astronaut; Wanda Austin, engineer and former CEO of the Aerospace Corporation; Mary Barra, engineer and CEO of General Motors; Randa Milliron, founder and CEO of Interorbital Systems; and Megan Smith, the nation's third chief technology officer, who served in the Obama White House.

Be a mentor. A mentor is uniquely positioned to help a girl elevate her sights, to realize that she has within her the power to be and do more. A mentor is someone who is accomplished in a specific field and enjoys teaching about his or her experiences and giving back to others. Most successful people have universally had some sort of mentor early in life or in their career.

Why wait? You can mentor a girl. You don't have to be a CEO or expert! Discuss your experiences and provide feedback and guidance. Be the president of her fan club and help her gain the confidence to pursue her passions.

Look for mentoring opportunities online, like Million Women Mentors, or ask schools about mentoring opportunities. I often go to schools and speak to girls and classes, or I volunteer to mentor students. Frequently I will mentor my friends' daughters.

6. HELP ELIMINATE GENDER BIASES

Learn about your unconscious biases. Unconscious biases are social stereotypes that each of us hold about certain groups of people, without being aware that we are doing so. Many girls and women experience these types of biases at home, in school, and through our everyday media.

One thing I recommend to parents, teachers, and organizational leaders is that they take the Harvard Implicit Association Tests. They are free online tests that will make you aware of your own unconscious biases, because we all have them. After you have taken the tests, you can start to become more aware of how these play out in your life and work. You can start to change, and you can start to have open conversations with others about unconscious bias.

Recognize gender learning differences, and teach in ways most effective for how girls and boys learn. The more I have studied how girls' brains learn differently than boys', the more puzzled I am by books and articles about children that fail to mention or account for these differences. Girls are more inclined to respond to specific stories and problems in math, for instance. Boys tend to have better spatial relations, while girls are more likely to need 3-D catch-up. Girls' language skills and maturity often exceed those of boys of the same age. These differences are well documented, so try to incorporate them in your teaching.

Pay attention to the "only woman in the room." Many times I find myself to be the only woman in the room. It can still be intimidating and I still find myself shrinking and hesitant to bring up my ideas. Let's make sure that as teachers, employers, and peers we create a diverse and comfortable environment for all to speak up. If you notice a girl being interrupted, pause the offending speaker and ask that the girl continue her thought. Or if you notice a girl not raising her hand in class or not participating, make sure that you get her input. Ask her in private why she is not participating, and if she is comfortable, make sure to call on her in class.

Enlist men to raise consciousness of unconscious bias. The technology fathers I've interviewed are "on the case." They observe women in the workplace holding back, lacking confidence, not stepping up to the opportunities that could be theirs for the asking. It frustrates and puzzles them even as they mentor and advocate for women.

Luckily, I have seen companies and cultures changing, as men have been stepping up to "call out" inappropriate behavior and to write letters to their boards about the lack of women. As a man with a daughter, or an important girl or woman in your life, it's important that you speak up so that we can address the problem. Make sure that when you are hiring or looking for others to join your team you are spreading your net far and wide to other genders, races, and ethnicities.

7. ENCOURAGE A GROWTH MIND-SET

Compliment girls' efforts, not their intelligence. We have a generation of increasingly anxious kids. It's hard to experience a creative release when so much rides on grades and test scores, and failure is stigmatized.

To instill a growth mind-set, follow Carol Dweck's lessons on talking with your children. Instead of saying, "Perfect, an A, you're so smart!" change to, "You worked really hard, and you did it." I say things to my kids about being hard workers and great learners. I talk about their effort and acknowledge that things may be hard, but they just need to practice, or adjust the way they are learning, and they can learn anything.

It's a subtle change that takes practice—but I believe in you and you can do it.

8. ENCOURAGE ENTREPRENEURIAL INSTINCTS

Turn together time into entrepreneurial skill-building time. Make something together, or help your child sell something she's made. A seven-year-old sister and her younger brother wanted to sell an airplane they had made. The girl thought their three-hundred-dollar price was too high, considering it was a modified corrugated box that only kids could fit in. Their mother thought so, too, but said nothing. And sure enough, as passersby listened to the pitch, they questioned the three-hundred-dollar sticker price—especially since it didn't fly. Some of them couldn't help laughing. The price was a failure—but the project was successful when their mother bought it for three dollars. "If I'd objected to the price and persuaded them to lower it, they'd have thought I'd caused them to leave money on the table, and they wouldn't have learned nearly as much as they did getting feedback from other adults."

Think of the possibilities for a girl to sell things she has made—plants she has grown from cuttings, paintings, bookmarks she's designed, or decorations she's crocheted. Or it can be a service that's digital and intangible, like demonstrating to a relative how to play a video game or put together a digital photo album. Right now my girls have been into selling slime and are trying their hands at dog sitting and dog walking.

Start an idea journal. Kids come up with the most amazing ideas. Help your kids start an idea journal to write out and/or draw their ideas, or any problems they see around them. Have them write down their goals and what they want to do in life. I believe that impractical doesn't mean impossible. As your kids write or draw their ideas, goals, and dreams they can come back to them and build upon them. And someday, when the right technology or right window of opportunity opens up, they can go back and actually turn that dream or idea into a reality.

9. HELP GIRLS GAIN EXPOSURE TO THE WORLD OF MONEY AND BUSINESS.

Take a girl to work. You're more than just a parent; you're a driven, smart, and career-minded person, too. Be sure to show your kids that side of you, and get them actively involved in your work. Now, don't go so far as to let them file your reports or send an e-mail to your boss, but if you're forced to bring work home on the weekends, take a minute or two to walk them through exactly what you're doing. Tell them the why, show them the how, and let them see just where hard work can get them.

Teach kids about money. How many of us wish we were taught more about money and how to manage it when we were younger? Start teaching your kids that things have a value and that you need to work or provide a service in order to earn money to buy those things. Teach kids how to handle and exchange money. Talk about saving, spending, donating, and investing. Have kids do chores, special jobs, or projects to earn money. If they are older, suggest an internship. I use a great app called iAllowance, where our kids can see how much they have saved and spent and how much they have to donate to causes they care about.

10. SOLVE MEANINGFUL PROBLEMS

Solve problems that help people and the planet. Studies show that girls become more engaged in learning when they see how it is applied to helping people and the planet. STEM subjects become more concrete and engaging when girls understand how to apply them. Find ways to tie science and math to real-world problems. Go to engineeringchallenges.org and look at the list of the Grand Challenges for Engineering for pressing worldwide problems that need solutions, like improved medical care or getting water to people without it. If a girl is interested in coding, tie it to a problem she cares about. Maybe she can develop an app that helps people with obesity. If a girl is interested in the environment and is a good artist, maybe she can develop and sell small sculptural figures where the proceeds go to a nonprofit supporting the environment. Or maybe she starts her own nonprofit. And it can be as simple as finding a way to help in your home, your school, or your community.

ACKNOWLEDGMENTS

THIS WORK WOULD NOT HAVE BEEN POSSIBLE WITHOUT THE HELP AND DEDication of many wonderful people. I am grateful for all those with whom I had the honor of working to complete this work of passion.

First, I would like to thank HarperCollins and Associate Editor Sofia Groopman for their support and confidence in this important piece of work. This book would not be the success that it is without their expertise, dedicated editorial assistance, design assistance, and marketing support.

I would like to thank my research assistant, Susan Engelking, for her tireless help in organizing, conducting, and transcribing interviews and helping shape those interviews for the book. I would also like to thank my editorial assistant, Desiree Prieto Groft, for her tremendous editorial and organizational skills, and for being my taskmaster and cheerleader during the challenging times.

I would like to thank my editor, Karl Weber, for his wonderful work editing the book and helping shape and craft the true vision and message of the book. I truly appreciate his patience with me while working on my first book and his mentorship in helping me navigate the process of publishing.

I would like to thank my agent, Tom Miller, for his assistance, feedback, and mentorship. I would like to thank Bill Schley for his mentorship, for introducing me to the world of writing books, and for his feedback on the initial direction of the book, title, and subtitle.

Nobody has been more important to me in the creation of this book than my family. I would like to thank my parents, who shaped my thinking for the creation of this book. My mother, Elaine Sanchez, always served as a female role model for me in her career and helped instill my sense of curiosity and creativity. My father, Adolfo Sanchez, instilled my sense of drive and the idea that I could accomplish anything.

Most important, I would like to thank my loving and supportive husband, Pat Condon. This book would not be possible without Pat's undying support, encouragement, and understanding of the time commitment and ups and downs of writing a book.

Finally, I would like to thank my four wonderful children, Javier Glangchai, Cate Condon, Maribel Glangchai, and Carter Condon, who provided the inspiration for the book and my desire to teach kids an entrepreneurial mind-set.

APPENDIX: SOME TIPS ON RAISING A VENTUREBOY

I'VE DEDICATED MYSELF PARTICULARLY TO HELPING GIRLS OF ALL AGES discover the joy and creativity of mastering science, math, and entrepreneurship. But in today's world, boys, too, need to be encouraged to nurture their inner spark of entrepreneurial energy—while recognizing the equal potential of their female friends and classmates.

Like VentureGirls, VentureBoys understand the power of science, technology, engineering, math, and the entrepreneurial skills that help people apply the STEM disciplines to everyday life. They also respect and honor the talents of all people, male and female, which means they're prepared to work constructively and creatively with colleagues of both genders and of every background in the excitingly diverse workplaces of tomorrow.

APPLY THE INSIGHTS FROM THIS BOOK EQUALLY TO YOUR SONS AND YOUR DAUGHTERS

ALL THE ADVICE I'VE PROVIDED IN PART THREE OF THIS BOOK IS JUST AS valid when it comes to raising boys as girls. As a mom of two girls and two boys, I use these ideas with all of my children, and I can see their positive effects. So if you have one or more sons, you can and should use the ideas in this book to help stimulate their interest in STEM and entrepreneurial thinking. In other words, help your sons learn about the entrepreneurial process; start teaching them about STEM and problem-solving at an early age; foster their curiosity; give them permission to get messy; teach them to have an attitude of resilience when it comes to failure; help them channel their idealism into creative thinking about the world's big challenges; provide access to role models that will inspire them; and get the whole family involved in creating an environment your boys will find encouraging.

Are there any dramatic changes you need to make in applying the advice from this book to a boy rather than a girl? Not really. In fact, the biggest adjustment you'll need to make is likely changing the pronouns from "she" and "her" to "he" and "him."

ENCOURAGE BOYS TO FOLLOW THEIR INTERESTS WHEREVER THEY LEAD

SEXISM DOESN'T HURT GIRLS AND WOMEN ONLY. IT ALSO HURTS BOYS AND men—in part, by imposing needless, arbitrary limits on what's considered acceptable behavior for them. So if you want to raise a boy who is free from the burdens of sexism, you should be supportive of his interests and dreams, even if they violate societal stereotypes about boys and men.

If your three-year-old boy likes to play with dolls, kitchen pots and pans, and a toy vacuum cleaner rather than blocks or action figures, that's fine. If your grade school son is more interested in learning ballet or playing the violin than in soccer or camping, that's fine, too. And if your high school–age son is talking about majoring in French or fine art rather than engineering or business, he deserves your support in that choice—just as his sister would, no matter what path she might favor.

In all these cases, however, I'd urge you to expose your son or daughter to the importance of STEM fields and the creative problem-solving skills involved in entrepreneurship. As I've explained throughout this book, it's not just scientists or business founders who need to know about these subjects. In today's fast-paced, tech-driven world, everyone from painters and actors to lawyers and history teachers needs a basic comfort level with STEM and entrepreneurial thinking. So make sure your children of both genders are aware of these subjects and, most important, are raised to appreciate how interesting and enjoyable they can be.

RAISE YOUR SON TO RESPECT GIRLS AND WOMEN

THE ERA WHEN AMERICA COULD AFFORD TO HARBOR PREJUDICES OF ANY kind is long past. To compete successfully in today's world, our country, our communities, our businesses, and other organizations all need to engage and energize the talents of people of every background, no matter their gender, race, religion, ethnicity, or sexual orientation. So it's important for all of us to teach our kids to be respectful and fair toward everyone they come into contact with.

That specifically includes raising children to transcend sexism, recognizing the equal value of males and females in every walk of life—and it's at least as important for boys as it is for girls. After all, the son you are raising with high expectations for a lifetime of achievement may one day be the CEO of a company that relies on the skills and creativity of talented women just as much as on the abilities of men. So teaching him to understand the importance of equal justice for both genders and to live his life accordingly is one of the most valuable lessons you can give him.

Of course, the best way to teach a boy to respect girls and women is not by lecturing him but by setting a personal example. Look closely at your own behavior and the unspoken, perhaps unconscious assumptions that shape it. If you find yourself making an occasional thoughtless remark that reinforces a sexual stereotype, or unthinkingly treating males and females you know differently for no reason other than their gender, ask yourself why—and make a real effort to change the way you act.

Kids learn what they see around them. If you model behavior that is truly bias-free and respectful of all people, they'll learn to take those attitudes for granted . . . and they'll become better adults as a result.

HELP YOUR SON EXPERIENCE ROLE MODELS OF BOTH GENDERS

ANOTHER COROLLARY OF THE RULE THAT "KIDS LEARN WHAT THEY SEE around them" is the importance of giving kids a chance to see admirable people of many kinds . . . including both women and men who are dynamic, ethical, inspiring leaders. That means when a woman astronaut comes to your town to give a talk at the local science museum, it's great to bring your daughter to meet her and get an autograph—but bring your son along, too. By the same token, if a family friend who works at a high-tech startup offers to give your son a tour of his lab, invite your daughter to join the excursion.

The same kind of inclusive thinking should apply to your family's media diet. When your children are little, bedtime storybooks needn't be segregated by gender. Girls can draw inspiration from the life story of Thomas Edison and the adventures of Harry Potter . . . and boys can learn a lot from the experiences of Marie Curie and the science-inspired fantasy tales of Madeleine L'Engle, author of *A Wrinkle in Time*.

In the same way, just as older girls can be fascinated by movies about male entrepreneurs, like *The Social Network* (2010) and *Steve Jobs* (2015), boys can be moved and inspired by films with heroic, problem-solving female leads, like *Erin Brockovich* (2000) and *Joy* (2015).

TEACH YOUR SON TO TAKE CARE OF HIMSELF AND OTHERS

One of the most persistent gender stereotypes we need to break down is the association of women with "caregiving." Not that there is anything wrong with caring for people. Just the opposite—it's vital, valuable work in which all human beings ought to share, whether in a professional context or in their home and family lives. When work that centers on caring for human needs is stereotypically assigned to just one gender, the impact is often negative. During the decades when women in our society were automatically shunted into careers like nursing, schoolteaching, social work, hospitality, and child care, it meant their life choices were restricted and their occupations were widely denigrated as "women's work," often leading to lower salaries and poorer working conditions. At the same time, men who might naturally have gravitated to such jobs felt forced to make different choices, meaning that everyone's opportunity for a better work/life fit suffered.

For all these reasons, it's important for gender equality to be applied to caregiving work, and that people working in these fields be given dignity, respect, and rewards equivalent to those provided to people in other lines of work.

Caregiving at home also deserves greater respect than it sometimes receives. In every family, there are basic jobs that need to be done that some might consider menial but that involve meeting fundamental human needs—jobs like cooking, cleaning, shopping for necessities, doing the laundry, and caring for those who need extra help, such as children, the elderly, and the disabled. Here, too, our society has tended to assume that this is "women's work." Thankfully, that assumption is changing, although too slowly. One big way to accelerate the trend is for us to raise boys and girls alike to view caregiving as worthy, important work in which every family member must share.

When you raise sons to understand that they are expected to spend as much time doing household chores as their sisters, you are doing them a favor in several ways. You are teaching them resilience, discipline, and hard work; you are giving them the opportunity to master skills they will need to know in order to survive and thrive when they live on their own (from cooking a tasty omelet to washing their shirts without shrinking them); and you are helping them to learn about the practical demands of life in the real world, which is the main driver of creative problem-solving for the world's most effective entrepreneurs.

EXPOSE YOUR SON TO THE IDEALISTIC ASPECTS OF STEM AND ENTREPRENEURSHIP

I'VE EXPLAINED IN THIS BOOK THAT MANY GIRLS ARE ESPECIALLY EXCITED about the possibility of using STEM and entrepreneurial skills to make the world a better place—to help the poor, protect the environment, alleviate hunger, cure diseases, and so on. The same applies to plenty of boys.

In our society, we tend to stereotype male scientists, engineers, and business founders in two ways—either as socially awkward nerds obsessed with arcane technical topics, or as greedy, power-hungry megalomaniacs obsessed with money. Both stereotypes are exaggerated and unfair. Many boys and men share the same drive to improve society and address serious social ills that girls and women feel. And, of course, it's entirely possible to combine an idealistic vision of creating a better world with both a fascination with science and an interest in money. People are multifaceted, and their personalities shouldn't be reduced to a single simplistic characteristic.

When talking with boys about the worlds of work and possible career options for them to consider, don't restrict the conversation to "cool" jobs involving the obvious "boy toys"—lasers, rockets, computers, and robots. Like girls, many boys are more likely to be excited about the possibility of creating innovative ways of helping millions of people. That's a dream to be encouraged—after all, our world can sure use the help!

LOVE HIM JUST THE WAY HE IS!

ABOVE ALL, THE MOST IMPORTANT THING YOU CAN DO FOR A SON THAT YOU hope will become a VentureBoy is the same thing you can do for a daughter—love him just the way he is!

Our society often imposes expectations on young men that can be, in their own way, as oppressive as the stereotypes we impose on women. Boys often feel driven to fit a preconceived image of what makes a "real man"—tough, aggressive, competitive, physically imposing, decisive, hard-edged, stoical, unemotional. Sometimes these demands are made explicit, through lectures delivered by well-meaning dads, granddads, uncles, and older brothers, or by role models like gym teachers, scout masters, and coaches. More often the expectations are conveyed implicitly, through media images (from John Wayne in the 1950s to Dwayne "the Rock" Johnson today) and through sexist messages—as when a parent uses a word like *sissy* or *fag* as an insult, or tells a boy who is scared or upset, "Be a man—stop that crying!"

Those who pass along these expectations usually don't mean any harm. But they help to convince millions of boys and young men that their real personalities are "no good," and that they must somehow force themselves to play the role of the tough-guy character our society appears to revere. Too many men end up being trapped in this painful pretense for a lifetime.

If our society is to thrive, we don't need more males who feel driven to lives and careers of macho posturing (often at the expense of the women around them). We need people of both genders who are free to express their deepest creative dreams, embodying the full range of ideas, emotions, and drives within them. That sense of creative freedom, nurtured through unconditional acceptance and love, is what truly characterizes a VentureBoy or VentureGirl . . . and as parents, relatives, friends, and mentors of the young people around us, nurturing that freedom is perhaps the greatest gift we can offer.

RESOURCES FOR FURTHER LEARNING

BELOW IS AN ANNOTATED LIST OF RESOURCES THAT READERS CAN EXPLORE for more ideas about how to nurture and encourage the VentureGirls in their lives.

ORGANIZATIONS

WHILE DEVELOPING VENTURELAB, I WAS HAPPY TO LEARN ABOUT DOZENS of other organizations dedicated, in whole or in part, to supporting girls and women studying STEM subjects and pursuing careers in related fields. Here are a few with the widest reach.

ORGANIZATION	REACH	DESCRIPTION
4-H Clubs	Grades K to 12	4-H is one of America's largest youth development organizations, empowering young people with leadership skills through hands-on projects in school, after school, and through school and community clubs and 4-H camps.

ORGANIZATION	REACH	DESCRIPTION
American Association of University Women (AAUW)	Limited grades K to 12, university and professional	AAUW has been empowering women as individuals and as a community since 1881 through STEM initiatives for girls, university initiatives, research, public policy, and educational funding.
American Medical Women's Association (AMWA)	University and professional	AMWA is an organization that functions at the local, national, and international levels to advance women in medicine and improve women's health. It achieves this by providing and developing leadership, advocacy, education, expertise, mentoring, and strategic alliances.
Anita Borg Institute (ABI)	University and professional	ABI is a social enterprise founded on the belief that women are vital to building technology that the world needs. They bring women technologists together to learn, celebrate, and thrive at their annual Grace Hopper Celebration of Women in Computing conference.
Association for Women in Science (AWIS)	Professional	AWIS promotes women leaders in STEM by driving systemic change through research, advocacy, and career-focused initiatives.
Black Girls CODE	Youth	Black Girls CODE is devoted to showing the world that black girls can code, and do so much more. By reaching out to the community through workshops and after-school programs, Black Girls CODE introduces computer coding lessons to young girls from underrepresented communities in a multitude of programming languages.

ORGANIZATION	REACH	DESCRIPTION
Con Mi MADRE	Grades 6 to 12 and adult	Con Mi MADRE strives to help young Latinas to graduate high school as college ready. In its Post-Secondary Preparedness program, girls and their mothers are encouraged and supported to maintain good grades, take AP coursework, and have a deeper understanding of post-secondary expectations, as well as increase financial literacy, confidence, and their support system.
DECA Idea Challenge	High school and university	Distributive Education Clubs of America (DECA) prepares emerging leaders and entrepreneurs for careers in marketing, finance, hospitality, and management in high schools and colleges around the globe. The DECA Idea Challenge is a fast-paced, hands-on learning experience that dares students around the globe to generate an innovative new use for a commonplace item in just eight days. Students must organize into teams, access the challenge item online, collaborate as a team to produce an original and sustainable use for the item, and pitch their invention in an engaging YouTube video presentation.
Design for Change	Grades K to 12 and university	Design for Change equips children with the tools to be aware of the world around them, believe that they play a role in shaping that world, and take action toward a more desirable, sustainable future.

ORGANIZATION	REACH	DESCRIPTION
Girl Scouts of the USA	Grades K to 12	Girls Scouts is the preeminent leadership development organization for girls. Girls can get involved in a collection of engaging, challenging, and fun activities like earning badges, going on awesome trips, selling cookies, exploring science, getting outdoors, and doing community service projects.
Girls in Tech (GIT)	University and professional	GIT is a global nonprofit focused on the engagement, education, and empowerment of girls and women who are passionate about technology. Their programs help women advance their careers in STEM fields.
Girls Inc.	Grades K to 12	Girls Inc. inspires all girls to be strong, smart, and bold through direct service and advocacy. Their Operation SMART program in particular develops girls' enthusiasm for and skills in STEM through hands-on activities.
Girls Learn International (GLI)	Youth and adult	GLI educates and energizes students in the global movement for girls' access to education. The GLI Program supports the empowerment of students as they discover that through their own creative initiatives, dedication, and passionate leadership, they can create real solutions that address the obstacles facing girls and women in the United States and around the world.

ORGANIZATION	REACH	DESCRIPTION
Girls Who Code	Grades 6 to 12	Girls Who Code is a national nonprofit organization dedicated to closing the gender gap in technology by teaching girls to code through clubs and summer immersion programs across the United States.
Girlstart	Grades K to 12	Girlstart provides a year-round, intensive suite of STEM education programs for K–12 girls. Girlstart's core programs foster STEM skills development, an understanding of the importance of STEM as a way to solve the world's major problems, and an interest in STEM electives, majors, and careers.
I Am That Girl	Youth and adult	I Am That Girl is a 501(c)3 organization helping girls to transform self-doubt into self-love by providing a safe space to connect and have honest conversations about things that matter.
Kode with Klossy	Ages 13 to 18	Kode with Klossy empowers girls to learn to code and become leaders in tech. The organization hosts girls' coding summer camps, awards career scholarships to young women developers, and helps create a national community changing the role of girls and women in tech.
L'Oréal Foundation: For Women in Science and For Girls in Science	High school and up	For Women in Science encourages the vocations of girls in high school, supports women in research, and recognizes excellence in a field where women are underrepresented. For Girls in Science is a unique program advocating for young girls to consider science as a future career path.

ORGANIZATION	REACH	DESCRIPTION
Ladies Learning Code	Third grade to adult	Ladies Learning Code is a not-for-profit organization with the mission to be the leading resource for women and youth to become passionate builders—not just consumers—of technology by learning technical skills in a hands-on, social, and collaborative way. It offers workshops for all ages with chapters across Canada.
Million Women Mentors	Ages 6 to adult	Million Women Mentors' mission is to support the engagement of two million STEM mentors (male and female) to increase the interest and confidence of girls and young women to persist and succeed in STEM programs and careers by 2020.
Moms as Mentors	Grades K to 8 and adult	Through a variety of hands-on workshops, Moms as Mentors provides moms with the tools and opportunities they need to be mentors in their daughters' daily lives, ultimately helping their girls to grow into confident and influential women.
National Center for Women & Information Technology (NCWIT)	Grades K to 12 and adult	The National Center for Women & Information Technology (NCWIT) is the only national nonprofit focused on women's participation in computing across the entire ecosystem, helping nearly nine hundred organizations recruit, retain, and advance women from K–12 and in higher education through industry and entrepreneurial careers by providing support, evidence, and action.

ORGANIZATION	REACH	DESCRIPTION
National Coalition of Girls' Schools (NCGS)	Adult	The National Coalition of Girls' Schools (NCGS) is the leading advocate for girls' schools, connecting and collaborating globally with individuals, schools, and organizations dedicated to educating and empowering girls.
National Girls Collaborative Project (NGCP)	Adult	The National Girls Collaborative Project seeks to broaden the participation of girls and women in all fields of STEM education by supporting research, dissemination of research, and extension services in education that will lead to a larger and more diverse domestic science and engineering workforce. NGCP provides a directory of girl-serving STEM programs and acts as a resource for community organizations to advance gender equality in STEM fields.
She Geeks Out	Adult	She Geeks Out supports a welcoming network, enables mentorship, supports girls, advances women, and encourages every woman to proudly fly her geek flag. Through workshops, education, and networking events, She Geeks Out fosters diversity and inclusion.
Society for Women Engineers (SWE)	Grades K to 12 and adult	SWE's mission is to stimulate women to achieve full potential in careers as engineers and leaders, expand the image of the engineering profession as a positive force in improving the quality of life, and demonstrate the value of diversity. It also offers a wide variety of K–12 outreach events and programs.

ORGANIZATION	REACH	DESCRIPTION
STEMinist	Adult	STEMinist focuses on women in STEM and aggregates and features stories about women in STEM from across the web in order to increase the visibility of women in STEM, promote and elevate the perspective of women in these traditionally underrepresented fields, and encourage younger women and girls to pursue careers in STEM.
Strong Women, Strong Girls	Youth and adult	Strong Women, Strong Girls empowers girls to imagine a broader future through a curriculum grounded on female role models delivered by college women mentors, who are themselves mentored by professional women.
TeachHer initiative (UNESCO, United Nations)	Adult	TeachHer is a public-private partnership aimed at encouraging adolescent girls to pursue Science, Technology, Engineering, Arts and Design, and Math (STEAM) careers. TeachHer works with target Member States, UNESCO regional field offices and institutes, and NGO leaders in STEAM training to implement and promote programs that will support girls' education in STEAM. The focus will be on developing a master corps of gender-sensitive STEAM teachers who will tangibly increase the number of adolescent girls interested in pursuing STEAM careers, along with ongoing professional development and networking for teachers.

ORGANIZATION	REACH	DESCRIPTION
Technovation	Youth	Technovation is a nonprofit that offers girls around the world the opportunity to learn the skills they need to emerge as tech entrepreneurs and leaders. Every year they invite girls to identify a problem in their community, and then challenge them to solve it. Girls work in teams to build both a mobile app and a business plan to launch that app, and present at the World Pitch Summit.
VentureLab	K to 12 and adult	VentureLab is building a movement to spread the entrepreneurial mindset around the world to empower youth with the tools needed to become the next generation of innovators and changemakers. VentureLab's mission is to enable and inspire anyone to utilize an open-access youth entrepreneurship curriculum to unlock student potential and prepare youth, especially girls, to succeed in technical, creative, and entrepreneurial fields.
Women in Technology (WIT)	Adult	WIT has the sole aim of advancing women in technology—from the classroom to the boardroom. WIT meets its vision through a variety of leadership development, technology education, networking, and mentoring opportunities for women at all levels of their careers.

ONLINE RESOURCES

THE INTERNET OFFERS AN AMAZING VARIETY OF SITES THAT GIRLS CAN USE to learn about STEM and to develop their skills in science, technology, engineering, math, and entrepreneurship. Here are some of the best.

RESOURCE TYPE	WEB ADDRESS	DESCRIPTION
Educational and science videos	http://pbskids.org/scigirls/home	*SciGirls* is a show for kids ages 8 to 12, showcasing bright, curious, real tween girls putting STEM to work in their everyday lives.
	http://thekidshouldseethis.com	Smart videos about science, art, nature, animals, space, tech, and more, for curious minds of all ages, as well as a free resource for parents and teachers.
	https://www.ted.com/playlists/86/talks_to_watch_with_kids	From the TED nonprofit devoted to spreading ideas, this playlist offers fun, informative, and captivating talks to inspire young minds.

RESOURCE TYPE	WEB ADDRESS	DESCRIPTION
Cool maker websites	https://www.thingiverse.com	A design community for discovering, making, and sharing 3-D-printable items, all encouraged for free use under a Creative Commons license.
	https://www.instructables.com	Website offering ideas for countless hours of tinkering, soldering, stitching, frying, and making just about anything.
	https://diy.org	A safe online do-it-yourself community where kids can discover new passions, level up their skills, and meet other fearless geeks.
	https://makezine.com/projects/	A project source for the maker movement, where tinkerers, teachers, parents, and professionals can find cool projects to try.
Coding websites	https://code.org	Website offering courses and resources for students and teachers from a nonprofit dedicated to increasing participation in computer science by women and minorities.

RESOURCE TYPE	WEB ADDRESS	DESCRIPTION
Coding websites (*cont.*)	https://www.khanacademy.org	A source for practice exercises, instructional videos, and a personalized learning dashboard for self-study inside and outside the classroom.
	https://teamtreehouse.com	Site offering courses in web design, coding, and more. Free for the first seven days.
	https://www.codecademy.com	Educational site providing a curriculum for interactive instruction in coding.
Crowdfunding websites	https://www.kickstarter.com	Crowdfunding site that helps designers, artists, filmmakers, and other creators find resources and support for their projects.
	https://www.gofundme.com	World's largest crowdfunding site, with a community of more than forty million donors.
	https://www.indiegogo.com/	Crowdfunding site offering clever and unconventional products that solve everyday problems large and small.

RESOURCE TYPE	WEB ADDRESS	DESCRIPTION
Websites to make simple and easy websites	https://www.wix.com	Three sites that provide resources to enable users to create their own websites for free.
	https://get.weebly.com/	
	https://www.site123.com	
Websites for doing market research	https://factfinder.census.gov/faces/nav/jsf/pages/index.xhtml	Source of vital data about your community—population, income, demographics, and more.
	https://www.surveymonkey.com	Site that provides tools for designing and administering online surveys and tabulating results.
Websites for making mockups and wireframes	https://balsamiq.com	Rapid wireframing tool that reproduces the experience of sketching on a whiteboard, but using your computer.
	https://www.invisionapp.com	Site that lets you design, review, and user-test products through intuitive tools for prototyping, task management, and version control.
	https://www.omnigroup.com/omnigraffle	Site for creating precise, beautiful graphics: website wireframes, electric systems, family trees, software maps, and more.

RESOURCE TYPE	WEB ADDRESS	DESCRIPTION
Websites for making mockups and wireframes (*cont.*)	https://proto.io	Site for creating fully interactive, high-fidelity prototypes for apps, without the need for coding.
	https://marvelapp.com	Interactive site for designing and prototyping in collaboration with others.
Websites for 3-D printing	https://www.3dhubs.com	World's largest network of manufacturing hubs, offering services in more than 140 countries.
RESOURCE TYPE	**TITLE**	**DESCRIPTION**
Cool apps	Blockly, Wonder, Path, Go	Coding challenges, missions, and play for use with the Dash and Dot toys.
	Stop Motion Studio	App for stop-motion moviemaking.
	Park Math HD	Teaches early math concepts based on Common Core state standards.
	Minecraft PE	Using pixelated graphics and a character you create, assemble blocks to build anything from a roller coaster to a city.

RESOURCE TYPE	TITLE	DESCRIPTION
Cool apps (*cont.*)	Ozobot Evo	Create private games, secret codes, and robotic equations with friends. For use with the Ozobot toy.
	Keezy	A musical instrument with eight colored tiles that let you record sounds and play back the tunes you create.
	TinkerBox	Use tools like conveyor belts, chains, platforms, and motors to build original machines and share with friends.
	DIY	App that provides thousands of challenges to explore and learn new skills.
	Instructables	App offering more than a hundred thousand tutorials by DIY creators on everything from cooking to outrageous inventions.
	iMovie	Easily convert photos or video clips into movies to share with the world.
	BloxMob	Mobile builder teens can use to create apps with no need for coding.

COOL TOYS

THERE ARE A GROWING NUMBER OF COMMERCIALLY AVAILABLE TOYS THAT are great for learning and exploring the world of STEM as well as just plain fun. Here are a few favorites.

TOY	DESCRIPTION AND AGES
Snap Circuits	Snap Circuits makes learning electronics easy with exciting projects, such as FM radios, digital voice recorders, AM radios, burglar alarms, doorbells, and much more. Recommended for ages 8 and up.
Ozobots	Evo, a robot available from Ozobots, entertains with autonomous LED lights, sounds, and movements. Evo uses infrared proximity sensing to avoid obstacles and app-enabled RC controls to explore the world with you. Recommended for ages 8 and up.
Dash and Dot	Fun-loving robots ready to play out of the box. They respond to voice, navigate objects, dance, and sing. Recommended for ages 5 and up.
Puzzlets	Puzzlets is a physical bluetooth accessory for your tablet or computer used to play Puzzlets-specific games. Each game focuses on a traditionally challenging STEM subject, such as coding, math, or color theory. Ages 6 and up.
Lego Mindstorm EV3	Classic robot-building toy with Bluetooth radio that lets builders control their robots via an app, and a new sensor suite enables creations to navigate and react autonomously. Ages 10 and up.

TOY	DESCRIPTION AND AGES
Legos	You can never go wrong with traditional Legos. They are great for stimulating the imagination. Ages 2 and up.
littleBits	A platform of easy-to-use electronic building blocks that empower you to invent anything, from your own remote-controlled car to a smart-home device. The Bits snap together with magnets, no soldering, no wiring, no programming needed. Ages 8 and up.
Makey Makey	Makey Makey is an invention kit for the twenty-first century. Turn everyday objects into touchpads and combine them with the Internet. It's a simple invention kit for beginners and experts doing art, engineering, and everything in between. Ages 8 and up.
3-D printing pen	With a 3-D pen, available from a number of suppliers, you can create your favorite toys. Whether it is a lovely animal or a car, use a 3-D pen to turn it into a model that can be played with in your hand. The possibilities are endless. Recommended for ages 12 and up, because the pen tip gets hot.
Electrically conductive ink	Electrically conductive ink is available from a number of suppliers and can be used for birthday cards, or fabrics, or whatever you like to create a circuit. Ages 8 and up.
Arduino	Open-source electronic prototyping platform enabling users to create interactive electronic objects. Ages 8 and up.

TOY	DESCRIPTION AND AGES
3-D printer	3-D printing, or additive manufacturing, is a process of making three-dimensional solid objects from a digital file. There are many types and brands of 3-D printers, including Ultimaker and MakerBot, which are tabletop devices you can use at home. Ages 8 and up.
Squishy Circuits play dough kits	Squishy Circuits uses conductive and insulating play dough to teach the basics of electrical circuits in a fun, hands-on way. Let your creations come to life as you light them up with LEDs, make noises with buzzers, and spin with the motor. You can use provided recipes or recipes online to create your own conductive and insulating dough. Ages 3 and up.

NOTES

Introduction

1. Sir Ken Robinson, quoted in George Land and Beth Jarman, *Breakpoint and Beyond: Mastering the Future Today* (Scottsdale, AZ: Leadership 2000, 1998).

1. Where Are All the Girls?

1. Interview by the author with Nick Hahn, March 2016.
2. Klaus Schwab, "The Fourth Industrial Revolution: What It Means, How to Respond," World Economic Forum website, January 14, 2016, https://www.weforum.org/agenda/2016/01/the-fourth-industrial-revolution-what-it-means-and-how-to-respond/.
3. See, for example, Bruce Goldman, "Two Minds: The Cognitive Differences Between Men and Women," *Stanford Medicine*, Spring 2017, https://stanmed.stanford.edu/2017spring/how-mens-and-womens-brains-are-different.html.
4. Dr. Stacy L. Smith, Marc Choueiti, and Dr. Katherine Pieper, *Gender Bias Without Borders: An Investigation of Female Characters in Popular Films Across 11 Countries*, Geena Davis Institute on Gender in Media, 2015, https://seejane.org/wp-content/uploads/gender-bias-without-borders-executive-summary.pdf.
5. Ibid.
6. *Science and Engineering Indicators 2016*, National Science Foundation, https://www.nsf.gov/statistics/2016/nsb20161/#/.
7. *Women, Minorities, and Persons with Disabilities in Science and Engineering*, National Science Board of the National Science Foundation, January 2017, https://www.nsf.gov/statistics/2017/nsf17310/.
8. Interview by Dane Anderson and Susan Engelking, research associates of the author, with Maria Klawe, December 2015.

9. Interview by the author with Grace Frye, March 2016.
10. "Science Not Immune from Gender Bias, Yale Study Shows," *Yale-News*, September 24, 2012, http://news.yale.edu/2012/09/24/scientists-not-immune-gender-bias-yale-study-shows.
11. *Women Technologists Count: Recommendations and Best Practices to Retain Women in Computing*, Anita Borg Institute, 2013, http://anitaborg.org/wp-content/uploads/2013/12/Women_Technologists_Count.pdf.
12. Interview by the author with Graham Weston, March 2016.
13. Rebecca Ratcliffe, "Nobel Scientist Tim Hunt: Female Scientists Cause Trouble for Men in Labs," *Guardian*, June 10, 2015, https://www.theguardian.com/uk-news/2015/jun/10/nobel-scientist-tim-hunt-female-scientists-cause-trouble-for-men-in-labs.
14. Sharon Begley, "He, Once a She, Offers Own View on Science Spat," *Wall Street Journal*, July 13, 2006, https://www.wsj.com/articles/SB115274744775305134.
15. Smith, Choueiti, and Pieper, *Gender Bias Without Borders*.
16. Justin Wolfers, "Fewer Women Run Big Companies Than Men Named John," *The Upshot* (blog), *New York Times*, March 2, 2015, https://www.nytimes.com/2015/03/03/upshot/fewer-women-run-big-companies-than-men-named-john.html.
17. Ibid.
18. Kieran Snyder, "The Abrasiveness Trap: High-Achieving Men and Women Are Described Differently in Reviews," *Fortune*, August 26, 2014, http://fortune.com/2014/08/26/performance-review-gender-bias/.
19. Interview by the author with Catherine Crago, February 2015.
20. Ann Cuddy, "Your Body Language May Shape Who You Are," TED Talk, June 2012, https://www.ted.com/talks/amy_cuddy_your_body_language_shapes_who_you_are.
21. Catherine Hill, Christianne Corbett, and Andresse St. Rose, *Why So Few? Women in Science, Technology, Engineering, and Mathematics*, American Association of University Women, 2010, https://www.aauw.org/files/2013/02/Why-So-Few-Women-in-Science-Technology-Engineering-and-Mathematics.pdf.
22. Londa Schiebinger, *Has Feminism Changed Science?* (Cambridge, MA: Harvard University Press, 2001).
23. Interview by the author with Bruce Porter, January 2015.
24. Carol S. Dweck, PhD, *Mindset: The New Psychology of Success* (New York: Random House, 2006).
25. Interview with Nick Hahn.
26. Interview with Graham Weston.
27. Interview by the author with Jason Seats, March 2016.

28. "23 New STEM and Outdoor Badges Enrich Girl Scout Programming, Which Data Shows Helps Girls Excel in Life," Girl Scouts of the USA Press Room, July 25, 2017, https://www.girlscouts.org/en/press-room/press-room/news-releases/2017/23-new-stem-outdoor-badges-enrich-programming.html.

2. Daring, Risking, Growing

1. Interview by the author with Bri Connelly, December 2015.
2. Malcolm Gladwell, *Outliers: The Story of Success* (New York: Little, Brown, 2008).
3. Dweck, *Mindset*.
4. Lise Eliot, *Pink Brain, Blue Brain: How Small Differences Grow into Troublesome Gaps—and What We Can Do About It* (Boston: Mariner Books, 2010).
5. "If in Doubt, Innovate: The Nordic Region Is Becoming a Hothouse of Entrepreneurship," *The Economist*, February 2, 2013, http://www.economist.com/news/special-report/21570834-nordic-region-becoming-hothouse-entrepreneurship-if-doubt-innovate.
6. Jim Clifton and Sangeeta Bharadwaj Badal, *Entrepreneurial StrengthsFinder* (Washington, DC: Gallup Press, 2014).
7. Heather Long, "Where Are All the Startups? U.S. Entrepreneurship Near 40-Year Low," *CNN Money*, September 8, 2016, http://money.cnn.com/2016/09/08/news/economy/us-startups-near-40-year-low/.
8. *Generation STEM: What Girls Say About Science, Technology, Engineering, and Math*, Girl Scouts of the USA, 2010, http://www.girlscouts.org/content/dam/girlscouts-gsusa/forms-and-documents/about-girl-scouts/research/generation_stem_full_report.pdf.

4. Help Her Start Her Entrepreneurial Adventure

1. Interview by the author with Mike McDerment, January 2016.
2. "Leopard Poaching Statistics," *Poaching Facts*, http://www.poachingfacts.com/poaching-statistics/leopard-poaching-statistics/.

5. Start Her Young

1. Stephanie Brown, "Is It Okay for My Toddler to Eat Play Dough?" verywell website, July 2, 2017, https://www.verywell.com/is-it-okay-for-my-toddler-to-eat-play-dough-290074.
2. Lisa Rivero, "Be More Creative Today: Five Ways to Sustain Creativity at Home and School," *Psychology Today*, March 10, 2012, https://www.psychologytoday.com/blog/creative-synthesis/201203/be-more-creative-today.
3. Eliot, *Pink Brain, Blue Brain*.

4. Leonard Sax, *Why Gender Matters: What Parents and Teachers Need to Know About the Emerging Science of Sex Differences* (New York: Harmony, 2006).
5. Deborah Tannen, *You're Wearing That?! Understanding Mothers and Daughters in Conversation* (New York: Random House, 2006).
6. Sax, *Why Gender Matters*.
7. Sheryl Sorby, "Enlightening Minds," talk at Stem Solutions, *U.S. News & World Report* conference, June 30, 2015.
8. "Early Spatial Reasoning Predicts Later Creativity and Innovation, Especially in STEM Fields," Association for Psychological Science, July 15, 2013, http://www.psychologicalscience.org/news/releases/early-spatial-reasoning-predicts-later-creativity-and-innovation-especially-in-stem-fields.html.
9. Interview by Susan Engelking, research associate of the author, with Randa Milliron, July 2015.
10. Interview with Catherine Crago.

6. Make Playtime Curiosity Time

1. Jonathan Mugan, *The Curiosity Cycle: Preparing Your Child for the Ongoing Technological Explosion*, 2nd ed. (Buda, TX: Mugan Publishing, 2014), http://www.jonathanmugan.com/CuriosityCycle/curiositycycle_chapter_one_second_edition.pdf.
2. Interview by Susan Engelking, research associate of the author, with Sue Kolbly, December 2015.
3. Richard Feynman, "The Making of a Scientist," *Cricket*, October 1995.
4. Quoted in David Kohn, "Let the Kids Learn Through Play," *New York Times*, May 16, 2015, https://www.nytimes.com/2015/05/17/opinion/sunday/let-the-kids-learn-through-play.html?mcubz=0.
5. Robert S. Root-Bernstein and Michele M. Root-Bernstein, *Sparks of Genius: The Thirteen Thinking Tools of the World's Most Creative People* (Boston: Mariner Books, 2001).
6. Bill Gates interview, *OnInnovation*, The Henry Ford, June 30, 2009, https://www.thehenryford.org/docs/default-source/default-document-library/default-document-library/transcript_gates_highlights.pdf?sfvrsn=0.
7. Robert Scherrer, "How to Raise a Scientist in the Xbox Age," *Wall Street Journal*, December 14, 2015, http://www.wsj.com/articles/how-to-raise-a-scientist-in-the-xbox-age-1450137781.
8. Adam Bryant, "Lori Senecal on Coaching When the Bar Is High," *New York Times*, May 29, 2015.
9. Melia Robinson, "14-Year-Old Wins Google Science Fair Award with Ge-

nius Way to Use Corn Cobs," *Business Insider,* September 23, 2015, http://www.businessinsider.com/sripada-srisai-lalita-prasida-wins-at-google-science-fair-2015-9.

7. Please Get Messy!

1. Sir Ken Robinson, quoted in Jessica Shepherd, "Fertile Minds Need Feeding," *Guardian,* February 9, 2009.
2. Interview by the author with anonymous, December 2015.
3. Gladwell, *Outliers*.
4. Interview by Susan Engelking, research associate of the author, with dt ogilvie, October 2015.
5. "Tidy Desk or Messy Desk? Each Has Its Benefits," Association for Psychological Science, August 6, 2013, http://www.psychologicalscience.org/news/releases/tidy-desk-or-messy-desk-each-has-its-benefits.html.
6. "Messy Children Make Better Learners," *Science Daily,* December 2, 2013, https://www.sciencedaily.com/releases/2013/12/131202082318.htm.
7. Eleanor Barkhorn, "Messy Kids Learn More," *Atlantic,* December 6, 2013, https://www.theatlantic.com/education/archive/2013/12/messy-kids-learn-more/282095/.
8. Quoted in Rivero, "Be More Creative Today."
9. Ibid.
10. John Medina, *Brain Rules: 12 Principles for Surviving and Thriving at Work, Home, and School* (Edmonds, WA: Pear Press, 2008).
11. Interview by the author with anonymous, December 2015.
12. Interview by Susan Engelking, research associate of the author, with Gail Papermaster, October 2015.
13. Kevin Benson, "3 Reasons Improvisation Makes You a Better Entrepreneur," Bold Move Consulting & Coaching website, August 28, 2014, http://boldmoveconsulting.com/3-reasons-improvisation-makes-better-entrepreneur/.
14. Richard Branson, "Best Advice: Listen More Than You Talk," LinkedIn, February 2, 2015, https://www.linkedin.com/pulse/best-advice-listen-more-than-you-talk-richard-branson/.
15. Interview with Maria Klawe.
16. Eileen Pollack, *The Only Woman in the Room: Why Science Is Still a Boys' Club* (Boston: Beacon Press, 2015).
17. Interview with dt ogilvie.

8. Encourage Failure

1. Source of Sara Blakely story: Amy Wilkinson, *The Creator's Code: The Six Essential Skills of Extraordinary Entrepreneurs* (New York: Simon & Schuster, 2015).
2. Jonah Lehrer, *How We Decide* (Boston: Houghton Mifflin Harcourt, 2009).
3. Quoted in Alina Tugend, *Better by Mistake: The Unexpected Benefits of Being Wrong* (New York: Riverhead Books, 2012).
4. Ibid.
5. Kimberly Wright Cassidy, "Progress on the Gender Front in STEM," talk at Stem Solutions, *U.S. News & World Report* conference, June 30, 2015.
6. Julie Scelfo, "Suicide on Campus and the Pressures of Perfection," *New York Times*, July 27, 2015.
7. Quoted in Claire Shipman and Katty Kay, *Womenomics: Write Your Own Rules for Success* (New York: Harper Business, 2009).
8. Interview with Jason Seats.
9. Quoted in Deborah Perkins-Gough, "The Significance of Grit: A Conversation with Angela Lee Duckworth," *Educational Leadership*, September 2013.
10. Interview by the author with Stephanie Sullivan, January 2015.
11. Ibid.
12. Interview by the author with Diane Hessan, January 2015.
13. Ibid.
14. Ibid.
15. Interview by the author with Kelly Fitzsimmons, February 2017.
16. Gladwell, *Outliers*.
17. Interview by the author with Nan McRaven, February 2015.
18. Quoted in Root-Bernstein and Root-Bernstein, *Sparks of Genius*.
19. Root-Bernstein and Root-Bernstein, *Sparks of Genius*.

9. Channel Her Idealism

1. Daniel H. Pink, *Drive: The Surprising Truth About What Motivates Us* (New York: Riverhead Books, 2011).
2. Interview with Maria Klawe.
3. *Generation STEM*.
4. Harriet Lerner, *The Dance of Anger: A Woman's Guide to Changing the Patterns of Intimate Relationships* (New York: HarperCollins, 1985).
5. Interview by Susan Engelking, research associate of the author, with Pamela Ryan, June 2015.
6. Interview by Susan Engelking, research associate of the author, with Stacy Zoern, September 2017.
7. "30 Under 30: Social Entrepreneurs, Kerstin Forsberg," *Forbes*, April 5,

2013, https://www.forbes.com/pictures/ekeg45kfk/kerstin-forsberg-28/#1430ec85d2df.

8. "30 Under 30: Social Entrepreneurs, Sejal Hathi," *Forbes*, April 5, 2013, https://www.forbes.com/special-report/2013/millenials/millenials-sejal-hathi.html.
9. Pagan Kennedy, "The Tampon of the Future," *New York Times*, April 1, 2016.
10. Source of Mikaila Ulmer quotations: Mikaila Ulmer, "Talks at Google," YouTube, March 25, 2015, https://www.youtube.com/watch?v=1H4R5e64NDE.
11. Interview by the author with Anne Boysen, May 2015.
12. Lina Nilsson, "How to Attract Female Engineers," *New York Times*, April 27, 2015.
13. Interview with Randa Milliron.

10. Provide Role Models

1. Colette Pierce Burnette's story is based on an interview with her by Bre Clark, research associate of the author, in November 2015.
2. Lily Rothman, "What Actress Hedy Lamarr Said About Her Skill as an Inventor," *Time*, November 9, 2015.
3. Interview by Susan Engelking, research associate of the author, with Kennon Lydick, November 2015; interview by Bre Clark, research associate of the author, with Hayden Lydick, October 2015.
4. Interview by Bre Clark, research associate of the author, with Kathy Garza Smith, November 2015.
5. Scherrer, "How to Raise a Scientist in the Xbox Age."
6. Interview by the author with Susan Engelking, May 2015.
7. Interview by Bre Clark, research associate of the author, with Rachel Kast, November 2015.
8. Kara Sammet and Linda Kekelis, *Changing the Game for Girls in STEM*, Techbridge, April 2016, https://www.itu.int/en/ITU-D/Digital-Inclusion/Women-and-Girls/Girls-in-ICT-Portal/Documents/changing-the-game-for-girls-in-stem-white-paper.pdf.
9. Interview with Grace Frye.

11. Get the Whole Family Involved

1. *Women, Minorities, and Persons with Disabilities in Science and Engineering*, National Science Board of the National Science Foundation, January 2017, https://www.nsf.gov/statistics/2017/nsf17310/digest/fod-wmreg/minorities-by-degree-share.cfm.
2. Interview by Bre Clark, research associate of the author, with Teresa Granillo, November 2015.

3. Interview by Bre Clark, research associate of the author, with Karen Gonzalez, November 2015.
4. Interview by the author with Desiree Prieto Groft, March 2016.
5. Margaretha Lucas, "Identity Development, Career Development, and Psychological Separation from Parents: Similarities and Differences Between Men and Women," *Journal of Counseling Psychology* 44, no. 2 (1997): 123–32, http://psycnet.apa.org/record/1997-08136-001.
6. Interview by the author with Leslie Coles, October 2017.
7. Linda Nielson, "How Dads Affect Their Daughters into Adulthood," Institute for Family Studies, June 3, 2014, https://ifstudies.org/blog/how-dads-affect-their-daughters-into-adulthood.
8. Interview by the author with Nick Longo, January 2016.
9. Rana Faroohar, "Mary Barra's Bumpy Ride at the Wheel of GM," *Time*, September 25, 2014, http://time.com/3429651/mary-barras-bumpy-ride-at-the-wheel-of-gm/.
10. Ibid.
11. Matthew Panzarino, "Google CEO Larry Page Speaks at I/O About Competition and Negativity in Innovation," *The Next Web*, May 15, 2013, https://thenextweb.com/google/2013/05/15/google-glass/#.tnw_BKNMADPF.
12. Interview by the author with Frederick "Suizo" Mendler, January 2016.
13. Interview by Susan Engelking, research associate of the author, with John Wooley, October 2015.
14. Interview with Lane Kolbly.
15. Interview with John Wooley.
16. Lisa Evans, "Why Men with Daughters May Be the Key to Closing the Gender Wage Gap," *Fast Company*, June 30, 2014, https://www.fastcompany.com/3032432/why-men-with-daughters-may-be-the-key-to-closing-the-gender-wage-gap.

12. High School and Beyond

1. Valentina Zarya, "The World's Most Successful Women Share Their Career Advice," World Economic Forum Agenda, October 5, 2017, https://www.weforum.org/agenda/2017/10/the-worlds-most-successful-women-share-their-best-career-advice.
2. Tom Scanlon, "How to Build STEM Career Awareness at Your School," *NOVA* Education: Science of Learning, January 12, 2016, http://www.pbs.org/wgbh/nova/blogs/education/2016/01/how-to-build-stem-career-awareness-at-your-school/.
3. Malcolm Gladwell, *David and Goliath* (Boston: Back Bay Books, 2015).

4. Andrew Yang, *Smart People Should Build Things* (New York: HarperCollins, 2014).
5. Quoted in Rivero, "Be More Creative Today."
6. Ibid.

Conclusion

1. Amy Cuddy, *Presence: Bringing Your Boldest Self to Your Biggest Challenges* (Boston: Little, Brown, 2015).

INDEX

INDEX

ABOUT THE AUTHOR

CRISTAL GLANGCHAI, PHD, IS A SCIENTIST, ENTREPRENEUR, AND MENTOR with a passion for teaching and engaging girls in entrepreneurship, science, and technology. She is the founder and CEO of VentureLab, a nonprofit that runs experiential learning programs in youth entrepreneurship. She is the director of the Texas Entrepreneurial Exchange at the University of Texas at Austin. Dr. Glangchai recently served as the director of the Center for Entrepreneurship at Trinity University. Prior to that, she founded a nanotechnology drug delivery company and ran the Idea to Product Program at the University of Texas at Austin.